THE DIARY OF "HELENA MORLEY"

The Diary of

Translated from the Portuguese

THE NOONDAY PRESS

FARRAR, STRAUS AND GIROUX

NEW YORK

"Helena Morley"

by Elizabeth Bishop

Translation copyright © 1957 by Elizabeth Bishop
All rights reserved
First published in Brazil in 1942 as Minha Vida de Menina
English translation first published in 1957 by Farrar, Straus and Cudahy
This edition first published in 1995 by The Noonday Press
Published in Canada by HarperCollinsCanadaLtd
Printed in the United States of America

Library of Congress Cataloging-in-Publication Data
Morley, Helena.
[Minha vida de menina. English]
The diary of "Helena Morley" / translated from the Portuguese by
Elizabeth Bishop.
p.   cm.
Portuguese edition originally published: 1942. English
translation originally published: New York: Farrar, Straus and
Cudahy, 1957.
1. Morley, Helena—Diaries. 2. Morley, Helena—Childhood and
youth. 3. Diamantina (Minas Gerais, Brazil)—Social life and
customs. 4. Diamantina (Minas Gerais, Brazil)—Biography.
I. Bishop, Elizabeth, 1911–1979.   II. Title.
F2651.D5M6713 1995   981'.5—dc20   [B]   95–3582 CIP

FOREWORD

The Introduction to *Minha Vida de Menina* (*The Diary of "Helena Morley"*) that follows this note was written over twenty years ago and its possibly excessive length and detail are probably due to the pleasure and excitement I felt in translating the book and then actually seeing all the places, and even some of the people, mentioned in it. Since its first appearance in English translation, in 1957, both Dona Alice and Dr. Augusto Mario Brant, her husband, have died, and several of the friends mentioned in the Acknowledgments are also dead. But the diary itself lives on and on, continuing to be re-issued in Brazil. It has also appeared in French and, I think, in Japanese. (Dr. and Mrs. Brant refused, characteristically, to let it be translated into Russian.)

From what later visitors to Diamantina have told me, I think that my impressions, observations, and the information I was able to gather during my week's stay there in 1955, still hold fairly true: the fantastic landscape, the minute churches and houses, the narrow economy and the characteristics of the people have changed very little. Diamantina today seems to strike other visitors very much as it struck me then. However, it is more accessible: there is now a paved road from Belo Horizonte, or at least a *better* road than the old, almost impassable one, and I believe the plane goes and returns every day instead of—rather unpredictably—once or twice a week. I know quite a few people who have driven, or flown, there, as "tourists"—and in some cases the real attraction was to see the little town where the famous "Helena" grew up.

The small-scale Oscar Neimeyer hotel (for most of my stay I was its only guest) was closed for some years, but now, with the new "highway" and more regular plane service, it has opened up again. (Or had when I last heard of it; one shouldn't speak too confidently of such things in the interior of Brazil.) I have not been back to Diamantina, nor have I ever really wanted to go back. Remote, sad, and impoverished as it was, I liked the little town very much, perhaps because it seemed so close to the Diamantina of Helena's childhood, the writing coming off the pages of her diary, and turning to life again, as it had happened. I am superstitious about going "back" to places, anyway: they have changed; you have changed; even the weather may have changed. I am glad to see Helena's youthful book appear again; both it and my memories of Diamantina remain, as I'm afraid I said once before, in the earlier Introduction, still "as fresh as paint."

ELIZABETH BISHOP

Boston, Massachusetts
June 1977

"Minha Vida de Menina": the book and its author

When I first came to Brazil, in 1952, I asked my Brazilian friends which Brazilian books I should begin reading. After naming some of Machado de Assis's novels or short stories, or Euclides da Cunha's *Os Sertões*, they frequently recommended this little book. Two or three even said it was the best thing that had appeared in Brazilian letters since Machado de Assis, and then they were apt to launch into animated exchanges of their favorite stories from it.

In English the title means "My Life as a Little Girl," or "Young Girl," and that is exactly what the book is about, but it is not reminiscences; it is a diary, the diary actually kept by a girl between the ages of twelve and fifteen, in the far-off town of Diamantina, in 1893-1895. It was first published in 1942 in an edition of 2,000 copies, chiefly with the idea of amusing the author's family and friends, and it was never advertised. But its reputation spread in literary circles in Rio de Janeiro and there was a demand for it, so in 1944 a second edition was brought out, then two more, in 1948 and 1952, making 10,000 copies in all. George Bernanos, who was living in the country as an exile when it first appeared, discovered it and gave away a good many copies to friends, a fact to which the author and her husband modestly attribute much of its success. He wrote the author a letter which has been used, in part, on the jackets of later editions. Copies of *Minha Vida de Menina* are now presented every year as prize-books to students of the Convent of the Sacred Heart in Rio.

The more I read the book the better I liked it. The scenes and events it described were odd, remote, and long ago, and yet fresh, sad, funny, and eternally true. The longer I stayed on in Brazil the more Brazilian the book seemed, yet much of it could have happened in any small provincial town or village, and at almost any period of history—at least before the arrival of the automobile and the moving-picture theatre. Certain pages reminded me of more famous and "literary" ones: Nausicaa doing her laundry on the beach, possibly with the help of *her* freed slaves; bits from Chaucer; Wordsworth's poetical children and country people, or Dorothy Wordsworth's wandering beggars. Occasionally entries referring to slavery seemed like notes for an unwritten, Brazilian, feminine version of Tom Sawyer and Nigger Jim. But this was a real, day-by-day diary, kept by a real girl, and anything resembling it that I could think of had been observed or made up, and written down, by adults. (An exception is Anne Frank's diary; but its forced maturity and closed atmosphere are tragically different from the authentic childlikeness, the classical sunlight and simplicity of this one.) I am not sure now whether someone suggested my translating it or I thought of it myself, but when I was about halfway through the book I decided to try.

I learned that "Helena Morley" was still very much alive; that the name was the pseudonym of Senhora Augusto Mario Caldeira Brant and that she was living in Rio, well known and much loved in Rio society. Her husband was then, although almost eighty years old, acting as President of the Bank of Brazil for the second time. The poet Manuel Bandeira, an old friend of the family, kindly gave me an introduction. Armed with a friend, Lota de Macedo Soares, to serve as interpreter because my spoken Portuguese was very limited, I went to call.

Senhora Brant, or Dona Alice as I shall call her in the Brazilian way ("Helena" and "Morley" are both names from her English father's family), now lives in a large, stuccoed, tile-roofed house, on the street that borders the "Lagôa," or lagoon. It is a fashionable place to live. The house is set in a yard with flowerbeds, coconut palms, eight fruit-trees and a servants' house and vegetable garden at the back. A stuccoed fence and wooden gates protect it from the street. A large Cadillac is sometimes parked in the driveway, and its mulatto chauffeur wears a white yachting cap: Cadillac, chauffeur, and white cap are all contemporary Rio fashion. Nearby rise the extravagant Rio mountains and across the lagoon towers the one called the "Gavea," or crow's-nest, because its shape reminded the sixteenth-century Portuguese explorers of the lookout platforms on their little vessels.

On our first visit we were ushered into a large living-room, parlor, rather, with its silk and lace curtains closely drawn, luxuriously furnished: vases, bronzes, and clocks on small tables, rugs, a chandelier, chairs and sofas covered in gold-colored satin. This room is divided from the hall and another living-room opposite by a fence and gate-way of wrought iron, painted white. One of Dona Alice's daughters, Dona Sarita, appeared and started talking to my friend. Although they had not met before, very shortly they were identifying and placing each other's relatives, something that seems to happen in Brazil as quickly as it does in the south of the United States, when Dona Alice herself came in.

She is a large woman, very tall for a Brazilian, looking younger than seventy-six, her hair not yet entirely white, with a handsome, lively, high-cheekboned face lit up by two small but exceedingly bright and gay reddish-brown eyes. Her half-English blood shows, perhaps, in the unusual fairness of her skin, the fairness that made her liable to the freckles she used to complain of in her diary. She began talking, laughing and talking, immediately, and in no time at all we were telling each other stories and Dona Alice was leaning forward to pat our knees with the greatest ease and intimacy. (This warmth and ease in meeting strangers is a Brazilian characteristic especially charming to Nordic visitors.) At the first interview a great deal of the conversation was lost to me. However, I did gather that Dona Alice was proud of the book she had unwittingly written more than sixty years before, pleased at the thought of its being put into English, and still somewhat puzzled by its success in Brazil and the fact that George Bernanos, French people, and more recently, Americans, had seemed to like it, too. I could also recognize her re-telling of some of the anecdotes in the very words of the diary, or in more detail, and with a great deal of hilarity.

Presently Dr. Brant came home from the Bank of Brazil, a small, modest-appearing man of brilliant intelligence, who also looks much younger than his age. He is proud of his wife and it was he who had undertaken to put together all the old scraps and notebooks and prepare them for publication. He has been a lawyer, a journalist, and was five times elected to the National Congress; under the Vargas dictatorship he was exiled, and spent five years in France and England. He reads English; that day, I remember, he told me he was reading Boswell's *Journals*. In answer to my question he said no, that Dona Alice had never written anything since her early diaries, nothing, that was, but "letters, letters, letters!"

I don't believe we accepted the invitation to stay to dinner on this first call, but we did on our second, even though we had taken along two friends, admirers of the book, to meet Dona Alice.

Dona Sarita, another daughter, a son-in-law, a grandson of sixteen or so, a nephew—the number of people at the long table seemed to be constantly expanding and contracting. Dona Alice, very much a matriarch, sat at the head, Dr. Augusto Mario beside her at her left. She told stories, ladled soup, told stories, carved, told stories and served the multiple Brazilian desserts, occasionally interrupting herself to scold the maid, or the nephew, who used up a whole cake of soap, or so she said, every time he took a bath, in a sort of head-tone of mock-rage that disturbed no one in the slightest.

On one of our visits we were taken upstairs in Dona Alice's own elevator, to a panelled library and shown various copies of the book, the original of the letter from Bernanos, and some old photographs. By then it had been settled that I was to do the translation and I had hoped they might have some photographs of Diamantina and the people in the diary. They did have a few, but in poor condition. One was of Dona Alice's old home in the Old Cavalhada: plastered stone, two-storied, severe, with a double door opening onto a wide stoop. I said that I would like to get a copy of it for the book, but Dona Alice and Dona Sarita said Oh no, not *that* house, suggesting that I use a picture of Dona Alice's present house on the Lagôa in Rio. I'm not sure that my arguments for using the old photographs of Diamantina ever quite convinced them.

Diamantina is in the state of Minas Gerais (General Mines) and *mineiros*, miners, as the people who come from there are called, have the reputation for being shrewd and thrifty. There is a saying that the *mineiro* eats out of an open drawer, ready to close it quickly if unexpected company shows up. Dona Alice's hospitality belied this legend, but once when Lota de Macedo Soares went to see her she found Dona Alice seated in the upstairs hall darning linen, and was rather taken aback to be asked severely if she didn't employ her time on such chores when she was at home.

The diaries, I found, had been cut short where they now end by Dr. Brant because the next year marks his own appearance in them, and his acceptance as a suitor. I feel it is a pity he so firmly omits every incident of their courtship. By the time she was seventeen, "Helena" had already received five proposals of marriage from "foreign" miners living in Diamantina. Her girl cousins and friends had been reduced to hinting to her that if she didn't want any of her suitors perhaps she would let *them* have them. She had indeed become what she admits to yearning to be in her diary: "the leading girl of Diamantina." In true Brazilian fashion she chose a Brazilián and a cousin and at eighteen married Dr. Augusto Mario, whose family had been prominent in Diamantina since the eighteenth century. I am sure she has never for a moment regretted turning down those other offers, and that this is one of those rare stories that combine worldly success and a happy ending.

One story she told us, not in the book, was about the first time she received a serious compliment from one of the rejected suitors and at last became convinced that she was pretty, really pretty. She said that she had sat up in bed studying her face, or what she could see of it by the light of a candle, in a broken piece of looking-glass, all night long.

Dr. Brant has provided the following information about "Helena Morley's" English background:

"The family name is really Dayrell. Dona Alice's grandfather, Dr. John Dayrell, studied medicine in London. He married a Miss Alice Mortimer, the daughter of an Irish Protestant, Henry Mortimer, who was, or had been, a government official in Barbados, where he also had a sugar-cane plantation producing sugar and rum. His children were educated in London, and it was there that Alice Mortimer met and married Dr. John Dayrell.

"Dr. Dayrell left England between 1840 and 1850 to serve as physician to a gold mining concern at Morro Velho [Old Hill] belonging to the famous English São João del Rey Mining Company. A short while later there was a flood in the mine and work came to a halt. The other officials went back to England, but Dr. Dayrell, who had a 'weak chest,' remained in Brazil and went to live in Diamantina, a town 5,000 feet high and famous for its fine climate.

"In Diamantina he established himself as a doctor, acquired a *fazenda* [farm or country-seat] near town, and practised medicine for about 40 years. He and his wife were the only Protestants in the town. He had eight children, two born in England and the rest in Diamantina."

Richard Burton, in *Explorations of the Highlands of the Brazil* (Tinsley Brothers, London, 1869), speaks of meeting Dr. Dayrell in 1867, and also Felisberto Dayrell, the real name of "Helena Morley's" father, who was even then at work mining diamonds, as he is later, throughout the pages of his daughter's diary.

Diamantina

Like most children, Helena Morley seems to have taken her surroundings and the scenery of the region where she lived very much for granted. There are few direct references to them in *Minha Vida de Menina*. She does speak of the streams where she and her sister and brothers take baths, or catch the most fish, of places where there are wildflowers and fruits, or where she can set her bird-traps. And she says a good many times that she likes "the country better than the city," the "city" being, of course, the tiny provincial town of Diamantina. But whatever love of nature she has seems part utilitarian and part, the greater part, sheer joy at not being in school.

However, what impresses the occasional traveller who visits Diamantina these days first of all is its wild and extraordinary setting. Diamantina, the highest town in Brazil, is about 200 miles northeast of Belo Horizonte, the modern capital of Minas Gerais, a state bigger than Texas. At the time of the diary the railway had not yet been put through; now, sixty years later, trains still run but are already outmoded for passengers, and a once-a-day plane makes the trip from the capital in a little less than an hour.

I went there in May, when the worst of the rains are over but roads are supposedly not yet too dusty. After leaving Belo Horizonte the plane flies higher and higher, the land below grows rockier and rockier, wilder and more desolate; not a sign of life is to be seen. A high sea of waves and crests of steely gray rock, eroded and fragmented, appears; the rolling land between is covered with greenish grass, but barely covered. There are unexpected streams among the rocks; slender waterfalls fall into small black pools or the streams fan out glittering over beds of white sand. Never a village nor a house; only hundreds of the pock marks, or large pits, of old gold and diamond mines, showing red and white.

The plane comes down on a bare, slightly swelling field. There is nothing to be seen but a long red dust-cloud settling behind it, an open shed with names and comic heads splashed on it in black paint, and a wretched little house with a baby and a few hens against a ragged washing strung on a barbed-wire fence. But the air is crisp and delicious and the horizon is rimmed all around with clear-etched peaks of rock. The three or four passengers descend, immediately feeling that they are *up* and exclaiming about the change in temperature. There is no sign of Diamantina. The highest peak of rock, to the northeast, is the mountain of Itambé, sharp and looking deceptively near.

A lone taxi drives to town. A church tower suddenly appears between the brown-green waves of grass and the wilder, broken waves of gigantic rocks; then other church towers, and then almost the whole of the red-tiled cluster of roofs comes into sight at once. The town climbs one steep hill, extends sidewise over a lower one and down the other side. The highway enters from above along the line of the railway, passing under the striped arm of a police "barrier."

There are sixteen churches, most of them diminutive, no more than chapels; the Cathedral is new and very ugly. The famous churches of the gold-mining town of Ouro Preto are small, too, but with their baroque façades trimmed with green soapstone, their heavy curves and swirls and twin mustard-pot towers, they are opulent and sophisticated, while the little churches of Diamantina are shabby, silent, and wistful. For one thing, although they are built of stone, plastered and painted white, the window and door frames are of wood, in dark blues, reds, or greens, or combinations of all three colors. Ornamentation is skimpy or nonexistent, and belfries or clock-towers are square. The comparative poverty of the town is shown in the way, once the walls were up, the rest of the façade and the tower were simply constructed of boards and painted white to match the stone. Because of the steepness of the streets there is often a flight of stone steps at an angle across the front and off one side, and some churches are still fenced in by high old blue or red picket fences, giving them a diffident, countrified appearance.

The Church of the Rosário that figures prominently in Helena's diary, standing next door to her grandmother's house as it does, is still the most impressive. It is the Negroes' church, built by slaves in the middle of the eighteenth century; inside are three black saints: St. Benedict, St. Iphigenia, and St. Somebody; his name was unidentifiable. There are three crystal chandeliers, a great deal of red dust and faded blue paint, and a slightly rickety blue gallery for the black choir. The church has settled and everything is now askew. As in many old Brazilian churches, the ceilings are made of narrow boards, so that the scenes from the Life of the Virgin painted on them, copied from heaven knows what hand-me-down sources, are scored through by black lines. These ceilings have a sad appeal, like letters written in old copy-book handwriting on lined paper.

In front of this church there is a big tree of the *ficus* family. Looking up into its branches one is surprised to see a large black beam stuck in them, crosswise, then a rusty lantern and other indistinguishable rusty odds and ends that have no business being thirty feet up off the ground, in a tree. This is one of the town's modest "sights," and proves to be what is left of an enormous crucifix that once stood where the tree now stands. The air-borne seed started growing out from the side of the cross, grew upwards and downwards and took root, and now has taken over, broken up, and lifted the whole cross in the air: ladder, lantern, pliers, hammer and all.

These crosses are a common feature of the countryside around Diamantina, sometimes with all their accoutrements, sometimes bare or simply with stiff wooden streamers arranged over the arms and a flat tin rooster on top. The bird called *João de Barro*, John of the Mud, or Clay, builds his beehive-shaped adobe nests on the arms, and the hammock bird slings his woven ones underneath. One cross, on the high ridge of rock opposite the town, now burns brightly at night with hundreds of electric light bulbs. At Sopa (soup), where Helena's father went "to open a mine," there is a fine one, with a white skull and cross-bones on the black wood, silvered Roman centurions' helmets, and a flat rose-red "seamless garment" like a pattern for a child's dress. It stands near a small church known as the "Chinese church" because the eaves of the roof and tower are turned upwards in Oriental style, a common feature of Brazilian colonial architecture, traced directly to the Portuguese colony of Macāo. One becomes accustomed to it in Rio de Janeiro, but here far off in a desolate countryside it is strange to come across this church like a baby pagoda, and a crucifix almost as tall, loaded with its grim set of Christian iconography-toys.

The interiors of Helena's various churches are disappointing, cramped and musty, the Portuguese-style wedding-cake altars crowded with old artificial flowers and incongruously dressed, bewigged saints. The confessionals, however, are sometimes quaint and pretty: upright boards about five feet high; the priest sits on one side on a chair, the penitent kneels on the other; but the boards are gilded and painted in pastel blues and pinks, the upper part pierced with holes like a colander, or with long slits that make them vaguely resemble Biblical musical instruments, possibly some sort of organ. And the "masts" Helena speaks of as being set up on certain holy days lie in the sacristies or along the side aisles of their churches the rest of the year, big as telephone poles, painted in winding blue and white stripes.

I came upon the Church of the Amparo, that figures in the diary, unexpectedly, as it was getting dark. Its trim is dark peacock blue; on top a rusty rooster perches on a rusty globe; there is a minute balcony on either side of a large, faded coat of arms cut out of tin above the door, and over it a three-dimensional Dove of the Holy Spirit, dimly illuminated, nesting behind a quatrefoil window. Seen suddenly blocking the end of an alley-way, this church is stricken but dignified, like a person coming towards one whom one expects to beg, who doesn't beg after all.

Some of the church clocks by which Helena told the time have been removed. At about seven o'clock the light leaves the town rapidly and the surrounding sea of rocks, and the peak of Itambé, turn red. A few church-bells ring and then a great noise comes from the loud-speaker over the Cathedral door and reverberates all over town. *Ave Maria, gratia plena*; the town vibrates with it and the light bulbs on the high cross opposite snap into activity. It is the hour of the rosary, Helena's *terço*, which caused her so much "suffering" at family prayers and which is now broadcast every evening during the month of May. On Sundays the same loud-speaker is used to draw people to mass; at five o'clock it was blaring out *The Stars and Stripes Forever*.

In spite of these innovations and the Betty Grable film showing at the one cinema, the town has changed very little since the youthful Helena lived there and raced up and down its steep streets. Most of the streets have no sidewalks, some have narrow ones, two feet or so wide, long slabs of greenish stone raised a little above the cobblestones, the *pé de muleque,* or "ragamuffin's foot,"—that is, the confection we call peanut brittle, which it is supposed to resemble. Down the middle of the street runs another strip of long stones, set flush, much easier to walk on than the sidewalks that every so often stop altogether, or break up into steps. These footpaths are called *capistranas,* after a mayor of Ouro Preto, who introduced them there.

The houses are thick-walled and solid, in the middle of the town of two or even three stories, but as one gets away from the Cathedral they become smaller and lower and the tile roofs turn to thatched ones. The taller houses have balconies, formerly often completely covered in by the lattice-work cages, called *muxarabis* (from the Arabian *muxara,* a shelter), showing the influence of the Moors on the architecture and way of life of Portugal. From them the women could watch what went on in the streets, in an Oriental seclusion. On either side of the windows giving onto these balconies are little lanterns, globes of colored or milk glass, *luminárias.* (The word has been extended to mean a kind of small cream-filled tart, highly thought of by our diarist.) The same kind of globe, without lights, decorates the railings, and sometimes Tecoma vines or grape-vines are trained along the ironwork.

The window frames are curved at the top, with double sashes of a dozen small panes each. Here the trimming becomes confusing, since some of the wooden frames are marbleized or painted to imitate stone, and some of the stone ones are painted to imitate grained wood. A good many of the windows still have stencils on the lower panes, a form of folk-art that also served to protect the privacy of rooms right on the street. A paper stencil in a formalized leaf-and-flower or other design is held against the glass and patted with a rag dipped in white paint. The effect is very decorative, like frost on the window panes in northern climates, only geometrical. The wide overhang of the eaves contributes to the town's surprisingly Oriental air, and this overhang

is filled in solid with molding and is a favorite place for colored
stripes and other ornamentation. The houses are in admirably
bold or pretty colors. I particularly liked a crushed-strawberry pink
one, with a double staircase of blue, and window frames and under-
eaves marbleized in the same blue. There are mustard-colored
houses with bright yellow and dark green shutters, white with
dark blue and peach, mauve with dark blue and yellow. So that
passers-by will not be drenched in the rainy season, the mouths of
the rain-pipes are carried out two feet or more, across the sidewalks, and the funnels flare like trumpets. It is as if a band had
suddenly stopped playing. Sometimes they have tin petals or
feathers down them and around the mouth, and this decoration
is repeated in tiles set edgewise up the ridges of the roofs, dragon-
like and very "Chinese."

The grandmother's house still stands, to the right of the Rosário Church, but the Teatro Isabel, formerly on the other side,
has been torn down and in its place is a large baby-pink jail from
whose barred windows a drunken prisoner yelled at me incom-
prehensibly. The house is low, its stoop just a few inches off the
ground, a deceptively small-looking house with a sweeping, con-
cave old tile roof. The woman who lives there now knew *Minha
Vida de Menina* and its author and kindly showed me through.
The old rooms for slaves, extending along the street by the church,
are let out. Inside there is room after room, high, square, sadly
neglected, almost devoid of furniture. The walls are a yard thick,
wooden shutters can be closed and barred on the inside; the
ceilings are of boards or woven rushes painted white, the two
common Brazilian types. After a good many of these high dark
rooms we reached the kitchen, where a girl was cooking over an
open fire. Stoves here consist of a long iron plate with four pot-
holes in it, laid on the edges of a stone trough full of embers. A
wood called *candeia* is commonly used. It has a peculiar sweetish
smell, sickening until one gets used to it; at the dinner-hour this
sweetish stench hovers bluely over Brazilian towns and villages.

Behind the house the grandmother's former garden covers about five acres, sloping down to a brook and a jungle of banana trees. There are huge *jaboticaba* trees (see page 64), the same ones that Helena used to climb into for refuge. There are a few beds of lettuce and cabbages, and a grove of coffee trees, but everything is overgrown and gone to seed and it is hard to imagine how it must have looked in the old days, tended by the grandmother's ex-slaves. A big sociable pig stood up on his hind legs in his pen, to watch us.

One of the handsomest buildings is Helena's "Normal School," now the Grupo Escolar, and located in the middle of the town; big, white, rectangular, with bright blue doors and window-frames. Juscelino Kubitschek, the present President of Brazil and a former governor of Minas, was born in Diamantina. He had visited recently and a great canvas banner bearing his smiling face almost concealed the front of the building. There are also a Kubitschek Street and a Kubitschek Place with his head in bronze in it, less than life-size, as if done by the Amazonian head-shrinkers.

The market is a large wooden shed, with blue and red arches, and a sparse forest of thin, gnawed hitching-posts around it. The drovers are still there, with loads of hides and corn, but because of trains, better roads, and trucks, trade has dwindled to next to nothing since Helena's day. Near the Cathedral one is warned from the street or alley where the "bad girls" live. They are extremely juvenile mulattoes, sitting on their doorsteps with their feet stuck out on the cobblestones, gossiping and sucking sugar-cane in the sunshine. The live-forevers that Helena used to pick are still very much in evidence, in fact they are one of the town's few industries besides diamond-mining. They are a tiny yellow-white straw flower, less than half an inch in diameter, on a long fine shiny brown stalk. Tied up in bunches, the bundle of stems bigger than two hands can hold, they lie drying in rows on the streets all around the Cathedral, and freight-cars full of flowers are sent off every year, on their way to Japan. They are used, I was told, for "fireworks," or "ammunition," but I suspect that, dyed and glued, they merely reappear in the backgrounds of Japanese trays, plaques, etc. Brazilian-made fireworks play an important role in Diamantina, as they do in all provincial Brazilian towns, and are used in staggering quantities for religious holidays. I was shown a warehouse packed to the ceiling with firecrackers, catherine-wheels and Roman candles; the supply looked much larger than that of food-stuffs on hand at the same wholesaler's.

Diamonds and gold, but chicfly diamonds, still obsess the economy. The hotel manager (a new hotel, designed by Oscar Niemeyer, was finished in 1956), using almost the very words that Helena used in 1893, complained that he had to fly in vegetables from Belo Horizonte. "Here no one's interested in anything but gold and diamonds," he said. "They say they can't grow vegetables in this soil, but it isn't true. They think of nothing but diamonds, diamonds, diamonds." It is strange to see, on the side of a miserable little house, a blue and white enamelled sign announcing that here is a diamond dealer. I looked inside one of these houses and could see nothing but overhead a lurid plaster statue of St. George killing the dragon, with a small red electric light bulb glowing in front of it, and under it, on the table, a bunch of live-forevers and a fine pair of scales in a glass case. The scales are covered up at night, like the innumerable caged birds hanging everywhere. Curiously shaped stones, lumps of ores, clusters and chunks of rock crystal and quartzes are everywhere, too, used as door-stops and sideboard decorations. In the cold clear air, the town itself, with its neatness, rockiness, and fine glitter, seems almost on the point of precipitation and crystallization.

In the recently opened museum there are the usual polychrome saints and angels, sedan chairs and marriage beds, and then suddenly and horribly an alcove hung with the souvenirs of slavery: rusty chains, hand-cuffs, and leg- and neck-irons draped on the wall; pointed iron prods originally fastened to poles; and worse things. Driving about the region, the sites of the old slave encampments are pointed out. Trees, and a very fine short grass, supposedly from Africa, distinguish them, and they are usually beside a stream and near the pits of old mines. But now there is only the small Negro and mulatto population to show for all the million or more slaves who came here in the eighteenth and early nineteenth centuries.

I made an excursion to Boa Vista, where Helena's father mined. The mines are abandoned now, although they were worked on a large scale by foreign companies up until a few years ago. There is nothing to be seen but an immense excavation exposing soils of different colors (each with a different name; Burton's book gives an excellent account of them and the different methods of mining), and endless iron pipes. Boa Vista is slightly higher than Diamantina; although it is six or seven miles away one can see a church-tower. The road there is dirt, narrow, winding, and eventually the taxi scrapes over outcroppings of naked rock and splashes through streams. Battalions of grotesque rocks charge across the fields, or stand like architecture, pierced by Gothic-ruin windows. Large slabs balance on top of moldering turrets, with vines, bushes, and even stunted palm-trees on their tops. Helena Morley was not a fanciful child but I wondered at her riding on her borrowed horse, before sun-up, along this nightmare road, hurrying to get back to Diamantina in time for school.

I took with me a life-long friend of Helena's future husband, Dr. Brant, Senhor Antonio Cicero de Menezes, former local director of the Post Office service, now eighty years old, a very distinguished-looking man with a white Vandyke beard and moustaches, like an older, frailer Joseph Conrad. We came back through the hamlet of twenty or so houses that is Palha (straw) today and Seu Antonio Cicero said, in Helena's very phrase, "Now let us descend and suck fruit." So we sat in the tiny general store, surrounded by household and mining necessities: iron kettles and frying pans, salt beef and soap, and sucked a good many slightly sour oranges. A little boy brought them in a gold-panning bowl and Seu Antonio Cicero prepared them for me with his pocket-knife faster than I could suck. The storekeeper showed me a store room full of these wooden bowls, cowhides and tarry lumps of brown sugar and sieves for panning diamonds, piled on the floor, and boxes and boxes of dusty rock crystals, bound, he said, for the United States, for industrial purposes.

Near there we stopped again to watch a group of men looking for diamonds in a stream beside the road. The head of the group had four men, black and white, working for him; he gave me his name and asked me to print it; here it is: Manoel Benicio de Loyola, "diamond-hunter of Curralinho." They were shovelling in the shallow, sparkling water, damming it up, releasing it, and arranging piles of gravel on the bank. One of them took up a small quantity of gravel in the wide round sieve and held it just beneath the surface of the water, swirling it skilfully around and around. In a few minutes he lifted it out; the gravel was distributed evenly over the sieve in one thin layer. With the gesture of a quick-fingered housewife turning out a cake, he turned the whole thing upside down on the ground, intact. Senhor Benicio de Loyola then put on his horn-rimmed glasses, lowered himself to his knees in the wet mud, and stared, passing a long wooden knife over the gravel from side to side. In a second he waved his hand, got up and put his glasses back in his pocket, and his assistant got ready to turn out another big gravel pancake, while he and Seu Antonio Cicero talked about a large blue diamond someone had found somewhere a day or two before.

This is the simplest of all forms of diamond "mining." It goes on all around Diamantina constantly, and enough diamonds are found in this way to provide a meagre living for some thousands of people. One sees them, sometimes all alone, sometimes in groups of three or four, standing in every stream. Sometimes they are holding a sieve just under the water, looking for diamonds, sometimes they are sloshing their wooden bowls from side to side in the air, looking for gold. The bent heads and concentration of these figures, in that vast, rock-studded, crucifix-stuck space, give a touch of dementia to the landscape.

I also made an excursion to Biribiri (accented on the second and last "i"s), an enchanting spot, where Helena used to dance, and leap through St. John's Day bonfires. The factory, for weaving cotton, is still there, but nothing could look less like industrialization. One descends to a fair-sized river and the landscape is green and lush; there are many trees, and fruit trees around the blue- or white-washed stone houses along the one unpaved street. In the middle is the church, better kept up than any of the others I saw, trim, almost dainty. Indeed, it looks like an old-fashioned chocolate box. A blue picket fence encloses the flourishing flower-garden and over the door, below the twin towers, is a large rounded pink Sacred Heart with a crown of realistic ten-inch thorns, green wooden palm branches and blue wooden ribbons. Close around the church stand a dozen real palms, Royal palms, enormously tall and slender, their shining heads waving in the late afternoon sun.

"Helena Morley"

In one of his letters to Robert Bridges, Hopkins says that he has bought some books, among them Dana's *Two Years Before the Mast*, "a thoroughly good one and all true, but bristling with technicality—seamanship—which I most carefully go over and even enjoy but cannot understand; there are other things, though, as a flogging, which is terrible and instructive *and it happened*—ah, that is the charm and the main point." And that, I think, is "the charm and the main point" of *Minha Vida de Menina*. Its "technicalities," diamond digging, say, scarcely "bristle," and its three years in Diamantina are relatively tame and unfocussed, although there are incidents of comparable but casual, small-town cruelty. But—*it really happened*; everything did take place, day by day, minute by minute, once and only once, just the way Helena says it did. There really was a grandmother, Dona Teodora, a stout, charitable old lady who walked with a cane and managed her family and her freed slaves with an iron will. There really was a Siá Ritinha who stole her neighbors' chickens, but not Helena's mother's chickens; a Father Neves; a spinster English Aunt Madge, bravely keeping up her standards and eking out a living by teaching small obstreperous Negroes, in a town financially ruined by the emancipation of the slaves and the opening of the Kimberly diamond mines.

Some of the people in the diary are still alive, and the successors of those who are dead and gone seem to be cut very much from the same cloth. Little uniformed girls, with perhaps shorter skirts, carrying satchels of books, press their noses against the dining-room windows of the new hotel and are overcome by fits of giggling at seeing the foreigner eat her lunch—on their way to the school run by the Sisters of Charity, the same school that Helena ran away from. The boys still give them the same nicknames. (They call a freckled child of my acquaintance *Flocos*, "Flakes," but that is a new product in Brazil and Helena was spared it.) Mota's store, where she bought her boots, is now Mota's Son's store. There is still a garrison of soldiers, now outside the town; there is a seminary, and young priests walk in the streets and people talk to them through the latticed windows.

When the diary happened, Helena was tall and thin and freckled and always, always hungry. She worries about her height, her thinness, her freckles and her appetite. She is not a very good scholar and fails in her first year at Normal School. Her studies can always be interrupted by her brother, her many cousins, or even the lack of a candle. (The diary was mostly written by candlelight.) She is greedy; sometimes she is unfair to her long-suffering sister, Luizinha, but feels properly guilty afterwards, rationalize as she may. She is obviously something of a show-off and saucy to her teachers; but she is outspoken and good-natured and gay, and wherever she is her friends may be getting into mischief but they are having a good time; and she has many friends, old and young, black and white. She is willing to tell stories on herself, although sometimes she tries to ease her conscience, that has "a nail in it." She thinks about clothes a great deal, but, under the circumstances—she has only two or three dresses and two pairs of boots—who wouldn't?

She may grow tedious on the subject of stealing fruit, but it is, after all, the original sin, and remember St. Augustine on the subject of the pear tree. On the other hand, she seems to take the Anglo-Saxon sin of sins, "cheating," rather lightly. If she is not always quite admirable, she is always completely herself; hypocrisy appears for a moment and then vanishes like the dew. Her method of composition seems influenced by the La Fontaine she hates to study; she winds up her stories with a neat moral that doesn't apply too exactly; sometimes, for variety's sake, she starts off with the moral instead. She has a sense of the right quotation, or detail, the gag-line, and where to stop. The characters are skilfully differentiated: the quiet, humorous father, the devout, doting, slightly foolish mother, the rigid Uncle Conrado. Occasionally she has "runs" on one subject; perhaps "papa" had admired a particular page and so she wrote a sequel to it or remembered a similar story.

In matters of religion, Helena seems to have been somewhat of an eighteenth-century rationalist. She steps easily in and out of superstition, reason, belief and disbelief, without much adolescent worrying. She would never for a moment doubt, one feels, that the church is "a good thing." With all its holidays, processions, mast-raisings, and fireworks, its christenings, first communions and funerals, it is the fountain-head of the town's social life. Her father remains in the background, smiling but tolerant, while her mother pleads with him to go to church and constantly prays for all the family. Like him, Helena is at first skeptical of a schoolmate who dies and acquires a reputation for working miracles; then she veers towards her mother's party. Her religion, like her feeling for nature, is on the practical side.

She lives in a world of bitter poverty and isolation. A trip to the capital, Rio de Janeiro, where a few boys go to study, takes ten days: eight on mule-back to Sabará, and from there two days by very slow train to Rio. Supplies are brought to town by the drovers, on long lines of mules or horses. One of the greatest problems is what to do with the freed slaves who have stayed on. Reading this diary, one sometimes gets the impression that the greater part of the town, black and white, "rich" and poor, when it hasn't found a diamond lately, gets along by making sweets and pastries, brooms and cigarettes and selling them to each other. Or the freed slaves are kept busy manufacturing them in the kitchen and peddling them in the streets, and the lady of the house collects the profits— or buys, in her parlor, the products of her kitchen.

Now that I can join in my friends' exchanges of anecdotes from the book, and have seen Diamantina, I think that one of my own favorite entries is Helena's soliloquy on November 5th, 1893, on the meaning of Time (her style improves in the later years):

"The rooster's crow never gives the right time and nobody believes it. When a rooster crows at nine o'clock they say that a girl is running away from home to get married. I'm always hearing the rooster crow at nine o'clock, but it's very rarely that a girl runs away from home.

"Once upon a time I used to believe that roosters told the time, because in Boa Vista when you ask a miner the time he looks at the sun and tells you. If you go and look at the clock, he's right. So I used to think that the sun kept time during the day and the rooster at night. Now I realize that this was a mistake . . .

"In Cavalhada only the men have watches. Those who live in the middle of the town don't feel the lack of them because almost all the churches have clocks in their towers. But when papa isn't home the mistakes we make about the hours are really funny. . . . The rooster is mama's watch, which doesn't run very well. It's already fooled us several times." She goes on to tell about "mama's" waking her and Luizinha up to go to four o'clock Mass, because the rooster has already crowed twice. They drink their coffee and start out. "I kept looking at the moon and the stars and saying to mama, 'This time the Senhora's going to see whether the rooster can tell time or not.' The street was deserted. The two of us walked holding onto mama's arms. When we passed by the barracks the soldier on duty looked at mama and asked, 'What's the Senhora doing in the street with these little girls at this hour?' Mama said, 'We're going to Mass at the Cathedral.' The soldier said, 'Mass at midnight? It isn't Christmas eve. What's this all about?'

"I was afraid of the soldier. Mama said, 'Midnight? I thought it was four o'clock. Thank you very much for the information.'

"We went home and lay down in our clothes. But even so we missed Mass. When we got to church later Father Neves was already in the Hail Marys."

I like to think of the two tall, thin little girls hanging onto their mother's arms, the three figures stumbling up the steep streets of the rocky, lightless little town beneath the cold bright moon and stars; and I can hear the surprised young soldier's voice, mama's polite reply, and then three pairs of footsteps scuttling home again over the cobblestones.

Food

The staple diet of Brazil consists of dried black beans and rice, with whatever meat, beef or pork, salted or fresh, can be afforded or obtained. And black beans, instead of the "bread" of other countries, seem to be equated with life itself. An example of this: when the Brazilian football team went to play in the Olympic Games recently, thirty-three pounds of black beans were taken along for each man. And recently in Rio the court ordered a taxi-driver to pay alimony to his wife and children in the form of twenty-two pounds of rice and twenty-two pounds of black beans monthly.

They are boiled separately and seasoned with salt and pepper, garlic, and lard. The common vegetables, such as pumpkin, okra, *couve* (a kind of cabbage), are usually made into stews with small quantities of meat or chicken. As in other Catholic countries, salt codfish is a common dish. But black beans and rice form the basis of the main meal, the heavy lunch, usually served early, between eleven and half-past twelve. At the time of the diary lunch was even earlier, at half-past ten or eleven, and dinner was eaten at three or four o'clock. This explains why everyone is always ready to eat again in the evenings.

A dish of roasted manioc flour is always served with the beans and rice, indeed it is what the unqualified word "flour" signifies. It is sprinkled over the food, to thicken the sauce, and perhaps to add a little textural interest to the monotonous diet, since its nutritional value is almost nothing. It is also used in making various cakes and pastries. There is an impressive variety of these in Brazil, using manioc and cornmeal as well as wheat flours, coconut, brown sugar, etc., each with its own name, frequently religious in origin and varying from region to region. Helena mentions a dozen or more and there are whole books on the subject. Desserts are often *pudims*, usually, or unusually, heavy, and a great variety of fruit pastes, guava, quince, banana, etc., served with a small piece of hard white cheese. On a good Brazilian table, desserts appear, or always used to, several at a time. Cinnamon is the universal spice. Most Brazilians have very sweet tooths.

Breakfast is simply coffee, black or with boiled milk, and a piece of bread, although Helena varies hers strangely with cucumbers. Coffee is served after the other meals, at intervals in the day, and inevitably to callers at any time, in the form of *cafezinhos*, "little coffees," black, boiling hot, and with the tiny cup half-filled with sugar. (The sugar is only partially refined so it takes quite a lot to sweeten a cup.) It is made by stirring the very finely ground coffee into boiling water, then pouring it through a coffee bag. These brown-stained bags and their high wooden stands are a symbol of Brazil, like black beans, and they are seen everywhere, even in miniature, as toys. There are laws to ensure that the coffee served in the innumerable cafés is unadulterated and of the required strength. (In an American movie being shown in Rio a character was told that he'd feel better after he had "a good breakfast, porridge and bacon and eggs and coffee," and this speech was rendered by the Portuguese sub-title, "Come and take coffee.")

A glance at the photographs will perhaps explain what may seem like Helena's over-emphasis on fruit, or unnatural craving for it. Through June, July, and August, the long dry winters in that stony region, when everything is covered with red dust, with a constant shortage of fresh vegetables and the only drinking water running in open gutters as it was at that time, "sucking oranges" must have been the best way to quench one's thirst, and stealing fruit an almost irresistible impulse.

Money

Dr. Brant has given me the following information about the value of money at the time the diary was kept.

The *mil reis* (a thousand *reis*, the plural of *real*, or "royal") was worth twenty cents of U.S. money. (As a banker, Dr. Brant points out that the dollar has since been devalued, so that a *mil reis* would be worth ten cents of today's money. But as Helena says, we are speaking of "bygone days" and it seems simpler to keep it at the earlier evaluation.) Five *mil reis* would therefore be a dollar, 100 *reis* two pennies, and so on. Dr. Brant gives a list of approximate prices of goods and labor at the time:

A pound of meat: 10¢
A pound of sugar: 3¢
A dozen eggs: 4¢
A quart of milk: 4¢
A pound of butter: 12¢
A pair of shoes: $3.00
A good horse: $20.00
Average rent for a good house: $8.00 a month
A cook: $2.00 a month
Wages of Negroes employed in mining: 40¢ a day (paid to the whites who

rented them out. In the town, or in agriculture, Negro wages were less.)

Arinda receives about $100 for the diamond she finds, page 6, Helena makes $6.00 by selling her mother's gold brooch without a diamond in it, page 172 ff.; and the grandmother sends home a present of $10.00 to her daughter, on page 48, etc.

Acknowledgments

I am indebted to many friends and acquaintances for the help they have given me, both as sources of information about Diamantina and its life and vocabulary, and with the actual work of translation. Thanks are due:

In Diamantina, to Antonio Cicero de Menezes and his granddaughter; to Armando Assis, manager of the Hotel de Tourismo; and to many other inhabitants who showed me the way or went with me, invited me into their houses, and patiently repeated and spelled out the names of things.

To Vera Pacheco Jordão, who went with me to Diamantina and came to my assistance when my Portuguese failed me; to Manuel Bandeira; to Dora Romariz; to Otto Schwartz; and to Mary Stearns Morse, who typed the difficult manuscript.

To Rodrigo Melo Franco de Andrade, head of the Patrimonio Artistico of the Brazilian Department of Education, who took an interest in the book and who got out the Department's collection of photographs of Diamantina for me to choose from.

To my friend Pearl Kazin, who, in New York, received the manuscript and gave me invaluable help with it.

To my friend Lota de Macedo Soares, who reluctantly but conscientiously went over every word of the translation with me, not once, but several times.

To Dr. Augusto Mario Caldeira Brant, who also went over every word of the translation, and without whose remarkable memory for the customs and idioms of Diamantina in the '90's a great deal

of detail might have been lost. I am grateful to him for many sug-
gestions, and many of the footnotes are his.

But most thanks of all are, of course, due to Dona Alice herself
for her wonderful gift: the book that has kept her childhood for
us, as fresh as paint. Long may she live to re-tell the stories of
"Helena Morley" to her grandchildren and great-grandchildren.

ELIZABETH BISHOP

Sítio da Alcobacinha
Petrópolis
September, 1956

Principal Characters and Glossary

HELENA MORLEY'S FAMILY:

Alexandre, father

Dona Carolina, mother

Dona Teodora, grandmother, mother of Dona Carolina

Luizinha (diminutive of Louise), younger sister

Renato, older brother

Nhonhô, little brother (real name João, or Joãozinho, for John)

Aunt Madge, an "English aunt," one of the father's sisters

Dindinha (diminutive of *madrinha,* godmother), a godmother
     who is also an aunt, the mother's sister. Also called *Chi-
     quinha,* diminutive of Francisca.

Nhonhô, pronounced Nyo-nyo, is the slaves' corruption of the
     diminutive of *Senhor, Senhorzinho,* or "little master."
Iaiá, pronounced Ya-ya, is the slaves' corruption of the diminutive
     of *Senhora, Senhorazinha,* or "little mistress." These pet
     names are still heard, even for adults.
Inhá is another diminutive of *Senhora,* as are *Sinhá,* and *Siá.*

Women are politely addressed as *Dona,* followed by the given name (or pet name). Men are addressed by an elision of *Senhor, Seu,* followed by the given name, or if they have a university degree, as *Doutor,* followed by the given name. In modern Portuguese these titles are not capitalized, but to make the text less confusing to the eye I have kept to the older style.

In formal speech the third person, with *a Senhora* or *o Senhor* (or *Dona,* or *Seu*) is used, and not the familiar *você,* for "you." Helena Morley addresses her elders, even her parents, in this way, as well-brought-up children formerly did. In general I have used the English forms, but wherever it seemed to give the atmosphere better I have used the third person.

For the same reason I have kept the Portuguese proper names although it got me into difficulties, and I hope not too many inconsistencies, when it came to things like "Saint Francisco of Assisi," or "Saint João." I have tried to avoid as many other Portuguese words as I could. A *chácara* is a little hard to define. It means a house with extensive gardens, or even a small farm, but not necessarily in the country. The grandmother's *chácara,* mentioned constantly in *Minha Vida de Menina,* is at the edge of the town. Since "farm," "garden," or "country house," would all give false pictures, I have left that one word untranslated throughout.

After a consonant "h" in Portuguese is pronounced like "y" in English; at the beginning of a word it is silent. "X" is pronounced like "sh."

When I was a child my father encouraged me to form the habit of writing down everything that happened to me. Almost every day at school the Portuguese teacher expected us to write a composition, which could be a description, a letter, or an account of what we had been doing. I found it was easiest to write about myself and my very numerous family. These compositions, filling many notebooks and loose sheets, were hidden away for years and years and forgotten. Finally I began to go over them and arrange them for my own family, chiefly for my granddaughters. It was their idea, to which I consented, to make a book that might show the girls of today the differences between present-day life and the simple existence we led at that time.

I do not know if a reader of today will be interested in the daily life of a small city in the interior, towards the end of the past century, as seen through the eyes of a little girl—a city without electric lights, running water, telephones, or even a bakery, where we lived happily with very little except our everyday preoccupations. But how beautiful life was then! And how many stories of my aunts and uncles, my cousins, my teachers, my schoolmates and friends, how many of my own outbursts and complaints—things I no longer remembered after so many years—came back to me when I reread my old notebooks!

As I read these pages, forgotten for so long, tears of longing came to my eyes for my kind parents, my dear grandmother, and my wonderful Aunt Madge, the most extraordinary woman I have ever known, whose advice and whose example had such an influence on me.

No alterations have been made in these journals except for a few minor corrections and the changing of a few names for motives that will be easily understood.

And now a word to my granddaughters: you who were born in comfortable circumstances and who feel sorry when you read these stories of my childhood, you do not need to pity poor little girls just because they are poor. We were so happy! Happiness does not consist in worldly goods but in a peaceful home, in family affections, in a simple life without ambition—things that fortune cannot bring and often takes away.

HELENA MORLEY

Rio, September 1942

Letter from Georges Bernanos to the Author

Pax Hotel
Praia do Russell, 108
Rio de Janeiro, May 30th, 1945

Madame:

I was very touched by your thoughtfulness in sending me your book, although I believe you already know how much I admire and love it.

You have written one of those books, so rare in any literature, that owe nothing to either experience or talent, but everything to *ingenium*, to genius—for we should not be afraid of that much misused word—to genius drawn from its very source, to the genius of adolescence. Because these recollections of a simple little girl of Minas present the same problem as the dazzling poems of Rimbaud. As vastly different as they may appear to the stupid, we know that they are both of them derived from the same mysterious and magical fountain—of life and of art.

It is possible that you do not even know the value of what you have given us. As for me, who feels it so deeply, I would not know how to define it.

You have made us see and love everything that you saw and loved yourself in those days, and every time I close your book I am more than ever convinced that its secret will always escape me. But what does that matter? It is deeply moving to realize that the little girl that you were and the little universe in which she lived will never die.

Please accept my homage.

G. Bernanos

THE DIARY OF "HELENA MORLEY"

Thursday, January 5th

Today is the best day of the week.

On Thursdays [school holiday] mama wakes us up at daybreak and we tidy up the house and leave very early for the Beco do Moinho [Mill Lane]. We go down the lane, which is very narrow, and come out on the bridge. It's the best spot in Diamantina and it's always deserted. We never meet anyone there; that's why mama chose it.

Mama sends for Emídio from the *chácara*,* and puts the big tin basin of laundry on top of his head and the ball of soft soap on top of that. Renato takes pots and pans and things to eat in the little cart and we start off. Mama, Luizinha, and I go down under the bridge to wash the clothes. Emídio goes to look for fire-

* See p. XXXV

wood. Renato fishes for *lambaris;** I never saw as many as there are there. He just has to put on the bait, drop in the hook, and he immediately pulls out either a *lambari* or a shad. Nhonhô spreads birdlime on a twig and stays a little way off watching for birds. When he catches one he runs out and cleans off the poor little thing's feet with oil and puts it in the cage. Then he puts more birdlime on the twigs and after a little while another bird arrives, a linnet, or a sparrow.

We wash the clothes and spread them out to bleach and then mama makes our lunch, *tutu*† with rice and pork cracklings.

After we've finished washing the clothes and eating our lunch, mama keeps a lookout on the road to see if anyone is coming and we go in the river to take baths and wash our hair.

After that we beat the clothes on the stones and rinse them and hang them on the bushes to dry. Then we can go to look for berries and birds' nests and cocoons, and little round stones to play jackstones with.

When we go home Renato fills the cart with firewood and puts the pots and pans on top, and Emídio takes another bundle of wood on his head, on top of the basin with the clothes folded up in it.

Now that the mines aren't producing diamonds any bigger than a mosquito's eye, what a big saving it would make for mama if we could go to the bridge every day, because Renato and Nhonhô sell everything they bring back on the same day. Or if only we could stay at the mine with papa, mama wouldn't have to work so hard. But our educations are such a burden to mama that it kills me to think of it. It's wonderful that Renato will be finishing his exams the day after tomorrow and we can go to Boa Vista for our vacation.‡

* *Lambaris*: tiny fish.
† Small balls of black beans.
‡ Where the father is mining, six or seven miles away. They go on foot.

Tuesday, January 10th

Today Benvinda came with her sister to tell mama and papa of her approaching marriage to a boy from Serro* who was a soldier and was discharged because he had to have a leg cut off. We enjoyed the way she told us the story of her fiancé without a leg very much. She said, "Dona Carolina, I've come to inform you and Seu Alexandre that I'm getting married." Mama said, "I'm delighted. Is he a good boy? Do you know him well?" She said, "He's good, but I don't know him very well, because he comes from Serro, not from around here." Mama asked her, "What does he do?" She said, "I don't know. I know he used to be a soldier and he was discharged." Mama: "Discharged for what?" Benvinda: "Because he got a defect." Mama asked where the defect was. Benvinda answered, "In his foot, that is, not exactly in his foot, in his leg." Then her sister said, "Say it, Benvinda! He's only got one leg!" Mama: "Oh, the poor boy! But then he can't walk, can he?" Benvinda said, "Oh yes, Senhora, he can walk. He goes on crutches." Mama said, "But do you know how he's going to make a living, without a leg?" Benvinda replied, "No, I hadn't thought of that, but we'll live the way people always live, somehow or other. God will help us."

Saturday, January 21st

When I am envious of other people's good fortune, mama and grandma say, "God knows who's fortunate." Here in Boa Vista I've learned to believe it. I've already told grandma that she's almost always right about everything she says.

The thing that all of us, the boys and girls of Boa Vista, like to do best is, after we've had dinner and papa and Uncle Joãozinho have dismissed the workmen, to climb up and down the waste of the mine in our bare feet, in the mud, looking for little dia-

* "Mountain": a town forty miles from Diamantina.

monds and flakes of gold, because my uncle will buy them all. We hardly ever find a diamond but we always find flakes of gold.

We were all, all the children, going from one side to the other with our eyes fixed on the waste. Arinda was with us. All of a sudden she screamed and bent down and picked up a really big diamond. We all ran to the house to get papa and my uncle. He looked at it and said to papa, "Look, Alexandre, what a beautiful stone!" and gave Arinda five brand-new hundred *mil reis* notes. She ran off to her father's cabin with all of us after her. Her father, her mother and everyone was crazy with joy. Her father folded up the bills and put them in his pocket, took them out again and looked at them, and put them back again.

It made me sad to see the poor man and I decided it was really best that Arinda had found the diamond. There is nothing in her house but a cowhide for them all to sleep on, *coitados.**

Her father said that he was going to make more money with the five hundred *mil reis*; he was going to invest it in a mine in a place he knows is going to produce diamonds. I was sad when I got home and told this and papa said to my uncle, "That poor fool! I know where he's going to bury that money; it's in that hill at Bom Sucesso where we've mined already."

Arinda didn't even get a penny but she didn't care.

Monday, January 23rd

Yesterday I had a terrible scare. They're saying in Boa Vista that there's a very dangerous thief in the neighborhood who's already been in Diamantina and the soldiers couldn't catch him. He kills people in order to rob them and when the soldiers come, if he's in a house, he turns himself into a broom or a chair or something; if he's outdoors he turns into an ant-hill.† Everybody's terri-

---

* *Coitados:* "poor thing." A much-used word in Portuguese, always with an inflection of sympathy or tenderness. Diminutive: *coitadinho.*
† In this section of Brazil the landscape is frequently strewn with ant-hills which may be three, four, or even five feet high. They are so hard that sometimes they are sawed off, hollowed out, and used as stoves.

fied. Last night papa was at Uncle Joãozinho's on the other side
of the ravine, and we were all asleep, when a dog barked. Mama
ran to the door of our cabin and began to shriek, "Joãozinho! Cap-
tain Gasparino! Seu João Roberto!" We all woke up and ran to
the door to see what it was. She screamed at Renato, "Run to
Joãozinho's house and call the sheriff and the soldiers there!" She
screamed this. Our mouths fell open; we thought she'd gone
crazy. Then she whispered, "Shut your mouths and I'll explain."
And she told us that the man who turns into an ant-hill was close
by, because the dog had barked, and she was afraid he was after
my father to try to get diamonds. She screamed those names
loudly so that the thief would think those men were at
Uncle Joãozinho's house and run away. Papa arrived a little later
and he thought that mama's idea was very funny.

Wednesday, February 15th

Thank God Carnival is over. I can't say that it was very pleasant,
because grandma beat me, something she never does.

It's my fate that everyone who loves me makes my life miserable. The only people who have any authority over my cousins
are their fathers. Oh! If only it were like that with me! My
father is the person who annoys me least of all. If it hadn't been
for grandma's and Aunt Madge's interfering I'd have gone to the
masquerade ball at the theatre. Since the age of seven I've dreamed
of being twelve so that I could go to the ball. And now I'm almost
thirteen and I'm beaten for not going!

Aunt Quequeta was the one who made me want to go to the
ball, telling me about what they used to do in her day. A friend
of hers put on a masquerade costume, disguised her voice, and
flirted with her father all evening until he fell madly in love with
her and the next day instead of coming in to lunch he kept walking around in the garden with his head hanging down, thinking of
the masked woman. Another friend of hers let her husband go to
the ball first and she went later, masked, flirted with him, and he

fell madly in love with her, to such a degree that he kept sighing
the whole evening.

My aunts still have the hoopskirts they used to wear. How I
wish they still wore them! They don't wear anything like that now,
but I'd like to go like that even so.

It was Glorinha who gave me such a swelled head that I thought
I could go. I asked mama and she said, "If your grandmother will
let you I'll let you." I asked grandma, "Grandma, mama will let
me go. Will you let me go to the ball with Glorinha?" She said, "I
certainly will not!" I stamped my foot hard and I ran and threw
myself on her bed, crying. She came in and took off her slipper
and hit me twice, saying, "That'll give you something to cry
about!" I thrashed my legs around but I didn't get up.

But it was worth it because today I got the material for a dress
and a silver two-*mil-reis* piece.

Saturday, February 18th

It's three days today since I started going to School.* I've bought
my books and I'm going to begin a new life. The Portuguese
teacher advised all the girls to form the habit of writing something
every day, a letter or whatever happens to them.

I went to see my English aunts and there I met Marianna. She
was my school's most famous pupil and I've always heard my aunt
speak about her with admiration. She encouraged me and she said
that the secret of being a good pupil is to pay attention and take
notes on everything.

Aunt Madge said that my old teacher, Dona Joaquininha, told
her that I was the most intelligent pupil in her school, but that I
was lazy and I missed several days. That's true, because last year we
went to visit papa in Boa Vista a good many times. I don't know
whether I'm intelligent or not. Grandma, papa, and Aunt Madge
think so; but I only know that I don't like to study and sit still and

* The "Normal School," for training grade-school teachers. Equivalent to high
school in the United States.

pay attention. But anyway, I like to have them say I'm intelligent. It's better than if they said I was stupid, which is what I'm afraid they're going to say when they see I'm not going to be what they hope for, in Normal School. Today I saw what's going to happen. Everything seemed very difficult and complicated. But what I can do easily is learn by heart. Even if I can't understand it, I memorize everything. But how am I going to memorize anything in the Portuguese lessons? Logical Analysis—where can I study that? Well, in a few days I'll know how things are going to turn out. It isn't going to be hard for me to write, because papa has been making me write almost every day. There are two things I like to do, to write and to read stories when I can find any. As far as stories and novels are concerned, papa has already put them away. He says that now they're only for vacations.

I'm going to go to bed and ask Our Lady to help me study and make me more intelligent, so I won't disappoint my father, grandma, and Aunt Madge.

Sunday, February 19th

Siá Ritinha, the chicken thief from Cavalhada,* spent the whole evening here in the house, telling stories about people who got sick from eating cucumbers, and she finished by saying, "Dona Carolina, you mark my words. The cucumber is so poisonous that if it so much as touches the hem of your skirt, it's dangerous."

During the whole conversation I kept expecting mama to tell her that I won't eat porridge but that I eat two cucumbers with salt every morning. Mama said to me: "Do you hear what she's saying? Are you listening?" I wanted to ask Dona Ritinha, "And isn't it dangerous to steal your neighbor's chickens?"

---

* The Cavalhada is a large open square in Diamantina. Burton explains the name: "These clear spaces were so called from the Portuguese carousels, which, like bull-fights, once accompanied every festivity." H of B, Vol. II, p. 96.

Thursday, February 23rd

Leontino came to invite us to attend the inauguration of the telegraph they are putting in his house, and he said that Aunt Aurélia was waiting for mama and all the family with *acarajés*,* biscuits, and chocolates. We all went, Dindinha, too. Half of the people sat in the parlor and the other half in the dining-room at the end of the hallway, which is very long. Those in the parlor sent a telegram to those in the dining-room, and the answer was written in dashes that the pen made on a strip of paper that Sérgio read out loud, and it was perfectly right. Dindinha, mama and my aunts were open-mouthed to see how the messages were correct, the way the telegraph does it. We ate a lot of *acarajés*. Then there was a nice table with coffee, biscuits and chocolates, and the aunts left talking about how intelligent those children are. Aunt Aurélia does so many nice things, because she knows that everyone admires her children and is jealous of them. Mama herself would give her life to have us like Aunt Aurélia's children, who just live to study. But she's already convinced herself that everything Aunt Aurélia's children do better than we do is because their father is a shopkeeper and can keep his eye on them. Since our father lives off at the mine, and mama's always wanting to go there after him, we'll just have to be the way we are.

Saturday, February 25th

Today I had the greatest surprise of my life. Every Saturday grandma sends one of my brothers to the Bishop's Palace, which is near her house, to change a bill into the Bishop's *barrusques*.†

---

* *Acarajés*: small fried cakes of ground black-eyed peas, garlic, and red pepper.
† Note in M V d M: "Scrip issued by the tradesmen, manufacturers, and charitable institutions, to make up, it was said, for the shortage of money in circulation, and which was used like money. The Bishop's *barrusques* were issued by the charity fund of the diocese and given out by him. The name of this scrip came from a French financier, Barrusque, who introduced it into Diamantina."

She puts all the *barrusques* into a pasteboard box and sits in the dining-room, waiting for her poor women. She gives a new two-hundred-*reis barrusque* to each one. Her poor women are: Chichi Bombom, Frutuosa Pau de Sebo, Teresa Doida, Aninha Tico-Tico, Carlota Pistola, Teresa Buscapé, Eufrasia Boa Ventura, Maria Pipoca and Siá Fortunata.* Those are the ones who come in and sit down with grandma in the dining room and tell her their troubles. There are others, too, who stay out in the hall and at the street door. Grandma says to give to the poor is to lend to God. By now grandma should have treasure stored up in heaven, she lends so much!

I always stay right there listening to their complaints, pretending to do my lessons at the table, because I think it's very funny when they quarrel and try to get two *barrusques* instead of one. Today after grandma had given the others one *barrusque* each she took out two and gave them to Siá Fortunata, Bertolino's mother. Siá Fortunata said, "Give it to the others, Dona Teodora; I just came to pay you a visit today. I don't need any more, God be thanked. In a little while I'll be able to give alms myself." Grandma asked her, "Did you win in the lottery, Fortunata?" She said, "It's just the same as if I had, Dona Teodora. My son, God be thanked, has found a protector." Grandma didn't say anything, and she gave the *barrusques* to the others.

When they went out grandma exclaimed,† "I never in my born days!" and called Dindinha, "Oh! Chiquinha, come here! I'm so dumfounded I can't even get up!" When I realized something had happened I kept my ears open but I pretended not to listen because grandma doesn't like to talk about things when we're around. She said, "Is it really true, Chiquinha, what they've been

---

* Chichi Bombom, Fruity Greased Pole, Teresa Crazy, Annie Sparrow, Charlotte Pistol, Teresa Firecracker, Eufrasia Good Luck, Maria Popcorn, and Siá Fortunate.
† *"Forte coisa!"* This is the grandmother's favorite exclamation, literally "Strong thing," or "Fine thing!"

saying recently?" And she told Dindinha what Fortunata had said and added, "What an idiot, to talk that way! As if the police weren't here for such things!" At that point I asked her, "Grandma, tell me why you're so surprised. I'm so curious." She said, "It isn't suitable for children. Do your lessons." Burning with curiosity, I asked her again, for the love of God, to tell me. Then she told me, "Haven't you heard them speak about the business of the three boys they caught a little while ago with forged money? And when the warrant for their arrest came two of them escaped in the middle of the night, and one of them, named Floriano, killed himself? They say that Bertolino took the two who got away to a *fazenda* in Mata do Rio, and he got a lot of the forged money. They say he passed off the money on the way there and that he brought some to pass off here in the market to the drovers, *coitados*. There's so much gossip about I didn't believe it. But now his own mother is saying it, and we'll have to believe it." And she turned to Dindinha and said, "Now you must be careful and not accept any new bills."

Tuesday, February 28th

Today was the first time I saw the Holy Eucharist go into grandma's house.

It's sad to see the Eucharist going into other houses. But at the *chácara* it was almost like a party, although I did feel sorry for Andreza.

Some people receive the Eucharist without even cleaning house; I've seen it in other houses. But grandma receives it like a procession. She ordered a quantity of sand and coffee leaves for the street outside the house. She prepared the altar, lit the candles, and looked overjoyed to see the Eucharist coming into her house.

I was very sorry for Andreza who was very upset at receiving Communion in bed. She wanted to wait until she was better, to go and take Communion in church, but grandma didn't want her to.

Renato and Nestor* held up the cassock. Seu Broa [corn cake] didn't want to give them the candelabrum, he carried it himself.

The priest always brings the sacrament to grandma in the *chácara* even when she isn't sick, but it comes from the Church of the Rosário. This time it came from the Cathedral.

Saturday, March 4th

I arrive at the *chácara*, look for grandma, and find her sitting in the garden watching the Negro women make tallow candles.

"Your blessing, grandma!"

"God bless you, child. I was just looking at that bunch of ripe *araçás*† and wondering how you ever happened to leave them there to get so ripe."

"It's because the day before yesterday I just came at night and yesterday I couldn't come."

"So that's it. Did you have dinner with your Aunt Madge yesterday? I like you to do that. You can only benefit from the society of your Aunt Madge. What did she teach you yesterday?"

"So many things!"

"Tell me some of them."

"In the daytime she gives me lessons in manners and at night lessons in how to be economical."

"How's that? Tell me."

"She's always taking the opportunity of telling me about other people's bad manners and I see it's just in order to teach me. She talked about people who spit on the floor, scratch their heads in the parlor and interrupt other people when they're talking. She said that at dinner people shouldn't push their plates out of the way. We should drink the soup and sit there enduring it with the plates in front of us until the maid takes them away. And one shouldn't pick one's teeth at the table."

* A Negro boy at the grandmother's house.
† *Araçá*: small fruit of the guava family.

"You learn such a lot when you're with her! Now you must practise it."

"But grandma, how can I when I take my own plate off the stove and afterwards I wash it myself?"

"Well, when you grow up you can."

"By that time I'll have forgotten everything."

"And what about being economical?" grandma asked. "What did she teach you?"

"It's simply incredible! Not even Seu Herculano can beat Aunt Madge at being economical. She talked a lot about changing one's shoes before going out in the garden, and not sleeping in one's clothes and everything. But the best thing was about saving matches. She was going to take me home and before we left she called me into the pantry, took the lamp, put in a drop of kerosene, and said, 'If I put any more in it, Marciana leaves the lamp going as long as there's kerosene. So I put in just a little and she goes to sleep, and this lasts long enough.' Then she opened the box of matches and took out three and put them in a little box and said, 'If I put in one it might not light, and two might not light, either, but it wouldn't be possible for all three not to, so I leave three.' Then she locked up the pantry and we came home, talking all the way."

Grandma said, "See what an extraordinary woman your aunt is! That's how she lives so well on eighty *mil reis* from the school, runs the house, and supports her sisters, and you see how she keeps inviting people to dinner, too. That's her secret, child. Notice everything. Learn from her."

Thursday, March 9th

Papa thought it was funny when I said I was jealous of Luizinha's going out in the street with a handkerchief tied around her face.

I don't want to have a toothache because I see everyone crying

so much with it that I think it must be very painful. When
Naninha has a toothache she drives the whole house crazy. Aunt
Agostinha shuts herself up and prays and makes vows, for fear
that Naninha is going crazy. She screams and rolls on the floor
and beats her head against the walls until people think she's a lunatic from the asylum. The other day she screamed so loudly that
people came in from the street to help her; she cursed them all and
went and rolled in the garden.

Nobody knows what to do to make a toothache better. Since
what happened to Dona Augusta's daughter no one thinks of pulling the tooth out. For days she screamed with a toothache. Her
father got very discouraged and called the dentist to pull it out.
He pulled it and the poor little one was only better for a little
while and then she died a horrible death. She grew stiff all over,
her teeth locked, and her head bent backwards until she died.

Luizinha had such a bad toothache this week that she was
screaming with it. Mama made her wash her mouth with salt and
water, then she put snuff on the tooth, and then creosote, but
nothing helped. It was Siá Ritinha who cured it, in a strange way.
She gave her a physic, castor oil, and the next day her face swelled
up and she didn't cry any more. Today she wanted to go out on the
street without the handkerchief around her face but mama was
horrified at the very idea, for fear her face would harden that
way.* I think that's why Seu Cula's Belinha lives her whole life
with a handkerchief tied around her face. Today I wanted to go
out on the street with a handkerchief tied around my face the way
I see other people doing, but mama wouldn't let me.

Saturday, March 11th

We have lots of uncles and we call some of our older cousins
"uncle," too. Today papa said to mama, "We should go to visit
Henrique and Julião, we haven't seen them for so long." They are

* They believed that if the swollen cheek got chilled it would harden.

two old men who live a long way from our house. I liked the idea because it was a long time since I'd gone anywhere with papa. He said, "Let's go to see Julião first, and then Henrique." They both used to have money but they spent it all, and now they live very poorly. Uncle Henrique is mama's uncle and he's over eighty years old. Uncle Julião isn't so old and he's a distant cousin of mama's. First of all we went to his house. He told some very funny stories about the stupidity of Seu João Laurenço and also a story about a thunderbolt. The story about the thunderbolt came up because a storm was threatening and I was very afraid. He said that a man named Carneiro was in a store in Amparo Street one rainy day. Every time there was a flash of lightning the storekeeper said, "Saint Jerônimo! Saint Barbara!" This man named Carneiro began to make fun of him and the storekeeper said, "God punishes him who mocks." Carneiro said, "If God can do it, let's see Him." He had scarcely finished speaking when a thunderbolt came down and struck him dead.

From there we went to Uncle Henrique's house. This uncle is the queerest member of the family. He always keeps three things on his parlor table, without fail: a little keg of *cachaça,** another of cucumbers, onions and string-beans all cut up, and a plate of cracklings, which are marvellous. He spends the whole day sitting beside the table drinking and eating these things. When my father tried to advise him to drink less, because it's bad for him, he said, "What! Alexandre, I've been drinking since I was a boy and I am eighty-two years old; people who drink only orange-flower water will go before I do." My father said that that was the truth and he remembered that Uncle Henrique's brother-in-law, a much younger man, had died during the past year. Uncle Henrique said, "No. That isn't a good example. He was seventy. His time had come."

Aren't these uncles funny?

It was very dark by the time we got home.

---

* Cachaça: colorless, fiery liquor made from sugar-cane.

This year the Ash Wednesday procession, that hadn't taken place for many years, went through the streets. I don't know why they hadn't held such an important procession, with so many saints. There are so many saints that not even grandma or my aunts know them all. They say that they didn't parade for so long because some of the saints are missing and a lot have got broken. Seu Broa was saying to Uncle Joãozinho that at the Church of the Luz they'd had to put the head of one on the body of another, and ask around at the other churches in order to be able to send the procession on the streets. Saint Domingos went out with the cheese and the knife, and at grandma's they explained to me that one can tell if a couple is happy or not if the wife is able to cut the cheese exactly in the middle. But I don't believe that Saint Domingos really carries the cheese to make tests like that, and nobody could give me any explanation why Saint José has the Child Jesus on his arm and a ball in his hand. Grandma's Negroes used to tell me that the ball was the world, and if it fell to the ground the world would be destroyed. When I was little I used to believe it, but now I know that's silly. The snake was wound around Eve's body and she had an apple in her hand. Saint Roque had a big beard. Everybody said they'd never seen Saint Roque with a beard before. Seu Broa said that in the sacristy of the Luz, in the confusion of starting the procession they had got some of the heads mixed up. The penitents went behind the saints, beating their backs with whips, but the whips were made of straw. I liked the procession very much but my father said it looked like a carnival, and mama thought it was a bad sin of my father to say that.

The mysterious burglar is the talk of the town; at grandma's *chácara* they don't speak about anything else. They say that he disappeared but now he's come back again and that he's robbed lots of houses and stores and nobody has been able to catch him. When they try to take hold of him he can turn into anything he wants to. Today Emídio and José Pedro arrived at the *chácara* terrified, talking about the thief's exploits. He broke into a store in Rio Grande Street and stole a lot. The owner arrived while he was filling his bag and whistled. The people of Rio Grande Street, who had already been warned, rushed into the street to help catch the thief. He ran away with the people after him. When he got near the Church of the Glória, and they'd almost caught him, he turned into an ant-hill. Emídio and José Pedro told us about it, scared to death.

I'm doubtful about this story, because if they saw the man turn into an ant-hill they could have taken the ant-hill and locked it up in jail and it would have to turn back into a man again. I don't believe this story about a man turning into an ant-hill or a tree-trunk or anything else. But just the same he frightens us terribly. Every day there are reports that he has broken into a house or a store. We'll all sleep easier when this mysterious thief is caught.

Thursday, March 23rd

I've noticed that the conversation of grown-ups is always the same. Papa, when he isn't talking about the mining he's doing, and the great expectations he has of it, tells stories about Seu Lage, or Seu Agostinho Machado, or about the Englishmen who used to come to see my grandfather. They're always the same stories, all the time.

Uncle Conrado tells a story abut a wood-cutter who found a stone in Mata dos Crioulos and the man with him said it was a diamond. Because it was very big to be a diamond, the wood-cutter hit it with his axe to prove that it wasn't and it jumped a long way, leaving a splinter. The man brought the splinter to Diamantina and it turned out to be a real diamond. He took

Uncle Conrado to the place to show him the stone and they looked until they were tired but they could never find the stone again.

When he isn't telling this, or other stories we already know, Uncle Conrado keeps talking about the ages of my father and my aunts. Once when I was having lunch there, he said, "Your father must be over fifty. When I was a boy I used to buy pomade for my hair in the English Doctor's shop, there at the top of Direita Street,* and your father was the clerk. I was a school-boy and he was already shaving, and your Aunt Madge used to come in and she was already old enough to get married."

When I told papa he said, "That's one of Conrado's stories. When I used to help in my father's pharmacy he was already a diamond-buyer. He used to go around the mines buying diamonds for his brother-in-law, João de Mata. He used to come on horseback, tie up the horse at the door, and I was so in awe of him that I always gave him more pomade than the other clerks did. He was always a good five years older than I was."

I told Uncle Conrado this and he said that that was one of my father's stories; that when he was a diamond-buyer my father was already a grown man and was mining at Saint Gonçalo. Papa insists that Uncle Conrado is older. And they both stick to it.

I think they're funny to be so stubborn, each one wanting to be younger than the other. I feel just the opposite way; I'd rather be older than I am.

Palm Sunday, March 26th

Aunt Carlota bought a cow with a calf, to sell milk, and mama became one of her customers. Mornings she sends the milk to our house by the maid's little girl, Maria, a very smart little nigger. Everybody began to notice that the milk had a lot of water in it. Today mama said to the little girl, "Maria, tell Carlota that the

* Burton: " 'Straight Street' is exceedingly crooked, steep, and badly paved." *Op cit.*, p. 95.

milk is getting very watery. She should give more corn or beans to the cow to make the milk richer." The little girl said, "Watery? That cow's milk is so strong that Siá Carlota has to put water in it every day, to thin it."

Holy Thursday, March 30th

During Holy Week my family takes advantage of the children's not having to go to school to get together at the *chácara.*

Yesterday, Ash Wednesday, Iaiá Henriqueta read the Passion of Christ out loud while we all listened. Because it was a codfish day, grandma had three bottles of port wine opened for dinner. We all ate and drank until we were full; Aunt Carlota drank more than all the rest of us and her eyes got very tiny and her nose as red as sealing-wax. After dinner we all went to confession at the Bishop's Palace.

We children are never allowed to confess to Senhor Bishop because he asks lots of questions that we can't understand and my father says it's silly of mama to let us confess to a man already in his dotage. He's very old. Since there are lots of priests at the Palace, mama picked out Father Florencio for us. He is very nice and gives very small penances, but we leave the confessional worn out with all the stories of the lives of the saints that he takes the opportunity of telling, and advises us to imitate. As if it were up to us. I decide for myself; I admire good and holy people but I can't possibly stop being the way I am.

Aunt Carlota went to the Bishop to confess. He won't let anyone tell his own sins, he likes to ask them himself. Aunt Carlota said that she was feeling very dizzy and she would like to have the Senhor Bishop ask her so she'd only have to reply. He began:

"Do you ever speak evil of others?"

She answered, "Often, Senhor Bishop."

"Do you miss Mass on Sundays?"

"Often, Senhor Bishop."

"Do you wish harm to others?"

"Often."

"Do you steal?"

"Often."

Then he said, "You are very drunk. Go home and sober up and then come back again."

We were all helpless with laughter when Aunt Carlota told us the story of her confession.

Easter Sunday, April 2nd

Ever since Chininha came to spend her vacation at the *chácara*, pretending to be a saint all the time just to please grandma, my life has been a hell. At evening prayers I get so mad at her and hate her so much that I always have to confess it as a sin when I go to confession. When our mothers call us to come and pray, even if we're at the most exciting moment in a game, she's the first to run and fall on her knees at the *oratório*.* She rolls up her eyes at Our Lady, folds her hands, and puts on such a sanctimonious expression that anyone could tell she's just pretending. I'm getting pretty sick of her.

When she came from Montes Claros to enter the convent school, she was so badly brought up that mama wouldn't let me play with her alone. But with one year of school she's turned into such a saint that the aunts talk about nothing but the change in her and when anyone praises her she gets more hateful than ever.

At school she's got used to kneeling a great deal, and now evening prayers are a torture for all of us cousins. After we've said the rosary and a lot of prayers, she always has the idea of going on praying for the souls of relatives who were dead long ago. I told her I didn't believe that prayers were really of any use in getting souls out of purgatory and that she only did it to make up to grandma. She went and told on me and grandma said she was surprised at my saying such things. Then I said, "Grandma, grandpa and my uncles and those people have been dead so long! If they've

* *Oratório*: any small chapel, altar, niche containing a statue of a saint, etc.

been in purgatory all this time they must be used to it, and we aren't going to help by praying on our knees all that time, the way Chininha wants to." Grandma said that no one ever gets used to purgatory; that Chininha was learning to be a saint with the nuns, and that I only want to run around and play.

I never spent such a disgusting day in my life as Good Friday. Chininha pretended she was sad about the death of Jesus Christ and she went to read the Passion of Christ out loud to grandma, the way they do at school, and we all had to sit and listen to her. Everybody knows that I am no saint, but when I'm in a group with others just like me, nobody notices. And now comes all this horrible pretending so the aunts will notice her. But grandma, thank God, doesn't let anyone speak against me to her very much.

Good Friday was a fast day for everyone in the house. I'm very unhappy about making sacrifices. I don't like to make sacrifices. But when I know I have to, I can fast. In the morning, at seven o'clock we take a cup of weak coffee which amounts to nothing at all. At ten o'clock we have lunch: codfish with pumpkin, black beans and mush; things we only eat to make us hungrier. During the day we have the same very weak coffee. Dinner at four o'clock and nothing more.

If Dindinha hadn't had a big kettle of green corn cooked for dinner, I think I could have fasted until the end. But the devil got into the kettle of corn and tempted me. I immediately planned to do something wicked. I thought, "I'm going to eat one ear, secretly, and afterwards I'll confess it to the priest." I took out the ear and went to eat it behind the Church of the Rosário. Chininha missed me and followed me, and then she went running to tell grandma that I'd lost my indulgences. She told her tales, but she got disappointed because grandma said, "Poor child, she was hungry. It doesn't matter, Chininha, she'll earn the indulgences some other time."

When I learned about it I had my revenge because I ate two more ears while she watched me, dying with envy. Hurray!

Friday, April 7th

Every Thursday Maria gives Didico to Luizinha and me for the whole day. We do our work, go walking, and do everything with him. He is sitting up already and is sweet enough to eat. I think I love this baby so much not because he's so cunning but because his father and mother are crazy. But only when people aren't around; when they're with us they speak so nicely that we even can't believe the things they do. Rodrigo goes home again and begins to fight and they keep on fighting until he goes out and she throws anything breakable she can find at his back.

She breaks every single thing in the house made of crockery or china on his back. I was awfully sorry yesterday when she threw the water jug at him; the water soaked him and the jug broke in the street. He didn't even turn around; he went out all wet, without saying a word.

When I am there holding Didico and he comes in, I run out. Now that I've seen one of their fights I don't want to see any more.

But Maria Flora is good; she loans us the baby for the whole day and we can take care of him just as if he were our little boy. We divide it between us: I give him a bath in the morning, Luizinha in the afternoon; I give him his porridge in the morning, she gives him his lunch; I feed him in the afternoon, she gives him dinner. At night we sing him to sleep and we carry him home and put him in his little bed.

Early today Luizinha was already waiting for them to open the door to take the baby, then we went to grandma's. It was the day for picking the coffee.

Nico and Renato have made up a game to play there now that's simply heavenly. They took a cow-hide up on the bank behind the *chácara*. One of them pulled the other on the cow-hide until it got smooth enough to slide down the bank and now it's so slippery that we can slide down it beautifully. None of the grown-ups have discovered it because if they knew about it they'd put a stop to it immediately. We say we are going to pick coffee and we take the basket, but we found out how we could steal the coffee that's already been picked and bring it back all over again, and then we go to the bank to slide.

Today I realized that there just couldn't be another baby as good as Didico. I and Luizinha decided to take the poor little thing to slide with us. I don't know how it happened; the baby rolled off in front of us and fell on an ants' nest. We went rolling after him, and the hide stopped on the way. We both of us fell into the ants' nest, too, and almost squashed the poor baby. We just missed mashing him because he had landed in a bunch of long grass. When we managed to get up and pull him out, he was a sight, *coitadinho;* covered with blisters and with big-belly ants sticking to him all over his little body. But he is such a good baby that he even cries quietly. We hadn't thought about getting back up and God must have helped us climb back up that bank carrying the baby.

We spent a dreadful day, bathing his blisters with salt water for fear that someone would see them and Maria Flora wouldn't let us take care of Didico any more. But fortunately by evening there wasn't a mark on his body.

Sunday, April 9th

I've seen many things in my life, but today was the first time I ever saw a tattle-tale priest.

I was in the doorway when I saw Father Augusto coming down from the Palace and coming towards grandma's. Because I know how much grandma likes priests I ran to meet him and kiss his hand. I took him into the parlor, happy about the pleasure it was going to give grandma, and never thinking ahead of time about what he'd come to do. I went to get grandma. We went into the parlor with her holding onto her cane on one side and my arm on the other, very proud of the visit. Mama, Dindinha, Iaiá, and Aunt Agostinha went to the parlor, too, to talk to the priest.

I left them all there and went back to the back of the house. We take every opportunity we can to go sliding on the bank. I called everybody: Nico, Renato, Nhonhô, Luizinha, and Rita, and we flew to the end of the garden. We had only slid once, we swear, when there were all the grown-ups at the top, watching what we were doing.

Then we guessed what had happened. Iaiá screamed to Quintiliano,* but because he's old and can't climb down the bank, Nico and Renato had to climb up with the hide. It takes just a minute to slide down, but it's hard to go back up. If it hadn't been for that the rest of us wouldn't have gone back through the house. But someone always wants to spoil our fun.

Quintiliano rolled up the cow-hide and took it away and Dindinha told him to keep it locked up in the harness-room.

Grandma scolded a lot and said it was a shame to see Father Augusto, so kind and good, leaving his duties to come and warn her that if she didn't watch out one of us might be drowned in the stream that runs down below, in back of the *chácara*.

We explained how the thing worked, but it wasn't any use; they didn't want to believe us. I said to grandma, "Father Augusto didn't come out of kindness, no, grandma. He came to tell tales. His tongue itched and he came; that's what happened."

And that's how we lost the best game we've ever discovered.

Wednesday, April 12th

Today I came home, threw my books on the table, and ran to the kitchen. Mama had saved coffee and *couscous* for me. I was drinking my coffee when I remembered to ask mama if she had collected the eggs from my hens. She said, "I got the yellow hen's egg, but the speckled hen hasn't been on the nest yet. I'm afraid they've stolen her." I dropped the coffee bowl and ran. Mama called, "Wait a minute. Don't do anything foolish!" But I rushed

* Apparently a Negro gardener.

out blind with rage. That hen is the best one I've ever had in my life. She lays a lot of eggs without ever getting broody. With her eggs I've already bought a pair of stockings and a tooth-brush, and I've eaten a lot, too. Now she's starting to lay again, but she'd only laid two eggs. It was Dona Gabriela who gave me this hen. And it was the one that was stolen!

In Cavalhada everybody says that Siá Ritinha steals hens to make dinner for the commander of the barracks, who boards with her. I went out blind with rage, and I wished I had the courage to tell it all to her face. But mama called after me, "Think, child! For the love of God, think what you're doing! Those women are dangerous!" So I decided to keep calm and to ask questions without showing too much how angry I was. I went to her house and only Américo was there, in the doorway. I asked him, "Américo, have you seen my speckled hen? She hasn't come home yet and I know she was going to lay an egg." He said he hadn't seen her. I said, "Mama's afraid she's been stolen. Who could be a chicken-thief, here in Cavalhada, is what I'd like to know. If anybody, man or woman, stole that hen I'm going to put a curse on them, and I have faith in God that He will hear me and that the thief will suffer in this life, beside the punishment he'll have to undergo in hell. I have faith in God."

That's what I was saying to Américo at the door when Inhá came to the window and asked me, "Do you mean all these things you're saying to Américo for us, by any chance? Do you think we stole your hen?" I answered, "I was speaking for the benefit of the thief who stole my hen. If the shoe fits, put it on." I left and came home. Mama said, "Now you'll see, we won't be able to keep a single hen after today."

Monday, April 17th

Ever since I was little I've been hearing my father say, "I must teach this girl English. She's a perfect little English girl, but she can't be one without knowing the language." He only talked about it and then he went off to the mine and forgot all about it. Now that he's teaching English at the high school he said to me, "Let's begin classes Monday." Today was Monday and I presented myself for my lesson.

My father thinks that I have unequalled intelligence. No one can even speak of anyone else's intelligence when he's around without his coming out with the same remark: "Daughter, if you'd just settle down and study one hour every day, I'd like to see the person who could get ahead of you." I listen to this the same way I listen when they say I'm pretty, because I know the story of the owl.* But today I felt I disappointed him and I feel sad about it. What makes my father go on thinking such nonsense? I've never given him the slightest proof of intelligence. I've only received two prizes at school. Just in music and gymnastics. Why does he keep on thinking I'm intelligent? It serves him right!

Today he began by saying that English is easier than Portuguese because the verbs aren't complicated the way they are in Portuguese; there are very few rules, and everything depends on the pronunciation, and I must have inherited that. We were going to begin by reading a book. He read first. I didn't understand a thing and he said that didn't matter and told me to repeat it. I couldn't. He read it a second time and told me to say that T H E the way he wanted. I said it about ten times and he kept saying it wasn't right. I saw it was impossible to get it right and I told him I didn't want to learn English any more; he says it's easier than Portuguese, and maybe it is for other heads, but not mine. Mine is very hard; English can't get in.

My father looked at me in amazement and said that we'd try again tomorrow.

Shall I have to go through this every day?

---

* Who thought her children were beautiful (La Fontaine, "L'Aigle et le Hibou").

Thursday, April 20th

The Cunhas are two old women who live shut up in their house
and only go out in the street at nine o'clock at night, to take the
air. They always walk close up against the walls of the houses, one
behind the other. They are old maids and nobody ever sees them
on the streets in the day time. Papa needed some men for the work
he's doing at Bom Sucesso, and he made inquiries and learned that
the Cunhas have two Negroes who used to be their slaves, and they
rent them out to work and divide the money with them, because
that's the only way they can support them. So papa and mama
thought of going to the Cunhas' house, in Bonfim Street, to hire
their Negroes. There they told them that the Negroes were already
hired, and in the middle of the conversation they mentioned that
they had two brothers, named Geraldo and Anacleto, who were
living there at home, too, without working. After they said that the
Negroes were hired, mama hadn't been paying any more attention
to the sisters' conversation, letting papa listen to them alone. But
when she heard them speaking of two unemployed men who were
in the house, mama said, "Then why don't you give us Geraldo
and Anacleto?" The women were shocked, and papa had to explain
that mama was distracted and had thought that their brothers
were Negroes, too.

Saturday, April 22nd

Yesterday was a holiday and when we opened the door Leontino
was already waiting for us to go to spend the day with them at
Prata. I and Luizinha went. I think that place is adorable, the river
is full of waterfalls and the pool is bigger than the Glória in the
Rio Grande.

What encourages us to go to the country on a picnic with
Uncle Conrado and Aunt Aurélia is the quantity of good things
she takes along: cakes, tarts, meat-pies, all the things she makes to

sell. She's a very good pastry-cook, as good as Siá Generosa.* If it weren't for that I wouldn't go. Of what other earthly use is it for us to go with them? We can't go wading at the river's edge. We can't climb trees. We can't go off to look for fruit. We can't do anything.

Uncle Conrado takes fishhooks and bait along and we all have to stay there on the bank of the river, without moving, waiting for catfish that never even nibble.

I'd like to have them spend a day with my father and mother at Rio Grande, just to see what a picnic in the country is like!

From everything they say, I feel sorry for my cousins, with that finicky father. At their house everything is on the dot and according to rule, even manners and words and everything. It's funny— my cousins are shocked at my father's and mother's not bringing us up right, they say, and not even going out without us two, I and Luizinha. But by the afternoon I'm more tired than if I'd been working all day long, pretending all the time I'm as well brought-up as they are.

I don't know whether my cousins are as sorry for me as I am for them. Probably.

I think that God punishes well-brought-up people. I've never seen my uncle bring home even a catfish. My boy cousins hunt for birds and don't even get a sparrow. But when we go to the country, Renato and Nhonhô bring home catfish and shad to eat and sometimes enough to sell, and never let a linnet or any other bird get away. They almost always catch linnets.

I asked Renato if he knew why it is he has such good luck fishing and Uncle Conrado never even catches a catfish and he said, "Certainly. He uses a ball of cotton rolled in manioc paste for a bait. Catfish aren't fools; they want worms. He could spend his whole life with his hook in the water; if he caught anything it would be an accident."

* The grandmother's cook.

Thursday, April 27th

Something happened today at grandma's that had never happened before. A Negro girl named Magna is married to a Negro from Africa named Mainarte. She's very smart. She didn't want him to live in idleness in back of the vegetable garden the way he was living, so she arranged for a little farm in Arraial dos Forros* for the two of them. She works around as a cook, and she makes Mainarte work for other people. He collects manure to sell for gardens; he brings around barrels of water in the mornings and evenings; gets sand in Almotolia† for people to scour their houses with; and gets straw from the drovers to stuff mattresses. And they get along that way.

At the *chácara* they talk all the time about how mean Magna is to poor Mainarte. There's scarcely a day goes by that she doesn't give him a beating. He went to complain to grandma, and asked her to speak to Magna. Grandma spoke to her and she answered, bold as brass, "It was the Senhora herself who made him lazy, in her house, and now she wants me to support a good-for-nothing? Either he works or I'll beat him. I can't stand laziness."

A few days ago at the *chácara* we heard the news that Magna was in jail and Mainarte was in bed, at death's door. She'd beaten him and tried to strangle him. Then grandma said, "I never in my born days!" And she called for Chico Guedes, the one they call the "lawyer," and asked him to get Magna out of jail. He went and made a fuss, and got Magna out. Magna knew it was grandma who had paid to get her out and she went to thank her. Grandma said to her, "You wicked woman, do you want to lose your immortal soul? To try to take the life of the husband God gave you to be your helpmate!" Then she asked her, "Why did you want to kill that poor man who wouldn't hurt a flea?" And Magna answered, "No, Senhora! He's just the kind that dies easy! I only squeezed his throat and he stuck

* Camp of the Freed-Men.
† Oil-pot.

out his tongue in order not to answer me. I didn't mean to kill him, no, Senhora."

Thursday, May 4th

How lucky it is that grandma lives at the *chácara!* The house is so near the Church of the Rosário that Senhor Bishop, seeing how fat and heavy grandma is, gave her permission to hear Mass from her bedroom window, and when she takes Communion the priest carries it over to her.

Yesterday was the day of Santa Cruz. My cousins only go to the party late, but I make the most of it from the time they begin to put up the decorations.

I'm the one who goes to get all the poinsettias and last year I had to make all the little lamps* from orange-skins because there were very few clay ones. This year Seu Claudio's daughters asked for alms and bought a lot of clay ones.

On the day of the Santa Cruz we don't rest a minute. Each one wants to work and help more than anyone else. My brothers help cut and put up the bamboo poles. I and Luizinha gather the poinsettia leaves and coffee leaves. Ivo Arara† lends the sticks and the boards. Seu Claudio's daughters fill the lamps with oil and set them on the shelves. Grandma orders a lot of sand, and I and Luizinha spread it on the floor and strew the coffee leaves over it.

This year Dona Ana Teles, the doctor's wife, came to help Seu Claudio's daughters.

It is a happy day for us. All my uncles and aunts and cousins get together at grandma's. The Negroes make a supper for us, chicken with blood gravy, roast pork, rice and manioc.

There are still a lot of Negroes living at the *chácara* who were slaves in the old days and who didn't want to leave when the law of 13th of May‡ was passed. Grandma supports them all. Tomé

* Usually small clay vessels with wicks, burning raw castor-oil.
† *Arara:* macaw.
‡ Emancipation of the slaves, May 13th, 1888.

was the only one grandma sent away because she says he was a witch and he was doctoring Andreza with a tea made from roots, so that she'd marry him. The Negro women, the ones that don't drink, are very good, and in order to make money they make manioc turn-overs, "dreams," and *acarajés* for the church holidays and to sell at the door of the theatre. Grandma buys lots of these things from them and we eat them all evening long.

The worst day for me is the day after a holiday. Mama's sorry for me because she says I'm never going to be happy in life as long as I keep wanting to enjoy everything; life is made up of suffering. But I'm not going to be so foolish as to make such a wonderful life into a life of suffering.

I can't write any more because papa's complaining about its being time to go to sleep.

Thursday, May 11th

Aunt Agostinha had a birthday and everyone from our house and all the family went to have dinner with her. The parties in Jogo da Bola Street* are very nice because the house is big and long, and it has grass in front where we can run and play.

When the family is all together the children always stay away from the grown-ups; I've tried staying with them once in a while but I couldn't stand it. The uncles who aren't away from home only appear at dinner-time or in the evening, and the aunts only talk about the church or the market. I don't see how they can stretch out the conversation the way they do about brown sugar, or salt pork, or black beans. What they adore is a game of cards: "Politaina" in the afternoon, or "Thirty-One" in the evening. Repeating gossip is a sin that grandma and my aunts never commit. They don't remember that other people exist in Diamantina, outside the family.

We children go and walk by the cemetery until dinner-time and in the evenings we play forfeits and dance to the piano.

* Street of the Ball Game, or Bowls.

But every day something has to happen and this time it was something very funny:

My aunt had some green corn grated to make a drink and cakes for dinner. After putting the corn through the sieve there were a lot of husks left, that couldn't be used. The little Negro girl, Jovina, took the husks and put them in a pot with salt and brown sugar, boiled it, and ate it all up.

The parlor of the house at Jogo da Bola Street is very big. One door opens into the hall and the other into the garden. We were all there together when the little Negro girl came running in, jumping up and down and screaming with pain, "Help! Help! I'm bursting! Help!" Nobody could understand what was the matter. She crossed the room and rushed into the garden, running round and round and screaming in the utmost agony, "Help! It's the corn husks!" Then we understood immediately; her stomach was bursting. We got a chicken feather, she tickled her throat with it and threw up more than two pounds of half-cooked corn husks.

Then the poor thing felt better. When that was over we were able to laugh.

Friday, May 19th

Mama never fails to have a penny tucked away to give to the man who goes around every Friday in a red cassock crying out at the doorways, "For Mass for the souls of the dead!" I have a horror of his coming around without our having a penny for the dead. But the other day we were upset because the man called out and we didn't have it. Mama said, "Give him an egg; he can sell it." I handed him one and then I saw that he already had a lot of eggs in his bag and I was glad to have given him one, too.

Today I was at Seu Ferreira's house, playing with Clementina, when the man in the red cassock called at the door, "For Mass for the dead!" Dona Germana answered, "May they help us!" And the man went by. Then I asked them, "Aren't you afraid not to give alms for the souls of the dead? The other day when he went by our house I didn't have a penny so I gave him an egg." Seu Ferreira said, "You gave it to him to eat. Didn't you notice what he calls out at the door?" I said, "Yes. It's 'For Mass for the dead.'" Seu Ferreira said, "You're wrong. He says 'For me and the dead.' But the dead will wait a long time before he gives them anything."

Sunday, May 21st

I think the day of the Holy Ghost is one of the best holy days we have. The music going on for nine days, and the going around with a banner to the houses of everyone who makes promises, brightens up the town for days in a row. For three years in succession now I haven't missed marching in the procession carrying wax.* Grandma takes a vow every year and when the feast of the Holy Ghost comes I have a new dress to wear when I carry the wax. And it's the only way I have of making my cousins envious, too. Dindinha talks to grandma sometimes about sending another cousin, but she doesn't want to.

This year, besides grandma's wax, I had to carry a "miracle" for papa, too, a wax leg with red stains for wounds on it. Mama promised this leg when papa was kicked in the shin by a donkey in Boa Vista.

In the Sacristy of the Church of the Amparo, the walls are covered with "miracles": heads, arms, legs, and even whole babies of wax, so well-made and so full of sores that they look real.

I want my father to be the Emperor† very much, but I've already given up hope that he'll be drawn.

Whether the feast is beautiful or not depends on the Emperor. This year it was much gayer and there were lots more fire-works than the year before. Seu Manuel Cesar took the greatest pains with everything. I can still hear the fire-works.

* To make candles for the church.
† The man drawn by lot to take charge of the celebration.

I like all the holy days of Diamantina, but when they're in the Church of the Rosário, which is right next to grandma's *chácara*, I like them even more. It seems as if the *festa* belonged to us. And this year it really did.

An ex-slave of grandma's named Júlia was drawn by lot to be the queen of the Rosário, and the king was a very exuberant Negro whom I didn't know. Poor Júlia! She's been saving up her money for a long time to buy a little piece of land. She spent everything on the festival and now she's in debt.

Now I've seen how expensive it is for the poor Negroes to be king and queen for a day. First Júlia had to spend a lot for the dress and the crown. Then she had to give a dinner for all her court. The queen has a train-bearer who walks behind her holding her robe that has a long train. The train-bearer was a Negro from the *chácara*, too, and she helped with the dinner. I think that the enthusiasm of the blacks for such a short reign is wonderful. None of them refuses the honor, even knowing what it will cost!

What happened to Júlia's dinner was very sad. There's a gang of boys in Diamantina who make a game of stealing from people. They are boys from good families; Lauro Coelho [Rabbit] is one of them. They broke into the *chácara* a few days ago and did such awful things that I wished I were a man so I could get revenge for grandma!

They jumped over the garden wall in the night and stole all the ripe fruit; they cut down the green fruit and left it there. They pulled up all the vegetables, the beautiful cabbages, and threw them around the beds. They picked the pumpkins, cut them up in pieces, and threw them around. Iaiá was keeping one enormous pumpkin to see how big it would grow and to save the seeds, and they cut it in pieces. You should see what they did.

Grandma has her own way of taking things. First she says, "I never in my born days!" Then she adds, "But it could be worse."

And didn't those wicked boys, those thieves, steal the suckling pig for poor Júlia's dinner! We think they boosted a little boy into the parlor through the window, which is low, and he stayed there hiding until the room was empty for a minute. The pig was a beauty! Full of *farofa*,* with toothpicks decorated with frilled tissue-paper, and olives and slices of lemon on his sides and a rose in his mouth.

Poor Júlia almost cried!

Thursday, June 1st

When I had learned to read, Aunt Madge, who thinks that only English things are any good, got a book called *Power of Will*, by Samuel Smiles, for me to read out loud to her. When that was finished she gave me another one, *Character*. I had to read it and then repeat every single little thing to her. The two books really said exactly the same things: Economy, Good Manners, and Force of Will.

I'm positive that these books were useless to me. I haven't acquired a drop more will-power than I had already. Anyway, character doesn't change. I'm not any better than I was before. I think I learned just one thing but, since he didn't teach me anything else, I'm not sure that it was Samuel Smiles who taught it to me: I think I've learned to be economical and keep what I have.

We each have two or three hens. My brothers and sisters just wait for them to lay and sometimes they even pull the egg right out of the hen and cook it in a spoon, or make egg flip. But I, since I read those wretched books, I save up my eggs. When I have a whole dozen I sell them. Once I bought a tooth-brush and once I bought a pair of stockings. If grandma sends us a cheese or a box of quince paste the others eat all their share the first day, but I keep mine and eat it a little at a time; but I always end up by giving

* A stuffing made of manioc flour browned in lard, with or without hard-boiled eggs, sausage-meat, etc.

some to them. Papa sent a box of *mangabas** from Boa Vista and they ate theirs and then they stole the ones I'd saved. The rest spoiled. They get the best of everything, but I have no hopes of changing myself any more now. Mama likes my being so saving and she told me to ask Aunt Madge for the books so that Renato could read them. He began and didn't even finish one chapter. Mama kept insisting, "You have to read them, at least to learn how to save things, like Helena." Renato said, "Mama, the fingers of the hand aren't all alike. Helena could be this Smiles' own daughter, haven't you noticed that? She read his book and even memorized it because it's just like her. But I'm the opposite; I don't like to read. And if I did like to I wouldn't waste my time on Samuel Smiles, no indeed. I'd read Jules Verne, who's much better and more entertaining."

Sunday, June 4th

Grandma's the best person in the world. If I were she I don't think I'd put up with Fifina the way she puts up with her. Mama says that Fifina used to have money, but she had the idea of marrying a boy who was ten years younger than she is, and he took all her money and spent it and disappeared and left her with one *conto.†* She put that in the hands of the Bishop, to gather interest, and she earned her living doing odd jobs, darning socks, mending clothes in people's houses, just enough to pay for a little room and a kitchen. Seu Leivas promised to pay her double interest so she took the money from Senhor Bishop and handed it over to him. But she's never seen a penny of the interest until today and she hasn't any hope of seeing the capital again, because Seu Leivas owes everybody money and hasn't any to pay them back. Besides this, when she goes to have dinner at his house she's always scolded at the table because she does the same thing there that she does at

* Small fruit.
† A *conto* is a thousand *mil reis;* in 1893 it would have been $200.

Grandma's. She lines her plate with black beans and manioc flour
and puts the rice and meat and whatever else there is on top. She
eats the things she likes best and leaves the black beans on the
plate. She said that she did this at Seu Leivas' house and he told
her not to do it again, that he didn't like that; that when the food
was on the platter the cook could eat it, but if it was on the plate
it got thrown out. But grandma puts up with everything. Fifina has
a room of her own and she used to spend the day every day in
different houses, but one night she happened to be at the *chácara*
when there was a storm, and Iaiá had a bed made up for her in her
room. Fifina liked it and she hasn't left yet. Now she never goes to
anyone else's house. She leads a life of luxury.* She plays cards in
the bedroom with Iaiá all day long, and is very demanding. She
ordered Reginalda to fill a water-jar, and then called her again and
ordered her to fill it again because it had dirt in it. At the
chácara there's a big water-tap right beside the dining-room door,
but Fifina is so lazy she can't even fill a pitcher for herself.

The Negro women were saying in the kitchen that if they knew
how to put a hex on anybody they'd put a hex on Fifina. I thought
they were right, and today I was even angrier with her than the
Negroes are.

Grandma got a box of "Pearl" biscuits, which are heavenly
they are so good, and she gave me the whole box. Fifina saw it
and immediately she said to me, "Let me see if they're good!" I
let her take one, and if I hadn't pulled the box away, she'd have
taken them all. I hid the tin on the shelf in the bedroom, to take
home and eat and make them last. In the evening, when I went to
get them, I only found half of them. Without knowing who had
robbed me, I was furious. Rita told me that she saw Fifina coming
out of the room with the end of her shawl full of something and
that she kept taking something out and eating, and that it couldn't
be anything except the biscuits.

I was good and mad and I wanted to go and scold Fifina, but

* Literally: "A little life of gold."

grandma held me back, saying, "Don't be angry, child. It isn't worth it."

But I'm going to get even with Fifina some day, even if grandma scolds me.

Saturday, June 10th

Now the family has discovered the game of "Thirty-One." When they play at grandma's I don't miss anything, because the Negroes always make a very good supper at nine o'clock and then I still have time to go home and do my lessons. At Uncle Geraldo's they only serve a slice of bread as thin as paper. I don't like to go to Iaiá's house, either, because she only serves biscuits and coffee.

Yesterday Luizinha, who's wonderful at finding out things, told me, "I know where Iaiá keeps the tin of butter. When the biscuits arrive let's go there and spread them with butter."

She took me to Iaiá's bedroom and showed me the tin on a shelf.

The coffee tray arrived with the biscuits and we each took two or three and went to the bedroom and in the dark we took the can and buttered the biscuits with our fingers. When we had made a hole in the butter in the can, I said to Luizinha, "I feel remorseful already. Iaiá's going to think it was Eva." Luizinha said, "No, silly; she'll think it was Nico."

That consoled me. We covered the can and put it back. When we took a bite of our biscuits we both gave a scream of horror and ran to spit it out outside.

It was the unsalted lard that Iaiá greases her hair with.

Saturday, June 17th

Yesterday Aunt Aurélia sent to invite the family there for dinner. We went. It was her birthday and her daughters wanted to celebrate with a play. They built a real stage and they and their brothers acted like real actors. They took their parts very well and were very funny. Uncle Conrado was like a turkey-cock about his children's play. I felt sorry for Aunt Agostinha who'd had a supper last week, too, for Lucas' play, and who was disappointed when she saw the difference between her children's play and Uncle Conrado's children's. Yesterday they had memorized a play and they showed everything as if it were taking place in a house. João Afonso was the husband, Beatriz the wife, Sérgio was a visitor, and Hortência the maid. Leontino was the Jew's horse* who moved the table and took away the flowers.

In Lucas' theatre he hung a sheet in the dark and had some dolls. Then he went in behind it with a candle and made the dolls dance. Then Nico turned somersaults on the stage. At the end he called Emídio up and asked us if we wanted to see a Negro turn white, and he threw flour in Emídio's face. Then he did something he learned from the clowns, he broke an egg on Emídio's head.

Lucas' play was just foolishness like that and Aunt Agostinha had thought it was awfully funny. Yesterday she saw that the other cousins were much more serious and she was jealous. Other people are always getting jealous of Aunt Aurélia.

Sunday, June 18th

Yesterday the family met at Iaiá's to play "Thirty-One." They were all at the table playing except Uncle Julião. When he comes he brings the whole tribe and one old maid daughter, very saucy, who answers very rudely to everything that's said to her, even in fun, even to her father and mother.

Nobody likes her.

We were all pleased that he hadn't appeared when suddenly all of them came in the door. Just as Uncle Julião came in he slipped and fell flat on the floor, all of him.

We all shut our mouths in order not to laugh and nobody said anything for fear of the rude daughter. Iaiá, trying not to laugh, began to talk about such things, and told about how last week she

* "In Diamantina, the name given to the scene-shifter in the theatre." (Note in *M V d M*)

had had a fall; she slipped and fell on top of Rita, and almost squashed her. Uncle Julião said, "Yes, but you fell on top of Rita. You were luckier than I was; I landed on the hard floor."

We all took the opportunity to laugh because we were already dying to laugh at his fall, which was very funny.

Wednesday, June 21st

The year of the famine I was very small, but I can still remember some things that happened then. If I had been bigger and smarter, the way I am now, I think we wouldn't have had to go through the things we did then, at home.

Nothing has ever impressed me as much as the famine that year. I remember to this day the candles that mama lit in the *oratório*, begging God to send rain. There was nothing to be bought in the city. The storekeepers sent people out on the roads to meet the drovers to buy what little they were bringing, in order to sell it for double or triple what it was worth. People who hadn't much money were starving. Every day everything went up more. Every day news came of people who had died in the country around.

Meat wasn't even mentioned. Grandma knew that Seu Marcelo had killed a pig and she sent someone to persuade him to give us an *arobe** at any price. To this day I remember our joy when we saw one of the Negroes from the *chácara* coming in with a plate of pork.

Sunday, June 25th

Early yesterday Leontino came to invite us for the feast of Saint João at Uncle Conrado's *chácara*, Romana. The house has an enormous vegetable garden with lots of fruit and the garden at the front has a wall around it. I don't know why Uncle Conrado leaves such a good *chácara* to live in a house in town that looks at a wall of the church.

* Portuguese weight of 32 pounds.

Uncle Conrado never fails to celebrate the feast of Saint João because *his* João is the goody-goody of the family. All the goodness that should have gone into the others, God put into one; the rest of them are like us, if not worse.

The celebrations there are marvellous because of the good things Aunt Aurélia makes and she spreads a big table with everything. But, since nothing is perfect, we have to endure Uncle Conrado's criticizing, which takes all the joy out of everything. I really don't know why my cousins like holidays. He gave the girls a few firecrackers, some Chinese squibs, and some pinwheels, and then he even helped light them so they wouldn't burn themselves. If a firecracker or a torpedo went off, there was Uncle Conrado, holding onto the girls so they wouldn't get burned. If one stays near the bon-fire one catches cold. Only Helena is idiotic enough to jump over the bon-fire! To roast sugar-cane and sweet potatoes—how awful! I only envied them one thing. I'm not sure that it's envy, exactly, because sometimes we think one thing and it's really something else. It was Uncle Conrado's having the celebration early and making my cousins stop at nine o'clock to study their lessons, in spite of its being Saturday.

If mama would only do that, I'd be a good student the way they are. But fortunately it never occurs to her.

Thursday, July 6th

I and Luizinha spent a day this week at Aunt Aurélia's with our cousins. They're very nice but they live shut up in the house in town, which doesn't have any view or any garden to play in and they can't stay out in the street. We have to play just at cooking for the dolls all day long. I used to enjoy it, but now that I'm thirteen years old I don't like to play at that any more.

They insisted so much on our staying that I stayed and helped my older cousins. My aunt makes things to sell, and they wanted to do it, too. She gave them some money and João Afonso bought peanuts to make peanut brittle and Sérgio coconuts for coconut cakes. We grated the coconut, shelled the peanuts, and began to make candy.

Sérgio's coconut cakes turned out very well but João Afonso didn't cook the peanut brittle to the right stage, and we all began to eat it and make fun of him. He's already bad tempered, but he got madder and madder and I don't know what gave him the idea of doing anything so silly. He climbed on the table and stamped on the peanut brittle in a rage, and broke it all to bits.

When the tray of coconut cakes was ready to send out in the street we told him, "Don't be silly and lose your money. Cook your peanut brittle over again, and send it, too. The people who buy it won't know and 'What the eye doesn't see the heart doesn't feel.'" So he did. He put it all in the kettle, melted it over again to the right stage, and turned it out on the table. This time it turned out splendidly. He counted the pieces and put them on Delmira's tray, to sell with the other things behind the Cathedral, a penny apiece, or three for two pennies.

Hidden on the balcony, we watched to see who'd buy. When somebody bought peanut brittle and went away eating it, João Afonso was crazy with remorse and he walked up and down in the parlor clutching his head and saying, "What a horrible sin I'm committing! My God, how bad I am!" And he kept calling to Delmira to bring back the peanut brittle but we wouldn't let her, and we convinced him that if people eat something dirty that's been cooked, it won't hurt them. None of us cared; we even enjoyed seeing other people eat stepped-on peanut brittle.

Sunday, July 16th

My father and mother were very pleased with me yesterday and papa even said, "Now I see that this girl can hold her tongue when she has to." But God alone knows how much it cost me. It even gave me a belly ache.

Papa came home from the mine and because it was Saturday he said, "Let's all go and play 'Thirty-One' at Henriqueta's. You can study tomorrow." We went to Iaiá's and Seu Paulino, who I'd always thought was an honest man, showed up there, too, I don't know why.

Papa told mama that everyone tries so hard to win at "Thirty-One" because they use pennies, that if they just used chips they wouldn't care about winning so much, but the pile of pennies is what makes them want to win. I know that's so because when I see a big heap of pennies I'm in agony I'm so afraid that the others will win them before my parents do.

I always stand a little way off watching the others play; I don't go near because they don't like it. Today I saw why. There was a pile on the table that had already been doubled three times. The excitement began and I began to suffer; I was keeping count of their plays from a distance. Mama made thirty. When it was Seu Paulino's turn I watched him play and counted to myself, "Twenty." He got an ace and I counted "twenty-one"; he got a four and I counted "twenty-five"; then he got a seven and I said out loud, "Thirty-two!" He turned on me and said, "A great big girl like you and you don't know how to count!" and he said to the table, "Thirty-one!" And he dropped the ace of clubs on the floor.

I was so shocked I was stunned. I never thought that a man who seemed so honest would cheat. I kept my mouth shut and went to relieve my feelings in the doorway, looking at the moonlight. I stayed there, thinking, and said to Luizinha, "Who knows, perhaps he did it because there's nothing to eat at his house." Luizinha said, "That explains it. Haven't you noticed how yellow Heloisa is?"

Wednesday, July 19th

In front of grandma's *chácara*, on the corner of Rosário Street, there's a house where they never even open a window. Only in the afternoon the door opens and Moisés de Paula comes out wearing a very old overcoat and walks to town with his hands behind his back. His brother and sister, Manuel Arrã and Modesta, live with him. Manuel Arrā has a little shop in the alley of Old Cavalhada where he only has cakes of brown sugar, tapioca, and peanut brittle for sale. Modesta isn't even allowed to stick her nose out the window.

Every year Moisés makes a beautiful *crèche* for Christmas, and on that occasion he lets us all go to see it. From the time I was little I've admired Moisés as I've never admired anyone else because of his lovely *crèches*, with the Christ Child in the manger, surrounded by figures and animals, all so well made.

We are all very curious to know about the life of these three beings living shut up in their house, without even opening a window. If one of the brothers goes out the door is shut immediately. So we planned to send our little cousin, Ester, to get in there with the excuse of asking Modesta if she had any lace to sell. She's a lacemaker. Ester went and spent some time inside with Modesta. When Moisés saw her coming into the dining-room he said, "Modesta, do we have an *eye-witness* in the house?"

Ester, who's very smart, ran to the *chácara* and told us and our curiosity was satisfied.

Monday, July 24th

Yesterday Siá Aninha, whose birthday it was, asked mama to dinner and told her that she should bring us because there would be a lot to eat. Dinners at Seu Antonio Manuel's house are very lavish. Because I'm smart I sat down at the first table, where everything is better. I stayed very quietly at the corner near the eaters and drinkers. The biggest glutton in Diamantina is Seu Antonio do Rego. The biggest drinker is our poor professor Leivas who always ends up drunk at every party.

I never thought I'd see what I saw yesterday at dinner.

After Father Augusto had recited some verses to the health of Siá Aninha, I was watching Seu Leivas and I saw him puff out his cheeks, with his mouth shut, making a very funny face. I was laughing helplessly and I didn't take my eyes off him. When he saw what he was doing, Seu Antonio do Rego grabbed a platter of roast pork with potatoes that was in front of him and hid it under the table. I was watching everything in amazement, without understanding, when something incredible happened. Seu Leivas puffed out his cheeks again; two spouts of beer came out of his nose and sprayed all the dishes that were in front of him!

They took Seu Leivas inside, covered the tablecloth and Seu Antonio do Rego put the platter on the table again, saying, "Well, this is saved, at least; let's seize the opportunity and eat it, before Leivas comes back!"

I couldn't finish dinner. It wasn't so much that it made me feel nauseated as that my fit of giggling didn't stop. When they began to sing the drinking songs I got up from the table and went to the room where the desserts were, where Caetaninho from the Bishop's Palace was keeping a special plate of blancmange and jam that he makes, which is delicious.

Wednesday, July 26th

Today I came home from school, threw my books on the table, and began to do my weekly chore: to iron our clothes. Mama sends them out to be washed and then keeps them for us to iron on Thursdays. I have the chore of ironing mine, mama's, and papa's. Luizinha has hers and my brothers'. Lots of times I have to help her when I finish mine. She's slow about everything.

Because tomorrow's our last Thursday to go to the country, I don't want to leave anything to be done.

I've ironed* up until now and I haven't finished everything. Tomorrow I'm going to get up early, tidy up my room, finish the clothes, and leave everything ready. Since we always leave at eight o'clock, I'll have time. I take my books and do my lessons outdoors. Mama doesn't want to have a maid because she says we must learn how to work.

We miss our little Negro, Cesarina, very much. She got lung

* Using a heavy charcoal iron with a short smokestack, rather like a tugboat.

trouble and mama didn't want to take care of her at home, *coitadinha,* because she says that that sickness is very catching. She's in Boa Vista and we've heard she's getting better. I was very pleased, because her mother died of consumption and I was afraid that she'd die, too. She's such a friend of ours and is nice to us.

Thursday, July 27th

Today was the day for Seu Ricardo's *chácara.* Mama likes the ladies there very much. One is Seu Ricardo's wife and the other his sister-in-law. The two are exactly alike; what one says the other repeats. The only unpleasant thing there are the dogs that bark a long time before anyone comes to open the door. We always buy fruit there; when there's fruit that won't last they send for us to come and get it. Today we went to buy sweet lemons; it's a wonderful fruit. They tell us to climb the trees, we eat all we want, and fill our basket, and they won't take any money. Then they treated us to their home-made wine which is very tasty, and biscuits and corn meal cakes.

All this affability is when we go with mama. When we go alone, —nothing.

Saturday, August 5th

I'm convinced that if only grandma would take charge of her own money, we wouldn't have such hard times, and mama and papa wouldn't be worried the way they are sometimes, merely because of the lack of a piece of dirty paper to which we attach more importance than to all the good things of life. Papa lives in hope of finding diamond-bearing gravel, but it's hope, hope, hope, all his life long. When he puts everything into the mine, like this time, there goes all the money and we're still in debt.

When I get my Normal School certificate I know everything's going to be better, because I'll go to the ends of the earth to get a school. I've made my plans, very well thought-out ones, so that we'll even be able to save money. But to leave my father to struggle, digging holes in the ground in the hope of diamonds that don't appear—I won't let him. Sometimes I think that Seu Zé da Mata was right about what he said to papa when papa asked him to join a mining company. He said: "No, Seu Alexandre, I'm not going to leave a business where I can see what I own, to go looking in the ground for something I never put there!"

Grandma suffers, knowing what we go through, although we never tell her, but I think she guesses. The little diamonds that papa found didn't bring enough to cover our expenses. Now what shall we do? I'm so afraid papa will have to sell our house, the way he already speaks of doing.

Today after dinner we went to grandma's before mama did, because when papa's at home she always goes later. Glorinha was there and the two of us were playing out in front. Grandma called me, and Glorinha, thinking that I might be going to get something, came after me. Grandma asked me, "What did you have to eat at your house today, child?" Before I could answer her, Glorinha was saying, "Grandma, I only had black bean *tutu*." Grandma said, "I didn't ask you anything. If you only eat black beans it's because you want to. Your father has plenty of beef. I asked Helena, poor lamb, because her father hasn't anything." Afterwards, grandma gave me a folded piece of paper, without Glorinha's seeing her, to take to mama. When mama opened it there was a fifty *mil reis* bill.

Thursday, August 10th

Yesterday I came back from grandma's very sorry for what happened to Glorinha, *coitada.*

When the Negroes of the *chácara* finish work they take away the key to the garden in their pockets; the garden is locked up for the night.

Today all the cousins were there together and something had had to happen. We all went out to the stoop and they immediately thought of the medlars and they helped Glorinha and me over the

wall to pick them. We got over, picked the medlars, and were
throwing them back to them. It was a dark night and we were
hurrying so we wouldn't get caught. When I'd picked enough I
jumped back over the wall. Glorinha, who is greedier, kept on eating. When she jumped she was so unlucky that she slipped and fell
and sat down on a horrible prickly pear. She began to scream and
the aunts came running to see what had happened. Glorinha was
carried inside and the spines were stuck in so deep that she
screamed when they were pulled out.

Fortunately nobody mentioned the medlars, and nobody knew
they were in back of it; otherwise there'd have been a tirade, how
"it was God's punishment, and richly deserved, too!"

Saturday, August 12th

If there's one house where I don't like to sleep it's Aunt
Aurélia's. I can't stand Uncle Conrado's being so orderly and
methodical, with a set time for doing everything. It may work all
right for my cousins' studying, but for everything else it makes me
sick!

Yesterday the cousins insisted that I and Luizinha go there for
the night. With the four of us together like that, it's impossible to
go to sleep; we only wanted to play, and with all our talking Uncle
Conrado wasn't asleep, either, and he kept calling to us all the
time to watch out. I'm the oldest of the four and I minded his
scolding the most. His own daughters didn't mind at all and kept
right on laughing and talking. At one point, because we'd put the
mattresses on the floor, a flea got into Beatriz's ear, and she jumped
out of bed completely wild, and ran into Uncle Conrado's room,
screaming, "There's something in my ear! I'm going crazy! Help!
Help!" Uncle Conrado got out of bed and said, "It's nothing,
child, nothing! Just a flea!" He tried to get it out, without any
result and Beatriz kept screaming, "Help me! I'm going crazy!" He
got even more excited than she was and begged us, "For the love of
God, give me a flea! Find me a flea to put in my ear to show this

girl that it doesn't amount to anything!" But nobody could find a flea. It was impossible. I hunted with might and main, just so he could put it in his ear and not keep saying such silly things. I never was so eager to do something disagreeable. But at the sight of the two of them, Beatriz screaming with her flea and Uncle Conrado wanting one, too, to put in his ear, I couldn't contain myself, I wanted to laugh so hard.

It's never happened to me but I imagine it must be horrible. Fortunately the flea came out, and we went to sleep in peace.

Monday, August 14th

A big family, with a lot of children, has moved into our neighborhood. One of the girls is a school-mate of mine and she is very pretty and nice. We all became friends immediately and they are always at our house. Mama doesn't want us to go to the neighbors' houses, but she likes to have us have friends who come to play with us on our doorstep. I like the girls and I think the whole family is nice, but their mother has a dreadful fault. When they've finished dinner she sits down on the stoop, on the street, with all her family, and that's the time she chooses to look for lice in her children's heads. We watch her, amazed, from our house. She takes a child by the neck and goes through his head killing lice with her finger-nail until he's tired of lying down. Then that one goes off and she calls another one, and that's the way she spends the most beautiful afternoons of the month of August, looking for her children's lice. I'm surprised that her daughters, who are my age, don't speak to their mother and tell her to stop. I was there yesterday and she gave me a piece of peanut brittle and told me to eat it. I excused myself by saying that I was going to bring it home, because I was feeling sick. But I thought of those lice and felt nauseated.

Friday, August 18th

Mama has some older cousins whom we call "aunt." One of them, older than mama, has been married a long time and she's never had any children. But for some time now, when my aunts and uncles are together, they've been talking about the baby that Aunt Raimundinha was expecting.

I'm in the habit of always listening to my aunts' conversation to hear the news, which always comes first, before the price of food. I kept hearing them ask each other, "Aren't you worried about Raimundinha's pregnancy? It's very dangerous at her age, and even more so, being her first." And they told stories of elderly women who had died having their first child.

When Aunt Raimundinha was with them she only talked about the baby, the layette, the joy it would be to have a child of her own, even at her age. It was God Himself who'd sent her a child, now that she and her husband were all alone. For some weeks now everybody has been getting more and more worried because the time for the baby to be born had gone by and everybody in the family was anxious. At home papa said to mama, "What's happened is that baby's dead and now it's going to be very serious."

Aunt Raimundinha calmly kept on waiting. Iaiá was so worried that she decided to call in the notary to have her make a will, and that frightened the family. Early yesterday the Negro woman from their house came to the *chácara* and said that she'd been to find the mid-wife. Today, since there hadn't been any news, mama and my aunts decided to visit her. She lives a long way off, and we all went, eager to see the baby. When we got there we found Aunt Raimundinha sitting up in bed, with lace-trimmed pillows, and without a big belly. My aunts asked for the baby, and with a mournful face she said, "It was air. Engrácia says she's been a mid-wife for thirty years and she never saw anything like it. She kneaded my belly like bread-dough and you can't imagine what happened."

Today grandma was explaining to me that people often have to do something wrong in order to avoid a greater evil. In order to get along with grandpa, sometimes she had to deceive him. His temperament was different from everyone else's in the family.

One of the things that grandpa was stubborn about was making soap on the *fazenda*. Grandma said that she couldn't spend her life at the *fazenda* buying soap. So when the *pequis** were ripe she ordered the Negroes to get loads of them to make soap with. When grandpa saw that quantity arriving at the house he asked grandma what she wanted with so many. She said, "It's to make candles with, Batista." Then he asked, "Can you make candles out of *pequis?*" She told him, "Very good ones." He said, "Then I want to see them when they're made." Grandma filled the copper kettles with *pequis*, made the soap secretly, and eventually grandpa forgot all about the candles.

In order to live peacefully with him, grandma said that she had to conceal anything that went wrong or anything that might have annoyed him, because when he got angry he locked himself up in his room and wouldn't come out. Once she had to climb through the window and make a fuss over him for a long time before he'd come out. I said to grandma, "I wouldn't have done that. He could have stayed in his room as long as he wanted to, and I'd never go and make a fuss over him."

I think that all the family just resigned themselves to going against their own wishes all the time, not to annoy grandfather. Because today why aren't any of the granddaughters as good as their mothers or their aunts? Grandma said that now everything is in a state of anarchy and everything is different. I said to her, "God be thanked, grandma. God help me if things were the way they were in your time."

---

* *Pequis:* small wild fruit, oily, with a strong odor.

Aunt Aurélia tells how, because she was the bravest, she told the others she was going into the parlor to ask grandpa for a dress length of white poplin for Christmas. Her sisters didn't believe her. Then she wanted to show her courage so she went into the parlor to ask grandpa; but she began to shake so that something awful happened to her. Then grandpa was sorry and ordered dress lengths for all of them.

I was saying to grandma that I say whatever I want to to papa, I tell him everything and I swear that if he ever did anything bad I would speak to him frankly about it. I could see that grandma thinks it's better that way because all she said to me was, "That's it, child. Times have changed."

Thursday, August 24th

Today I came home looking so different that Renato kept looking at me and saying, "Just look at her face!" Luizinha, who is a thousand times nicer than he is, said, "How pretty you are, Helena! Who fixed you like that?" I said, "Ester did." When I was talking with them on the stoop I said that I knew that I was homely but that it didn't bother me because Mama Tina* had brought me up knowing that "The homely lives, the pretty lives, they all lives." When I said that I was homely, Ester exclaimed, "You homely? Just let me fix you up and you'll see." I agreed, and she got the scissors and cut my bangs and combed my hair, then she put rice-powder on my face and when I looked in the mirror I saw that I wasn't homely at all. They laughed when I told them that what we do here is to grease our hair with chicken fat to keep it plastered down. She told me that I should wash my hair and then put it in curls and then go there for her to comb it. How nice that I've become friendly with Dona Gabriela's family. They're so kind! If it weren't for them I never would have thought to have my bangs cut and my hair combed in the latest style. Ester thought it

* Negro nurse. Her proverb is in Negro dialect.

was funny when I told her that Mama Tina used to say, "The pretty lives, the homely lives." She said, "It's true, but the pretty ones lives better." How happy I am today to be pretty at last!

Tuesday, August 29th

Why does everyone like to criticize the bad things we do and not to praise the good things? It doesn't seem as if my sister and I could be children of the same parents. I'm impatient, rebellious, impertinent, lazy, and incapable of being obedient and all the things they'd like me to be. Luizinha is as good as an angel. I don't know how anyone can be like her, so quiet. She never goes out of the house unless she's hanging on mama's arm. She never asks for anything. If I should say I'd ever heard her ask for a new dress, I'd be lying. And if she gets a dress and I want to take it away from her, she doesn't mind. Then everybody calls me a difficult child, but nobody praises Luizinha.

I'm going to write down here what I did to her, and not be ashamed, because only the paper's going to know.

For months she's been saving fifty *mil reis* that her godfather gave her, to buy a new dress. This year I've been thinking I should celebrate my birthday with a dinner party for my friends, because they invite me when they have birthdays. The Negro women at the *chácara* are all very good to me. Generosa, who's a very good cook, had already told me that if I could get the money to pay for the food she'd cook a very good dinner for me and I wouldn't have to bother about it at all. In my own imagination, I'm an only child. I'm already famous for it. The idea of Luizinha's money came to me. But because I didn't want to make her feel bad I prepared everything very well and I said to her, "Give me your fifty *mil reis* for my birthday party. If you make a dress with it, only you will get the benefit of it. But if you give me the money and I give the party, I'll get lots of presents and we'll divide everything." Luizinha agreed to do it. I gave the money to

Generosa. She cooked a banquet and there even was turkey. As presents I got: material for two dresses, a bottle of perfume, one of toilet water, a dozen handkerchiefs, a box of six cakes of soap, three pairs of stockings, and a tin of biscuits, besides the puddings and candies.

When the party was over my cousins began to butt in and take Luizinha's part, and wanted me to divide everything then and there the same night. But I didn't have the courage to deny myself anything and I said to them, "Tonight it's better just to divide the tin of biscuits and leave the rest for tomorrow."

Today Luizinha complained and I gave her one cake of soap, too, and one pair of stockings. She protested, but weakly. I know that eventually she'll forget about it. I know that I didn't keep my promise but I don't feel any remorse because I need the things more than she does. She almost never goes out of the house and then she only goes to the *chácara*, and I go out every day.

Thursday, August 31st

Today was the happiest day of my life. When I got home I found a big cardboard box on the table. "What's that, mama?" I asked. She said, "I don't know. It was delivered here and I left it for you to open yourself. See what the letter says; it's there on the table." I opened the letter and it said, "My dear Helena: I and Carlos haven't forgotten your birthday and the two of us join in sending you an outfit for that day that we hope you'll celebrate with all the joy and happiness that you deserve. I made every bit of it myself, even the embroidery, and we hope it will arrive in time. Your godfather and I send you the warmest embraces, praying God that you will continue to be as good and happy as you have been until now." This letter came inside another one for papa. What a pity the present didn't arrive before the twenty-eighth!

It was from my godmother who stayed at our house and took

her Normal School certificate when she was already grown up, and went as a teacher to Santa Maria de São Feliz, to live with Uncle Carlos, who's in business there.

My English grandfather's family is the best-organized family I've ever known. He had a lot of children and when they were grown he sent each of the brothers a sister to take care of and support. My godmother Quequeta was my father's. They are all still alive but only Uncle Mortimer has made a fortune yet. When they built the Normal School in Diamantina Aunt Madge was almost forty years old. But even so she entered the School and got her certificate. She lives with Aunt Efigênia and Aunt Cecília, who are good dressmakers, and when the fruit gets ripe they all go to the *fazenda* to make quince and guava paste. The "English ladies' guava paste" is admired even in Rio de Janeiro. Aunt Neném [Baby] never left the *fazenda* and she spends her whole life being sick, *coitada.* My godmother Quequeta was so envious of Aunt Madge that she went to Normal School very late, too, and now she's in Santa Maria earning money and sending me pretty things. I love all these aunts of mine so much!

There was a dress of white dotted Swiss muslin for me, a very pretty lace petticoat, a chemise, and embroidered drawers. A pair of button boots, three pairs of stockings, and a dozen handkerchiefs. The dress is so pretty that I can just see my success at the next party. It's all ruffles.

I'm going to take everything to show to grandma just to hear her say, "What fairy hands your aunts have!"

Saturday, September 2nd

Today Cesarina came in the front door, already cured of her weak chest, and we ran to welcome her with the greatest joy.

When Mama Tina died she left two children with mama, Cesarina and Emídio. Cesarina is very good, but Emídio began to teach Renato to steal other people's fruit. Then mama asked grandma to keep him at the *chácara* where there's more to do and he'd be away from Renato. Cesarina stays at home helping us with the work. But a while ago she began to spit blood and mama said that it was the phthisic that Mama Tina'd had, and she took her to Boa Vista, to Siá Virginia's house, and gave her some money to help cover her expenses.

Today she came back fatter and cheerful. When she's at home she makes us laugh all the time, but she helps us with the work and that's a good thing for mama and us. Now I'll have more time to study and write because she cleans everything very well and looks after my clothes.

Monday, September 4th

Every day I hear them saying: "So-and-so takes after his father or his mother." I think about it and sometimes I ask mama why none of us take after her or papa. I'm capable of making a sacrifice for a child, but I could never sacrifice my whole life for a friend, the way papa has for Uncle Geraldo.

When mama says that he never does anything in return, papa always answers, "Thank God it isn't necessary; I'm in good health."

Uncle Geraldo has been sick a long time and he didn't have the courage to go to be cured in Agua Quente* at Santa Barbara without my father. This month, after he'd settled his affairs at the mine, papa went with him and mama stayed with us. But mama can't be away from papa for very long. He hadn't been gone a week when she got a letter saying that he'd had an upset stomach, and she decided to go after him. I went with her to the *chácara*, to get grandma's blessing, and to go to school afterwards. We found Dindinha and grandma saying morning prayers. We joined in the responses and when they'd finished the rosary mama said to grandma, "I'm going to Santa Barbara. I came to tell you I'm going to leave the three oldest here and only take Joãozinho, because he's so small. I got a letter from Alexandre saying that his

* Hot springs twenty miles from Diamantina, frequented by people suffering from rheumatism.

stomach is bad. It's nothing but that dried beef that he shouldn't eat. But if I let it go it will get worse. You know how Alexandre is; he's only thinking about Geraldo's health and forgetting all about his own. And if he gets sick, he'll die like a sheep."

Grandma agreed and mama went after papa. We stayed at the *chácara* and I almost died, I missed mama so much. The *chácara* is full of people and we can't find a good place to study there. When it's something to memorize, it's easy, but arithmetic is harder. Grandma torments me all day long to study, but when I'm at the *chácara* I always find a lot to write, which is what I can do without paying much attention.

I like to have mama love papa so much, but I think that my cousins, whose mothers don't cling to their husbands so, lead better lives than we do. I never saw one of my cousins have to leave her home and go to stay at the *chácara* the way we're always doing, so mama can go after papa.

Wednesday, September 6th

None of grandma's grandchildren takes part in conversations with the grown-ups. Nobody in the family likes forward children. We all go to the *chácara* and begin to play on the lawn in front. Only Onofre likes to be treated like a grown-up and he won't play with us. When he comes here to the *chácara* with Uncle Geraldo, he stays sitting in the parlor like a man and joining in the conversation. Uncle Geraldo turns his back on him and everybody begins to criticize his bringing-up and say how disagreeable Onofre is. None of us likes him.

Today when I got back from school I found Onofre sitting in the parlor with grandma. He'd come to bring a message from Uncle Geraldo, and he and grandma hadn't been able to find a subject to talk about. Grandma told me to sit down, I think so that I could help her endure his visit. But I just sat there, too, without anything to say. Finally grandma asked, "You have a new servant girl haven't you?" He said, "Yes, Senhora." "Is she a good cook?"

He said, "I think so, because she picks over the black beans." At this reply I doubled up with laughter. I never thought there could be anyone who didn't pick over the black beans. Grandma scolded me, "You're laughing because you don't have a servant girl and you do things yourselves, properly. But what he's saying is perfectly true. It's something to have a cook who looks over the black beans. Almost all of them wash them without going over them."

Friday, September 8th

When I got to the *chácara* I missed grandma. "Where's grandma? Where are Dindinha and Iaiá? Where did they go?" Elvira answered, "They went to Sinhá Aurélia's. She had a miscarriage and Sinhá Teodora told me to tell you that you're to go there when you get home from school." I said, "Grandma knows we have to study, we have lessons on Saturday mornings. Wouldn't it be better if I stayed here, Elvira, and Emídio went to tell grandma I have to study?" She said, "No. You know that she gets uneasy when you aren't near her."

I thought to myself, "Heavens! I wish mama were here! How can I live like this, always being obedient and suffering, without saying a word!" I went running to Aunt Aurélia's house, hoping they'd give me something to eat, because I was dying of hunger. When I got there my aunts said immediately, "Don't give her anything to eat because it's almost dinner time and she'll spoil her appetite."

If there's one thing I desire in life, it's not to be as hungry as I am. I'm disgracefully hungry. I never had a day in my life when I didn't want to eat a lot. I even asked the doctor if there wasn't some way of not using my food up so fast, and he thought it was funny.

I waited without even talking very much, I was so hungry. Finally it was dinner time and the Negro, Maria, sat all the children on the bench at the big table in the kitchen and was bringing in the plates all ready for each one. When it was my turn she turned to me and asked me, "Sinhá Helena, do you want to eat, too?" I was surprised at the question and I said, "Oh no, I don't want to eat!" thinking that the stupid girl would understand me. I waited for my plate and nothing came. I called to Maria, "Where's my plate?" She answered, "Oh! Didn't you say you didn't want any? Now there isn't anything left."

I was so surprised I couldn't even speak. I did what mama says we should do when we undergo great suffering: offer it as a sacrifice to God, that it may please Him, and help us later when we need it.

I didn't want the dessert, yams and molasses. I don't know whether it was because I really wanted to make a sacrifice or whether I was in a rage. When dinner was over, grandma saw me and said, "You're pale, and your lips are white. What's the matter? Are you sick?" I said, "No, Senhora. Perhaps it's because I didn't have any lunch after school, or any dinner." Grandma said, "I never in my born days!"

Uncle Conrado's house is very full, but Aunt Aurélia is in bed and grandma doesn't feel at home there with cousin Bi, who's there keeping house. Grandma had to have her nap; she isn't able to leave her house and go back again twice on the same day any more. She said to Dindinha, "You know, Chiquinha, we can't stay here. These girls have to do their lessons." Then I knew what was coming. Dindinha said, "We don't have to go home for that, mother. Let's send for her and Luizinha's books, and they can study right here." Grandma whispered, thinking that only Dindinha would hear, "I'm my own mistress and I don't want to be bossed. I want to go and I'm going!" Dindinha looked at me as much as to say, "You'll be sorry!" We left, and as we were going away I heard Dindinha say to Aunt Aurélia, "What can we do, Quita? Inhá, with all her nonsense, clinging to Alexandre, goes away and leaves all her children with us, and then you see how mother behaves."

We went back to the *chácara* and I carried the little stool so that grandma could rest along the way. The only thing I can endure patiently in life is grandma's slowness in the street. The distance we could walk in five minutes takes her half an hour, holding onto Dindinha's arm, with her cane in her other hand.

When we got back to the *chácara* Dindinha only gave me half a piece of cheese and two bananas for dinner on purpose. I ate them and told grandma that I'd had lots of things to eat.

Monday, September 11th

Grandma has a saying that we have to put up with although it's very hard on us. She always says, "Mend your clothes and they'll last a year; mend them again and they'll last another month." Yesterday I was wearing my white dress that's already lasted me a long time, and it was torn. Because mama's in Santa Barbara, I took a chance and tore it some more and showed it to grandma, to have an excuse not to go with Dindinha to have dinner at Uncle Geraldo's, and to get a new dress. Grandma obeyed the saying and sewed up all the tears and I had to go out with the lace on my dress all mended. I hate to go to dinner at my uncle's house and I was already annoyed at having to go with Dindinha, without having to go wearing a dress with the lace all mended as well. And besides, my rich cousins enjoy seeing me badly dressed. Grandma won't catch me making an old dress last a year and then another month again.

Wednesday, September 13th

I did something so bad today! But I can't feel sorry about it because it wasn't my fault. Grandma was very grieved; she thought that Dindinha and Iaiá were right to be angry with me and scold me the way they scolded me.

It's all just because mama's away. I and Luizinha are sleeping on the floor in grandma's room. The house is full and I don't have a corner to do my lessons in. When I'm memorizing I memorize by pacing the floor, wherever I am; but for the French and arithmetic lessons, if I can't find a quiet corner I can't do anything. So, with the help of God, I found something simply wonderful. I went to pick mulberries and I climbed and climbed the tree up to the very top. What a discovery! At the top, right against the sky, the mulberry tree was so grown over with a vine that it looked like a mattress. I lay down on top of it and it was just like a bed. I decided to take my books up there and study and write there without being annoyed all the time. I'd tell grandma that I was going to study under the mulberry tree and then I'd climb up and stay there on top.

Today I came home from school, took my pencil, books, and notebooks, and went to the garden. I climbed the mulberry tree and stayed there studying and looking at the view from there which is perfectly beautiful! I arranged it in such a way that it made a bed and a table where I could study while lying down. You can't imagine what happened to me. When I had finished my lessons and exercises I should have climbed down and come away, but I forgot everything watching the clouds in the sky, and thinking and thinking, until I fell asleep.

When I woke up it was already dark. I climbed down quickly and went in. When I entered the parlor and saw grandma with the big rosary with the black beads in her hands, praying, I realized what I'd done without meaning to. Grandma only prays like that, not at prayer time, when something serious has happened. She, *coitada*, the only one who loves me, was so happy when she saw me come in that she didn't say anything to me; she only gave me my dinner. But my aunts went off into such tirades that grandma had to yell at Iaiá, "Stop it! That's enough of that! Let the child eat in peace!"

Sometimes I wonder how such a kind person as grandma can have such bad children as she has. My aunts want grandma to like their own pets. Dindinha wants everybody to like Nestor; Iaiá, Nico; and Aunt Clarinha, her grandchildren. It makes them furious that grandma only likes me. But this time I was smart; I told everything a little differently. I thought right away that if I told the story of the mulberry tree those two pests, Nico and Nestor, would tear down my bed and I'd be lost. My aunts kept saying, "Tell us where you were hiding, driving mother to distraction all this time! Everybody in the house has been looking for you for two hours. You deserve a good beating! You're possessed! We turned the house and garden upside down and couldn't find you! Tell us where you were!"

While I was listening to their raving I had time to think, and I answered, "I don't think you could have turned the garden upside down, because I lying in the clump of bananas beside the gate." They said, "And why didn't you hear us calling you?" I said, "Because I was asleep."

Grandma was pleased with me all evening and I saw that it was because I'd been scolded so without its being my fault.

Oh! What a nice grandmother!

Sunday, September 17th

I can't help seeing that Dindinha is right to be angry the way she is with grandma for going to so much trouble for me, when she is so old. But is it my fault?

Grandma always shows that she likes me better than she likes Luizinha, who is her own goddaughter. From the time I was little she's done things for me that mama never does and she pays attention to everything I say. Without realizing it she favors me so much over the others that it seems to me that she's the mother and mama's the grandmother. I tell grandma everything I think; if I'm happy I tell her and if I'm mad I complain to her. Now that she's getting older she babies me. If she's eating something, she gives me a bite; if she's going to walk in the garden, she calls me; if she wants to pick fruit, I have to go, too; and when it's time for prayers in the evening I'm the one who has to tell the rosary.

Yesterday I had to memorize my geography lesson. I haven't

any map, but even if I had I wouldn't study it, it's so much easier to memorize. The parlor was empty and I was in there reciting out loud, where I wouldn't be disturbed, pacing the floor. Grandma opened the door once or twice while I was doing it and said, "Stop now, child; that's tiring. And you're so thin!" But I said, "No, grandma. Let me memorize all the questions at once; it's easier to remember it later."

When I got through, grandma had a glass of milk and some cookies waiting for me. "Come and eat this, so you won't feel weak. You're so thin already and with this studying you're going to turn into a toothpick." I ate the cookies and milk; climbed into the *jaboticaba** tree, and sucked *jaboticabas* until I belched three times. I climbed down feeling very full and half-sick, something that never happened to me before. I went into the parlor with everything going around inside, and my belly began to ache. I went to lie down with the bolster across my belly, thinking it would go away, but nothing happened. When they noticed me I was rolling on the bed screaming and doubled up with pain. I began to sweat. Grandma arrived immediately with the castor oil. "Take it, child. This is what comes of mixing milk and *jaboticabas*. Take it." I smelled the oil and pushed the cup away. "I can't, grandma. I'll throw up." And I rolled on the bed.

When grandma saw she couldn't make me take it that way she said, "Take it, child, for the love of God, and I'll give you the material for a dress and you can pick it out yourself." I said, "No, grandma. It's impossible!" Grandma shouted, "Zé Pedro! Run to Mota's quick, and tell them to send me samples of the prettiest dress-goods they have!" Zé Pedro ran off and grandma kept saying, "Drink it, daughter. The cloth for the dress is on the way." At that point Iaiá said, "Why don't we all grab hold of her and hold her nose and pour the oil down her throat?" I howled, "Just you try!" Grandma said, "No. Nobody's going to do that. She's an intel-

* A black, shiny fruit the size of a hot-house grape. One bites into it, sucks out the inside, and spits out the skin and seed.

ligent girl and she knows she's not going to get better unless she takes physic."

Zé Pedro came back with the samples and not being able to choose because of the pain, I pointed at any one at all. When the dress was chosen, I said, "Now go and get me some medicine that's easier to take, too." Grandma agreed: "That's a good idea! We have some salts. Hurry up, Chiquinha, go and mix some in water and bring it here." Dindinha brought the salts and I said to grandma, "Now I'm going to wait for the dress first." She said, "It's on the way, child. Drink it up."

Zé Pedro came in with the material, I took the cup and swallowed the salts in one gulp.

Iaiá and Dindinha turned their backs, saying, "Pretty clever!"*

Saturday, September 23rd

Oh! What wonderful news, that mama's coming back from Santa Barbara!

Only to think that I am going to leave grandma in peace, without anyone's being annoyed with her on my account, is a relief. If grandma had her way, I'd live here; she's already talked about it many times to mama, to let me stay. But it was I who didn't want to; I don't like too much fuss made over me.

I don't like a lot of fuss. There's a man in our family, and I'm not going to name any names, even in my diary, who likes to hold my hand in his and flatter me, to please grandma. How I loathe it! It makes me shiver as if my hand were on a lizard's belly. Thank God he doesn't do it any more; I think he must have seen I didn't like it. Here at the *chácara* if I don't eat, it's to worry grandma; if I study, it's to worry grandma; if I disappear, it's to worry grandma. Can I spend my whole life in this torture? When I'm at home I come here, get grandma's blessing and disappear and go and play. Life is very strange. Nobody knows what a person is like inside, they just say what they want to be-

* Literally: "She's an eagle!" (a genius).

lieve. In my family, on my mother's side, there are only two people who like me, grandma and Aunt Agostinha. On papa's side I'm loved by all the aunts and uncles; but Aunt Madge makes my life miserable with fussing over me, too. Grandma likes her very much and won't let me pass a day without going there, even if it's just to get her blessing and go away again.

Dindinha and Iaiá are already showing their pleasure at getting rid of us on their faces. I'm more pleased than they are. Today I've already been to clean the house to be ready for mama and papa. I and Luizinha scoured the whole house with *pita** and sand, swept the yard and put flowers in the *oratório*. Renato chopped the wood and piled it beside the stove. We left everything shining. Godfather Carlos, my father's brother, thinking he'd already arrived, came in the house just when I and Luizinha with our skirts tucked in our drawers, and fastened with pins any old way, and with our legs showing, were decorating the altar and strewing flowers on the bed. I don't know why godfather thought it was so funny, but he laughed until he cried.

Wednesday, September 27th

Mama arrived from Santa Barbara, had dinner at the *chácara*, and we went home.

She brought a big cake of brown sugar, a can of milk candy,† a bunch of bananas, a bundle of "little girls' fingers" sugar canes, a bottle of pickles, and some peanut brittle. So many good things! It was almost worth having her go.

We slept late yesterday because mama kept us all up until eleven o'clock telling us about Uncle Geraldo's children. My uncle never puts on airs. Where do they get their silliness from?

---

* *Pita:* agave plant. When the leaves are crushed in water they give off a soapy liquid.
† *Doce de leite:* a popular sweet of milk and sugar boiled until it is like caramel.

Papa says it's because they were born big slave-holders and were always looked up to, "*Minha sinhá* this, *meu sinhô* that . . ." and that's what spoiled the family; that Uncle Geraldo thinks he's pretty important, too, but he's older and not so foolish. All the relatives go to his house but he never goes to their houses. He can't live without my father, but if my father got sick I'd like to see if he would come to keep him company all day long the way papa does for him. Mama says this to papa all the time but he pays no attention. Then mama says, "It's your father's weakness;* let him. It's better than if he drank."

Mama said that in Santa Barbara, when they went to Agua Quente in the mornings, Bibiana would make a bundle of the towels and clothes and say to Nhonhô, "Take it, Joãozinho. You carry it; you like to." Mama didn't mind. My brothers have been brought up to work. My father says that in England there aren't any Negroes and the whites do the work. He says that a man of the people, if he's intelligent and hard-working and honest, can get to be a minister of the Queen.

Mama said that she just let Nhonhô do everything and she even approved of it, so he wouldn't be lazy. The whole day long it was: "Joãozinho, go get this, Joãozinho, go get that," and mama let him do it.

They went to spend one day at Seu João Pereira's *fazenda*. He was very hospitable, he took them to the sugar-mill to drink *garapa*† and was very nice. When they were leaving he made a bundle of sugar cane for the children and said, "Who'll carry this?" Because it was sugar cane and they all wanted it, the others wanted to carry it. The sisters were a way off. Zezé put the bundle of cane on his head and they went off, very pleased. When they caught up with the sisters, what a to-do! Bibiana bosses the rest of them because she's the oldest. Bibiana called out, "What are

---

* Literally: "It's your father's *cachaça*."
† Drink made from sugar cane.

you doing, Zezé? Carrying a bundle on your head like a nigger from the *senzala!** Put it right down! Give it to Joãozinho to carry." Nhonhô took it and put it on his head.

If it had been my father who'd been there he wouldn't have minded. But mama was brought up with a lot of slaves, too. Grandfather was rich and had a great many slaves. Mama said that when she heard Bibiana use the words "nigger from the *senzala*" she was furious, and she shouted at Nhonhô, "Put that down! If they don't want to be niggers why should you be one?" And then she added, "And let me tell you, from now on you're not going to be anyone's servant! This is the end!"

I can just see mama saying this, when she got mad. Mama almost never gets mad, but I saw her once, and I can imagine just how it was this time.

Mama said that the hard feelings lasted. When she got home still angry papa said, "Why all this hard feeling? Our João is a perfect little Englishman; he couldn't look like a nigger from the *senzala*." And he told Nhonhô to keep on doing the things he'd been doing, going to the *fazenda* for the milk and everything else.

Thursday, September 28th

Today I went to take grandma half the things that mama brought from Santa Barbara. Grandma looked at them and said, "You got so many good things! But I'm not going to take any of them. Tell your mother I'm very much obliged, but I don't eat those things. Just leave me the *doce de leite* and take back the rest." I tried to insist on leaving them but grandma kept repeating, "No, no! Keep them for yourselves. But before you go, sit down here and tell me everything that happened there. Didn't she tell you anything?" "Yes, grandma, she told us everything. Something very funny happened." And I told her everything, just the way it happened.

We all know that Uncle Geraldo is the apple of grandma's eye.

* *Senzala*: slave quarters.

Nobody can say the slightest thing against him because grandma will scold immediately. When I finished my story grandma said, "I knew that if Carolina went there something like that would happen. She's very rude herself. She was the last of the children. Batista and I were getting along in years and she was always full of whims. Why did Carolina have to go and start a quarrel, and when she was Geraldo's guest, too? Alexandre could spend his whole life with them and nothing would happen. But in less than a month Carolina has to start a fight." I said, "But mama tells papa that he's silly, grandma; that he puts up with everything; but she's different, she sees through them." Grandma said, "He isn't silly, not at all. Your father's very good, and well-brought-up. It's she who's very rude."

I saw that grandma didn't like what mama had done at Santa Barbara; I stayed a little while longer and then I went home, taking the rest of the presents back. When I got home I told mama how grandma had been angry and she said, "If I'd known that mother was going to ask you I'd have told you not to say anything. Geraldo's a touchy subject with mother." I asked, "Why, mama? Because he's rich?" She said, "No, not because of that, because mother's richer than he is. It's because he's the oldest, and when he was little he was very sick. He was always very quiet and never gave any trouble. She's right. If you can't say anything good about Geraldo, don't ever mention him to her."

It made me sad to hear mama speak like that. I'd like grandma to love all her children equally.

Friday, October 6th

Renato woke up this morning with the mumps and a fever. His face was all swollen up to an enormous size. I like his being sick because our relatives all came to visit at the same time and the house was gay and full of people. Even Dindinha and Iaiá came; but grandma didn't. She only goes to her children's houses when an illness lasts a long time. Uncle Geraldo didn't come, either.

But since he's Renato's godfather he sent Joãozinho and Onofre to bring him ten *mil reis*.

Dindinha and Iaiá were here when they arrived and presented the ten *mil reis*. My tongue itched and I was crazy to speak out, because it was the first present he'd ever given Renato. I wanted to clap my hands and say, "What a miracle!" I waited until the two of them were leaving and then I whirled around and cried, "We don't have any bell, but let's beat a tin can. Today there's a holiday in heaven. Now that Renato's fifteen years old, Uncle Geraldo has remembered to give him a present. We all get presents from our godparents on our birthdays. This is Renato's first. Maybe his luck's going to change now, who knows?" Dindinha and Iaiá left without saying anything. In the afternoon I went to the *chácara* for dinner, as I always do. I sat down beside grandma and I thought she'd give me a tidbit, the way she always does. But this time she said, "Today I should put a hot egg in your mouth, so you won't be so talkative. I heard about your little speech. Just when I think you're improving and getting more sensible with age, another piece of your foolishness come along. You must stop it and learn to hold your tongue."

Grandma didn't have to say any more for me to see that Dindinha and Iaiá had been telling tales. They'd never miss a chance to make grandma angry with me. I sat there choking, with a lump in my throat, and tears began to fall in my plate. I left the table crying and ran to my house. I'd scarcely got here when Reginalda came running after me, "Sinhá Teodora told me to tell you to come back, if you don't want her to be angry with you." I can't disobey grandma, so I went back. I met her in the doorway, looking upset, with a book in her hand. She handed me *The Imitation of Christ*, saying, "Read this and learn how to be patient, and see how older people have to correct younger ones." Then she gave me a silver two *mil reis* piece, and some candy, and she just didn't know where to find more things to give me and she kept looking to see if I was still mad.

But I hated Uncle Geraldo more than ever. Grandma quarrels with everyone because of me, but it's only that tightwad* who makes grandma quarrel with *me* because of *him*.

Wednesday, October 11th

Some days I come home from school so sick of everything I haven't the slightest desire either to do my work or study.

Today, Wednesday, is the day I have the most chores. I have to begin to iron the clothes today so that everything will be ready for tomorrow. I know if I let it pile up it will only make it worse for me. But until now I haven't been able to do a thing. I began to iron a dress with ruffles and I got to thinking that so much work was ridiculous, that we should just wear baize skirts the way they used to in the old days.

So I spent the afternoon without doing anything. Because I'm never too lazy to write, I'm going to write down here a story of the old days, for the future, as papa says. Who knows if in the future there won't be many more inventions than there are today? José Rabelo spends his time weighing vultures on the scales, in order to invent a flying-machine. Wouldn't that be wonderful! Sometimes I feel envious when I see the vultures soaring up so high. How would it be if I could turn into a vulture? It would be awfully funny. But it would be better to discover something so that people wouldn't die. However, until we can fly, as José says we're going to be able to, it would be better to go back to the old days and wear baize or cotton skirts! What a good idea!

Grandma talks about the life she led in Lomba and I get so envious of her! If they wanted to write they caught a goose, pulled out a wing-feather, and made a point at the end. If they needed a dress they took some cotton, took out the seeds, carded it to straighten it out, and then spun it on the spinning wheel. When the thread was ready they put it on the loom and the slaves wove the cloth. Clothes were made by hand, because there weren't any

* *Munheca de samambaia:* a "fern-fist"; a young, tightly curled fern.

sewing-machines. There weren't any matches, either. The fire had to be kept going all the time. In Lomba when they got careless and the fire went out they had to roll up a ball of cotton and shoot into it, to light it. There was always trouble, of course. Even if they hadn't anything else, there were always guns to kill other people with.

Now that I've finished writing I see I was an idiot to want it to be the olden times again only so I wouldn't have to iron my dress with ruffles. That's why mama and my aunts like to work so much.

Speaking of ruffles, I remember something very funny about grandma. When she sees the parlor full of women waiting for dinner she asks Dindinha, right in front of them, "Chiquinha, my child, how are you going to manage the ruffles that shrink so?" Dindinha answers, "I've already un-shrunk them, mother." Then grandma can be quite calm, because that means that Dindinha has already put more water and cabbage in the black beans.

How funny grandma is, besides being so good!

Tuesday, October 17th

Although grandma never ate the "Beef of the Divine"* it's almost the same thing, living with a full house, *coitada.*

A man and his wife arrived as guests at the *chácara,* so Fifina had to go to the home of some of her cousins. Iaiá moved into a small bedroom and took the opportunity of telling Fifina that there was no more room for her. We were all extremely pleased to see the last of Fifina.

She went to spend a day with Aunt Aurélia and that night the same thing happened that happened at grandma's; there was a rain storm and she had to sleep there. As it was just for once, Aunt

* Note in *M V d M:* " 'Boi de Divino,' beef that the giver of the feast, or 'the Emperor of the Divine,' orders butchered in the square to be distributed to the poor. To eat the Beef of the Divine is to be a victim of beggars, of guests who stay on and on, etc."

Aurélia made up a nice bed for her in the guest room and treated her very well. She liked the room and stayed on.

This would be quite natural in the family's other houses. But Uncle Conrado isn't silly like the others and his house is very different. Aunt Aurélia works without stopping, the children study, and Fifina stayed in the parlor the whole day long, regardless, playing patience. Grandma said, "Do you want to know something? Conrado is kind, and Fifina is neat and quiet and knows how to amuse the children telling stories. It's quite possible that they'll get used to her and then we'll be rid of her."

Today Aunt Aurélia came with Fifina to the *chácara* after dinner and we were there, the children on the lawn and the grown-ups in the parlor. At nine o'clock Aunt Aurélia got up, half-stuttering and trembling at the trick she was going to play. She said good-bye to everybody: "Bless me, mother. Good-night, Chiquinha. Good-night, Inhá. Good-night, Fifina." And she left in a hurry, dragging her children after her.

So Fifina stayed with grandma again. What a blow!

Saturday, October 28th

Today was Aunt Carlota's birthday and we had dinner at the *chácara*. Nobody in my family drinks ordinary wine, even at the table. Only port wine, that grandma orders from Rio de Janeiro, that comes in enormous barrels called "tenths."* It is bottled on Christmas Eve and lasts the whole year long. We all like port wine, it is heavenly it is so delicious. But today Uncle Joãozinho was in town and he found out that port wine wasn't meant for the table but should be drunk separate from the food. So grandma ordered some wine bought that's made in town, at the Padres' *chácara*.

We sat down at the table and Iaiá Henriqueta filled her glass first and said, "I'm going to try the wine first. Your health, Car-

* Because they hold 100 liters, a tenth of a cubic meter.

lota!" and she took a big swallow. Then she stopped a minute and made a face and said, "Ugh! It's horrible, as sour as vinegar!" We thought she'd stop drinking it, but not at all! She said that and then she turned up the glass and drank it all in one swallow. Everybody at the table began to laugh. Uncle Joãozinho said, "It isn't physic, Henriqueta. It's for people who like it." But even so, horrible as it was and sour as vinegar, it went down everybody's throat, except grandma's, who didn't want to try it. The truth is that our family likes to tipple.

Tuesday, October 31st

Today was the end of the month of the rosary. It's the only month that grandma doesn't have us pray at her *oratório*. She says her beads alone with Reginalda and then we all go to the church. I don't know why the rosary is only said in the church during the month of October; nobody ever explained it to me. I'm going to ask Father Neves. I must confess that I like to say the rosary better in church than I do at the *chácara* with grandma. At the *chácara*, when they don't decide to say one more Our Father for all the dead people that no one knows anything about any longer, Aunt Iaiá stretches it out so slowly it's agony for us. The church is much more cheerful and there's no thinking up anything more; it's always the same thing.

If grandma should read what I'm writing she'd be horrified at me. She can't understand why we don't think that praying is the best thing in life. I only like to pray when I'm sad or when there's a thunderstorm. The only two things I simply can't miss are hearing Mass on Sundays and saying the short rosary at home when I don't say prayers at the *chácara*. If I don't hear Mass on Sundays, like when I'm at Boa Vista where there isn't any church and I can't go to hear it at Bom Sucesso, I have a nail in my conscience all day long. The rosary, too—I've fallen asleep without saying my prayers and waked up in the night to say them. After that I never skipped them again. I told grandma I was afraid to get used to saying the litany every morning the way she does, and afterwards not be able to go without saying it.

Wednesday, November 1st

Today I went to School leaving Luizinha at home sick. One of the things I don't like to do is to go to School alone, particularly when she's sick. I spend the whole day with something weighing on my conscience.

Luizinha is very obstinate. She obeys me very well but she's very greedy and eats things that make her sick, even secretly. She's already had a colic from guavas at Boa Vista and mama only succeeded in getting her over it by means of prayers and vows; and even that didn't teach her.

Yesterday she sold a dozen eggs and we went to School. On the way home for lunch we went by Xixi Bombom's house and saw a white guava tree, loaded down. Luizinha said, "I'm going to buy us two hundred *reis* worth of guavas." She went in and bought them. The woman gave us thirty and we divided them, fifteen apiece. We went down the street to our house eating them. On the way I began to remind her of Boa Vista and she said, "That was because I was little, I'm bigger now," and went on eating to the very last one. At home she ate lunch. But the night was something; she screamed with colic the whole night.

Here at home mama never attempts to give physic to anyone without Siá Ritinha. She came early today to give the physic and Luizinha got rid of such a quantity of guava seeds that mama was amazed. I ate all mine and they didn't hurt me because I didn't eat them all at one time the way she did, and I didn't swallow the seeds.

Fortunately she's well already and Friday we'll be able to go to school together. But I have no hope that the second lesson taught her anything. I know that if she finds any guavas she'll eat them on the sly. So I'm going around by way of Carmo Street in order not to pass Xixi's house, since her guava tree is really a temptation.

Thursday, November 2nd

Siá Ritinha came early to find out if Luizinha had had anything more in the night. She's always ready to give us medicine, especially if it's bad to take.

This Siá Ritinha is old and hunchbacked and she smells sour; she hasn't a tooth in her head and her face looks like a *maracujá* forgotten in the drawer. She talks to us in such a way that when we were little we trembled with fear of her. Now I'm smarter and I don't mind her the way I used to. But when I was little, and until I started going to Normal School, she was the bane of my existence. She wouldn't let me play with the little girls in the neighborhood. If I went out the door wearing a short dress, like the other girls, she used to make me go back again and change to a longer one. I remember that my cousins asked me why I minded her that way and once I answered them, "I mind her because I'm afraid she'll steal our hens."

I remember one day coming into the house furious because Siá Ritinha had ordered me to change my dress and mama changed it and said, "Why do you cross her, child? It's just because she's fond of you children."

I solved the business of the short dress by going around so that I wouldn't pass in front of her door. But I never managed to run and play in the Largo da Cavalhada with my black schoolmates. She'd call me and give me some eggs or *xuxus** for mama and say, "This is to get you away from that troop of little niggers. I've already told you that a girl like you shouldn't play with them! Your mother may not care, but I don't approve of it."

Siá Ritinha's bossing me made me mad, but mama used to say, "I like to have her watch you for me because I can't stay at the window keeping track of you. And besides, she's energetic and I'm not."

* Pronounced "shoo-shoo." An ubiquitous, watery, green vegetable.

In Cavalhada only the men have watches. Those who live in the middle of town don't feel the lack of them because almost all the churches have clocks in their towers. But when papa isn't home the mistakes we make about the hours are really funny. During the day we don't need a clock because we come home at the same time for lunch and dinner. And besides, we have the bugle at the barracks, which blows at nine o'clock. After that, the rooster is mama's watch, which doesn't run very well. It's already fooled us several times, and mama doesn't catch on. Some days I even wish our rooster and our neighbors' would die. But it wouldn't really help because others would take their place.

The rooster's crow never gives the right time and nobody believes it. When the rooster crows at nine o'clock they say that a girl is running away from home to get married. I'm always hearing the rooster crow at nine o'clock and it's very rarely that a girl runs away from home.

Once upon a time I used to believe that roosters told time, because in Boa Vista when you ask a miner the time he looks at the sun and tells you. If you go and look at the clock, he's right. So I used to think that the sun kept time during the day and the rooster at night. Now I realize that this was a mistake.

On Sundays mama wakes us up a little before four o'clock for early Mass. Today when mama called us, I was dead to the world, and I said to mama, "It can't be anywhere near four o'clock, mama. It seems to me I've scarcely been asleep an hour. I'm so sleepy I can't open my eyes." She said, "You can sleep after Mass. It's time to get up, because the rooster's already crowed twice."

I got up with my head nodding with sleep and washed my face. Mama'd already strained the coffee. We drank it and left.

In the street I can always tell whether it's early or late. I kept looking at the moon and the stars and saying to mama, "This time the Senhora's going to see whether the rooster can tell time or not." The street was deserted. The two of us walked holding onto mama's arms. When we passed by the barracks the soldier on duty looked at mama and asked, "What's the Senhora doing in the street with these little girls at this hour?" Mama said, "We're going to Mass at the Cathedral." The soldier said, "Mass at midnight? It isn't Christmas Eve. What's this all about?"

I was afraid of the soldier. Mama said, "Midnight? I thought it was four o'clock. Thank you very much for the information."

We went back home and lay down in our clothes. But even so we missed Mass. When we got to Church later Father Neves was already in the Hail Marys.

Thursday, November 9th

The only thing my father won't do to please my mother is go to confession. He does everything else that mama wants. He goes with her to church, to Mass, and everything. Mama doesn't want him to eat meat on Fridays, and he doesn't eat it. But she just can't get him to confession. Even I don't understand why. If my father had stolen something from somebody I'd think he was ashamed to tell it to the priest. But never, never did I see my father commit any little sin whatever.

All year long mama struggles with him to go to confession. During Lent it's a martyrdom; I really feel sorry for mama, and papa always says, "You all confess so much, and take Communion so much, and pray so much, that a little rubs off on me, too." Fortunately, papa is healthy, but if he had a bad heart and mama thought he might die suddenly, it would be horrible.

I don't think the way mama does. I don't say anything because about religious matters she won't permit any discussion. But I can't be afraid the way mama is because I think to myself, "If my father should go to hell, where will my uncles and all the men of Diamantina go, with the exception of Seu Juca Neves?" I know that God is just. I suffered a great deal when I was little on account of grandpa and I don't want to suffer now, too, because of papa. At Mistress Joaquininha's school if I had the littlest quarrel with a girl, she'd say, "My grandfather isn't like yours; yours went to the heaven for the English."* My grandfather wasn't buried in the church because he was a Protestant; he was buried in front of the Charity Hospital, and they speak of it in Diamantina until today. When he was about to die the priests, the Sisters of Charity, and even Senhor Bishop, who was very fond of him, argued with him to be baptized and confess so he could be buried in holy ground. He answered, "Any ground God made is holy." The vicar didn't want to toll the bells, but the leading citizens of Diamantina went to the churches and tolled all the bells of the town for the entire day. He was very charitable and much esteemed. When the sick couldn't pay, he sent the medicines, and chicken, and money, too. The whole city went to the funeral. When he died I was very small and until this day they speak of the charity of the English Doctor, as everyone called him. Could a man like that be in hell?

I used to suffer when the girls said that he was in the English heaven. I told papa and he said, "Tell them that it's where you're going, too, child, and that it's the heaven of the whites and not of the Africans." I always said, "Papa, if I hear you say one thing, and the girls and mama and everybody say another thing, it drives me crazy."

Sunday, November 12th

I never enjoyed anything so much in my life as something that happened today to Emídio. Uncle Joãozinho gave him a letter to take to Dr. Pedro Mata and he came back with a broken head. He showed his head to Uncle Joãozinho and said, "Look at what your doctor did to me!" Uncle Joãozinho asked him, "How did that happen?" He answered, "That crazy Pedro Mata gave me a

* Which signifies hell.

slap and I fell all the way downstairs." Uncle Joãozinho said, "Perhaps you spoke to him the way you're speaking to me, and called him 'Pedro Mata'?" Emídio said, "How does the Senhor want me to call him? Aren't I free and as good as he is?" Uncle Joãozinho couldn't keep from laughing, and he said, "That slap was well-deserved. I'm glad to see it. That'll teach you to talk back to white people, you shameless Negro!" I was glad, too, because he's very impertinent.

Emídio is a queer and lazy Negro. He puts his finger in the lamp oil and licks it as if it were molasses. The other day he had a bad toothache; he took an iron spit and put it in the fire until it was red hot and then he put it on the tooth and I heard the flesh hiss and I was horrified. He didn't complain about his toothache any more after that.

Monday, November 13th

I'm amazed at Renato's weakness in everything. He spends his life doing wrong, running away from home stealing fruit from people whose yards have fallen-down walls. Mama suffers and talks, but nothing helps. The other day we asked him why he grieved mama so much and he replied, "The devil tempts me." I was furious at this reply because I know that we can deliver ourselves from the temptations of the devil.

Yesterday I saw that he is much too weak and I felt sorry for him. I'm afraid that, with his bad companions, he'll really go wrong. Because whenever he wants something he simply can't resist.

Last night Uncle Geraldo came to grandma's. Dindinha went to the kitchen and brought a tray of meat turnovers that the Negroes were making to sell at the entrance to the theatre. She brought them in and gave out one to each child and each grown-up, and left the rest on the tray for my uncle and my father to eat with the port wine they were drinking. We were all talking. Renato, who's always famished, was sitting beside mama with his eyes nailed on the tray of turnovers. When there was only one left, he got up, went to the table, stuck the fork in the turnover, and went back again, eating it.

When we got home papa said, "You shamed me tonight, my boy. What made you take that turnover your uncle was going to eat? Couldn't you see he hadn't finished?" Renato said, "I know it was wrong, papa. I thought about it a lot before I did it, but I wanted it so much I couldn't resist."

His being so weak made me sad.

Monday, November 20th

Today I was very happy after a week of being mad. Grandma's spending a few days at Uncle Geraldo's house because he's sick. I have to go every day to get her blessing. If I should miss one day the sky would fall.

I've been wearing boots that are full of nails and they've hurt my foot so that I can't walk straight. I went to my uncle's house limping. Grandma was upset and kept talking about it, and she took the boots and had the nails hammered in, but they weren't any better. I went back every day the same way. What could I do? It kept bothering grandma and my rich cousins kept telling her, "It's just so you'll feel sorry and give her another pair, grandma!" I was so mad that I didn't go back there for two days running. Even in the evenings I stayed at home, studying. Grandma complained to mama; today I had to go back and I said to her, "I waited for my foot to get better and mama told the shoemaker to hammer in the nails, too. The cousins don't have to say anything more." Grandma said, "You're still limping. You have to keep making an effort. Go to Mota's store and tell Tião to give you some cheap boots." When my wretched cousins heard grandma's order they said, "Didn't we tell you? That's what she wanted." Grandma said, "It's none of your business!" And she turned to me and said, "Go, daughter. Go and get your boots."

They're all mad because I'm her favorite granddaughter. I went running to the store and I said to Tião, "Grandma says to tell you to give me the cheapest pair of boots you have." He said, "Not the cheapest, no. You deserve the most expensive ones." He brought out some boots with buttons, such as I could never even dream of having. And how soft on the feet! You'd think you were in your bare feet. I didn't want to take them and Tião kept saying, "Don't be silly, girl. Your grandmother is rich and you can tell her that I don't have any others here and I'll back you up."

I went out flying, to my uncle's house. Those fiendish cousins wouldn't believe there weren't any other cheaper ones, and they took away the boots and took them back to exchange them. But Tião stuck to what he'd told me and I got them.

I'm sure that tomorrow they'll really talk, but I won't be foolish enough to put on such beautiful boots to wear to School. But it's all right because yesterday I told grandma that my old boots didn't have nails in them any more and that my foot was healed already.

Sunday, November 26th

When I get married I wonder if I'll love my husband as much as mama loves my father? God willing. Mama lives only for him and thinks of nothing else. When he's at home the two spend the whole day in endless conversation. When papa's in Boa Vista during the week, mama gets up singing wistful love songs and we can see she misses him, and she passes the time going over his clothes, collecting the eggs, and fattening the chickens for dinner on Saturday and Sunday. We eat best on those days.

Monday, Uncle Joãozinho took my father to see about a mine in Biribiri and they were supposed to come back at the end of the week. Early Thursday morning we went to the window and there was papa's mule at the door, waiting to be fed. I had to admire mama's energy. She said immediately, "We must get ready to leave early tomorrow morning. Something's happened to Alexandre." And with her eyes full of tears she told Cesarina to kill two chickens for our provisions.

In the afternoon she put a clean dress in the suitcase for each of us, some clothes for my brothers, and she sent for José Pedro to carry it. Renato carried the basket of provisions. We went to bed early with our clothes beside us so we could get up at daybreak, get dressed and leave. Mama didn't even go to bed, saying that she couldn't sleep and would spend the time praying. We'd just got into a good sound sleep when mama woke us up. "Get up! The rooster's already crowed twice! It must be four o'clock. We can get as far as Pedra Grande before daylight." We got up, drank our coffee, and left, mama, my brothers and my sister, and the two little Negroes, Cesarina and José Pedro.

When we got out in the street the sky was very full of stars and the night was still very black for four o'clock. We kept walking and it didn't get any lighter. When we'd already gone a long way we heard the Seminary clock strike two. We all began to laugh except mama, the person who was responsible for it all, who didn't think it was funny. She said, "The time isn't the worst thing. It's a good idea to travel at night. But I'm afraid the road seems different. The Biribiri road is much wider than this one." We didn't know where we were any more but we kept on going. Finally mama said, "This road is really too strange. We'd better sit down and wait for daylight." She spread out the shawl on the ground for my brothers to lie down on, and sat down on a stone; then she put my head and Luizinha's in her lap, took out her rosary and began to pray while we slept.

When it was daylight, what an abyss! We'd taken the wrong road. We were in a place it didn't seem we could possibly get out of. It was the very top of the Serra dos Cristais [Crystal Mountain] and from up there we saw the road far below. We were on a precipice! We always have confidence in mama and her prayers, but she was silent and kept on praying. We asked her what we should do.

She said, "Wait. I'm praying to Santa Maria Eterna and I'll only know afterwards what I should do next." We waited. After a little she said, "Since we don't know the way it would be very hard to turn around and go back. What we have to do is have faith in God and keep on going, and try to find some way out of this by sliding down."

We looked like goats, and sometimes we slid down so far at one time that it was only at the end that we saw how ridiculous what we'd been doing was. Renato was trying to show off and he got hung up on a little tree. It broke and he fell in a hole in the side of the mountain and vanished in front of our eyes. At that point we began to cry and scream. Mama, with her eyes full of tears, looked up at the sky and prayed, "Santa Maria Eterna, Virgin of Virgins, help me on this occasion; deliver me from this affliction!" Then José Pedro asked for her umbrella, tied a leather strap onto it, and held it for Renato to take hold of and climb out. He tried and failed three times. Finally mama gave him the shawl to tie on, too, and Renato climbed out. We continued our rolling until we fell down onto the road.

I figured that our descent must have taken about six hours, because the sun was already high when we got down. When we looked at each other we had to laugh in horror. Our clothes were all muddy and in rags. And it was just then that mama saw that Luizinha's face was all swollen up with mumps! We were hungry and we didn't have anything left to eat; our provisions were finished. We went behind a bush, while mama watched the road, and changed our clothes.

While we were resting here a humming-bird with a white tail flew by very close. Renato waved his hat at the poor little thing and hit it and it fell dead on the ground. Mama said to him, "How mean! Wait and see what will happen to you. I could take my oath that you won't get any presents in Biribiri!" Every time we go to Biribiri we come home loaded with presents. Dona Mariana gives us dress-goods from the factory and my uncle gives us money and cans of candy.

After we had rested we went on to Biribiri. We were received with joy and astonishment. When mama told the story of how the mule had appeared and the adventures of our trip everyone laughed uproariously. It was only then that papa discovered that the mule had run away from the pasture and gone home.

We spent two days there and came home yesterday through town loaded down with the presents we'd all received. All except Renato, who didn't even get a handkerchief. There are still people who don't believe one is punished for killing a humming-bird. But I can't doubt it any more.

Monday, December 4th

Knowing that I and my sister have that failing of laughing at everything, how did papa have the courage to send a guest to our house the way he did? You can't imagine what our life has been like with this man in the house! Papa has been in Parauna for a week. He went to see a mine that a Frenchman wants to buy and asked papa if he'd go to see if it's worth it. There papa's the guest of this man he sent us. But you wouldn't believe it if I told you what his visit has been like.

We have a little Negro girl, Cesarina, very funny, who makes us laugh all the time at the things she says and does. On the day this man arrived something happened to us that couldn't possibly happen in any other house; there were only two tallow candles in the house. When mama discovered it there weren't any stores open. But these candles aren't any good; they don't last at all. One was used up before I'd even finished my lessons. Mama had the other one put in the guest room. In our house we only use kerosene in the kitchen and even the kitchen lamp was dry. When my candle came to an end I still had lessons to do; there was nothing else to do but send Cesarina to the guest room, to see if he'd gone to sleep. If he had, she was supposed to steal the candle without waking him up! She went and came back laughing so hard at finding the man still awake that she could only speak to us by making signs.

She held her hands up in the air and made spectacles with her fingers, meaning that the man had his eyes open. She made this sign and all the time she was having such a fit of the giggles that she couldn't speak.

We are idiots about laughing. We began that night and even now we can't look at our guest without a fit of giggling. We just have to see the man and then we remember Cesarina's spectacles and simply burst. Mama, *coitada*, doesn't know what excuse to give the man. She's said everything except that she has two lunatics in the house.

And I think that these attacks of laughing that we've had are due to our having as a guest a man who's never seen us before, and his being silent, without saying a word, in the house and at the table. Now mama's forbidden us to come to the table, but even in the kitchen we shake with laughter to see the man and mama sitting there in silence! I don't know what she'll tell papa. He's been here three days and it already seems like a week. I envy people who don't have giggling spells the way I have.

At the saddest moments, sometimes, when we shouldn't have had cheerful faces, we've laughed.

Thursday, December 5th

If there's one thing I'm jealous of, it's our teacher Sebastião's vineyard. I've never been in it, I've just seen it from outside. When the grapes are ripe I just die with envy of the quantity they have there; in Jogo da Bola Street a procession of women spends the whole day going to Seu Sebastião's place with baskets of grapes on their heads, to make wine. Some of them will give us a bunch, others are mean and won't give us any. But because there are so many people if we wait long enough we always get some.

I thought what Glorinha said was funny. She said: "Wouldn't it be wonderful if Seu Sebastião drank enough wine on the day of our exams and passed us all?" I replied that that had never occurred to me. I thought that being a friend of her family's the way he is, he'd never fail her. But I've seen that he is silly. He won't help you even if you flatter him; he's really mean. We'll have to study, there's no way out of it.

Saturday, December 9th

I didn't pass the first year and it was entirely due to bad luck and nothing else.

In the geography examination almost all of us cheat. We make concertinas;* it's so much easier. I made them all with the greatest care and I went to the examination with my pockets full of them.

The subject for the written exam turned out to be "Rivers of Brazil." Marvelous! I took out my little concertina and started to copy it, and told the others out loud that they should copy, too. I think that's what caught his eye. Seu Artur Queiroga came down from the platform and stood near my desk and I couldn't possibly go on writing. I put my concertina in my desk and put my hands on top. He said, "All right; go on!" I'd just been describing the Amazon River. I don't know what gave me the idea of saying what I said, that was what spoiled everything. He repeated, "Go on! Write!" I answered, "I can't, Seu Artur. I am drowned in the Amazon River." He gave a loud laugh that attracted the attention of the other examiners and they came to my desk, too. Seu Artur said, "I'm going to rescue you. Let's see if

* *Sanfona:* concertina; here means narrow strips of paper, folded concertina-style, on which the students wrote notes in order to cheat in their examinations.

you can go on if I get you out of the Amazon." And then he said,
"Run this way; receive these tributaries; debouch here . . ." But
it was impossible to follow him. It only amused the teachers and
the others went on cheating in peace and I and my class couldn't
do the exam.

I had to hand over the concertina and Seu Artur only asked
me to explain why I made that instead of studying. I answered
that I didn't know; that that was the way I'd been taught and I
thought it was a good system.

After this exam others went the same way. The teachers came
and distracted me while my schoolmates were peacefully cheating
away.

It was my bad luck. What can I do?

Monday, December 11th

Papa came back from Paraúna yesterday. The tests weren't good.
Papa says that he knew the mines there weren't as good as those
in Boa Vista and Sopa. He says that the Frenchman has already
ordered great quantities of machinery and that there's going to
be a different system of washing in diamond-mining now. The
big machines will mix everything and the diamonds will come out
separately. Papa thinks that in a good mine, where there isn't
water, it's going to be a good process, because they can bring the
water from a distance in iron pipes. I know I'm going to miss
seeing the men turning the pans out, and seeing the diamonds
sparkling in the sand. Only born miners, like our family, understand the pleasure it gives.

When Papa got back he asked mama if we had treated the
guest in our house well, and said, "He and his family couldn't
have done more for me at their house; they almost overwhelmed
me with attention. His daughters are homely and not very at-
tractive. I thought he'd come back enchanted with my girls, but
when he got back he was silent and didn't say a thing. I couldn't
keep from asking him if he'd seen my daughters and he told

me, 'I never saw their faces; they laughed from the minute I got there until I left.' "

Mama told him about the candle and said, "Even you can't imagine what it was like. These idiots didn't stop for an instant. I had to make them eat in the kitchen and I stayed and ate at the table with the man, trying hard not to laugh, too, the way they were doing in the kitchen."

Papa said, "I was the idiot, to forget the kind of daughters I have. Such pretty little girls, with this awful fault. You know, Carolina, we've got to find some way of putting a stop to these girls' giggling. It's a constant embarrassment to us. How many friends we've lost already because of it! In Boa Vista, Juca and Dona Mariquinha have turned against us on account of them— our friends for so many years. It's lucky I came back; on the other hand it would have been a trial for me to stay there, with Anselmo, after he'd been here, so different from the way he used to be with me. We have to find some way of putting a stop to it. It can't go on like this. I thought they'd improve with age, but they're getting worse." I took him at his word and said, "We will get better with age, papa, but forty years isn't thirteen and eleven." He said, "But you should know by now that much laughter is a sign of little sense."

Renato's taking geography tomorrow and I bet he doesn't pass. Early Thursday we're off to Boa Vista. Wonderful! I must make the most of this vacation.

Boa Vista
Wednesday, December 20th

Grandma swells with pride when she sees the things I write.

Mama never looks at what I write, but grandma wants me to read everything to her and to outside people, too. When I spend a few days at the *chácara* I'm on pins and needles to get home just because of that. *Coitada;* she's very intelligent, but she never learned to read and write well and so she still thinks it's something almost supernatural to write things down with a pen. The funny thing is that she isn't impressed when I tell her things. It's because she thinks writing is so much more difficult.

I'm going to tell about the big surprise I've just had in Boa Vista. The richest man here, and the only one who has a big and beautiful house, is Seu Joaquim Santeiro [saint-maker]. I've seen his parlor which has more beautiful holy statues in it than the Church. He has a Dead Christ there I'm sorry grandma can't see. She'll envy us, when I tell her about it, but she can't come, *coitada*. The Blessed Virgins are beautiful. Saint José, Saint Francisco, Saint Antônio,—he keeps on making them and filling the room with them, and he says that when he sells one he puts another in its place, so that the parlor's never empty. I go to his house every time I'm in Boa Vista and I never get tired of looking at them.

I wanted to know how Seu Joaquim Santeiro makes the holy statues. The other day we went there and he was in front of the house with a very sharp axe, chopping a tree trunk, with the chips flying. He didn't split it like fire-wood; he cut off pieces and there was the body, the legs, and everything, so that I was lost in admiration. Papa said, "Good morning, Joaquim. What are you making there?"

It's silly of me to write down here what he said and I know that grandma's going to be mad at me. But what can I do, since he did say it? He stopped using his axe, turned to papa, and said, "Good morning, Seu Alexandre. This is a devil of a Saint Sebastião that the Gouvea woman ordered a long time ago, and I've just now found this tree trunk, and it's giving me a hell of a lot of work . . ."

Sunday, December 24th

At the table my father is always repeating the reason why we're the poorest members of the family. In our family everybody has only worked at mining all their lives. Papa says that Uncle Geraldo asked him to join the Mining Society of Saint Antônio. He accepted, and joined with twenty *contos* that he had at that time. But mama was afraid of losing the money and she began to make a novena to Saint Antônio because the mine was named for him and she asked him to advise her, and if he didn't think papa was going to be successful, if he'd send her some sort of sign. On the day she finished the novena there was a knocking at the door and it was Seu Malaquias, an old miner, who was an authority on all the mines in the district. He came in and said to mama, "Dona Carolina, I've come to give you some advice. Don't let Seu Alexandre join that Society of Saint Antônio. That mine is all worked out." Mama was radiant with joy and she said, "Saint Antônio himself must have sent you here, Seu Malaquias. I've just finished a novena to him today that I've been making religiously, begging him to advise me." When papa came home and she told him the story, he gave up his share in the Society to Uncle Joãozinho and Uncle Justino, who don't believe in Saint Antônio.

Then mama tells of the suffering she and papa endured when the mine was opened and the diamonds began to shine like stars on top of the gravel. Papa went and bought the *corridos** of the mine and found a lot of little diamonds that he sold for sixteen *contos*. Uncle Geraldo, who owned the most shares in the mine, was the one who made his fortune.

I don't know how mama can keep on believing in Saint Antônio. She says, to console herself, that Saint Antônio knows what he's doing, and that perhaps the money would have brought her bad luck. I don't believe that money brings bad luck to anyone.

Saturday, December 30th

This week I've been kept in the house with a swollen knee. I got hurt by falling off a horse. I've suffered a great deal, not from my hurt knee, but by being imprisoned in the house; and when

* Here meaning the gravel that had been gone over once.

I'm in the country, too. How horrible it is to stay shut up in the cabin, knowing that there are so many wonderful things one might be doing outside! When I think that I could be fishing in the brook, or going after birds' nests and fruit in the woods, or trapping birds, and everything, and that here I am in this little house, seeing Renato and Nhonhô outside enjoying it all, I don't even know what I feel. If I knew how to write I'd have been able to write a big book, the days have been so long. Mama says I deserved this punishment for being a tomboy. All the same, it's a punishment. Everything that my brothers do, I want to do, too, and I can't rest until I've done it.

Monday papa sent Renato to get the horse from the pasture and I was jealous and went after him. On the way back I asked him to let me get on bareback, and he did. He did it out of meanness. I got on the horse and before I was sitting properly Renato switched him. The horse gave a jump and threw me on the stones. I got home with the greatest difficulty. If it had happened near the house I would have cried more and made a lot of fuss so my father would have punished him, but it was a long way off and I could only come groaning back to our cabin.

I used to be very jealous when I saw my brothers riding the horse bareback, but now I'm cured and I'll never get on again in my life since I've learned it's horrible to fall off and bruises one so much. I'm ending this year so badly! I only want to get better and rush out into the fields. How happy I'll be to be on the river bank, fishing with my sieve!

$$1 \quad 8 \quad 9 \quad 4$$

At Boa Vista
Sunday, January 7th

We went with mama to call on the teacher at Bom Sucesso. Boa Vista has no school; the children from here have to go to Bom Sucesso, almost a mile away. Every time Júlia meets mama she tells her: "I'm saving the school for Helena. I want to get away from here and go some place more up-to-date." I could see my future clearly: papa would keep on mining; the house would be sold and the money put into business for Nhonhô here; Renato, when he got his certificate, would go away to teach school, because he's a man; mama and Luizinha would keep house and raise hens, and I'd have the school.

Today when we got to Júlia's house, she said to mama, "Helena's plans have all vanished like a dream, Dona Carolina. Have you heard that I'm going to get married very soon now? I've already made arrangements for a substitute. Now it will be harder for Helena." I told her, "I haven't any hope of getting my certificate so soon, Júlia. If I failed the first year, imagine the others. And we can't see the future. Who knows? Perhaps when I grow up I'll meet a boy I like, like you, and I won't have to teach school." Júlia said, "Nothing could be more likely."

Wednesday, January 10th

Today we were sitting in front of the cabin, the whole family. Mama was picking over rice; Renato and Nhonhô were making bird-traps, I was darning my stockings and Luizinha was watching us work. All of a sudden I asked, "Why do you think we're alive? Wouldn't it have been better if God hadn't created the world? Life is nothing but work. We work, eat, work some more, and sleep, and then we never know if we're finally going to hell or not. I really don't know why we're alive." Mama said, "What a horrible thing to say, child! What have you been studying your catechism for all this time, if now you're going to tell me that you don't know why we're alive? Haven't you learned in it every single day that we live to love and serve God on earth and to see Him face to face in Heaven?" I said, "I learned it, mama, but I've noticed that only grandma's family and a few other people live in order to love God on earth and hope to see Him face to face in heaven. If you only knew how much I've suffered because of this business of loving God, you'd feel sorry for me. I haven't gone to confession once without telling the priest that I don't think I love God, because I only remember God in time of need. Father Neves says he doesn't believe it, and that he knows I love God because I never commit a mortal sin. I tell him that's because he doesn't think anything's a sin. Sometimes he even tries to make excuses for the sins I tell him, horrified at myself. When I and Luizinha stole the fruit that grandma would have liked so much, I expected to go to hell for it, but when I told Father Neves he said, 'It isn't a sin to steal from your grandmother.' I thought it was a sin, and I stole, and afterwards I was only afraid of hell; it never crossed my mind that I was giving offense to God." Mama said, "That's because you just go merrily along and don't try to think. When one thinks, one has to love God. I love Him above everything." Renato stopped working on the trap and said, "Do you know what I was just thinking? There isn't any such thing as heaven, or hell either; it's all just priests' talk. I think that life is just like a handful of cornmeal that's put on the palm of your hand; when somebody blows on it, it vanishes, and there's nothing left. When we're dead the earth swallows us up; there's no such thing as the soul." Mama was appalled and asked him, "Wherever did you get such ideas? I'm shocked at your saying such things! How can a boy as old as you are have such heretical ideas! God help me, what an affliction! How have I offended God that I should have a son like this! Blessed Virgin! I'm going to live only for your sake now, my boy." Mama told a story of a woman who had a son like that and she did penance by tearing her flesh with a nail so that God would pardon him. God pardoned him and he was ordained and became a very saintly priest. Renato kept on making the trap and without lifting his head he said, "But the Senhora doesn't have to tear her flesh with a nail, because I'm not going to be a priest. A crooked stick can't be straightened."

Sunday, January 14th

Grandma is very intelligent. She never studied and I never saw her open a book; only her prayer book. She didn't come to town to live until she was old, but how well she understands everything! She's interested in everything I tell her; she looks at my notes, something mama never does. She talks to me about when she was a girl, and I love to hear her.

When she and grandpa began their life in Itaipava, they were very poor; they only had two slaves. They only had baize coats to keep out the cold. They lived in a thatched house. Grandpa made a living mining; one day he'd find a diamond, another day, a little gold. And they lived happily like that. At that time, mining was against the law. When the dragoons went by, grandma hid the gold and diamonds inside her lace-pillow and sat throwing the bobbins. The dragoons came and looked and went away. Afterwards, mining was licensed and there weren't any more such scares.

Grandpa was from Serro and he was a lieutenant. When there was a war in Serra do Mendanha,* grandpa went, against his will, because he was on one side and grandma's brothers were on the other. He was shot in the arm and grandma still has his blue uniform, with gilded buttons, all stained with blood. When the war was over he came back to Itaipava.

At the time grandpa started working the mines at Lomba, grandma made a novena to the Blessed Virgin and she listened to her. When grandpa began working the mine he found a virgin *calderão*.† They were such big diamonds that a slave named Tito, who was a trusted friend, fell on his knees and raised his hands to heaven, exclaiming, "My Lord and Heavenly Father, if this wealth endangers my soul, let it vanish!"‡ Just then grandma arrived with grandpa's coffee, and she helped to pick up the diamonds; they were as big as grains of corn on top of the gravel.

Grandpa never wanted to leave that place. He sent his sons to be educated in Rio. The daughters only learned to read and write; but they all married in Lomba without ever coming to the city. The story of the wealth of Batista's daughters spread far and wide.

---

* Note in M V de M: "An allusion to the encounter between government forces and the liberals in Serro do Mendanha during the revolution of 1842."

† Note in M V de M: "Calderão: a concentration of diamonds formed in the depressions in the bed of a river in diamond-bearing regions." A *calderão* is literally a big pot.

‡ Burton, *The Highlands of the Brazil*: ". . . the wealth was such that sometimes an owner would exclaim, 'O my God, are You doing this to cause my loss?' "

Doctors* and rich farmers came from Diamantina, from Serro, and Montes Claros, to ask for my aunts in marriage, without ever having seen them, and it was grandpa who accepted them or rejected them, according to what he knew about them.

No girl would marry like that today. In spite of this I haven't seen anyone more happily married than mama and my aunts. Could it be because they weren't brought up in the city?

Diamantina
Saturday, February 10th

Since papa's been working at Boa Vista we've never come back so many days before the end of vacation the way we have now. But the cabin where we stayed last year was right in the way of the mine and it had to be torn down. So papa made an agreement with Seu João and Virginia, two very good Negroes, that they'd rent us a living-room and bedroom and give us our food. Mama, I, and Luizinha had the bedroom; papa, Renato, and Nhonhô the living-room.

We got along very well until their little girl got sick. Virginia slept in the bedroom next to ours. At night her little girl woke up crying with a bellyache. I jumped out of bed, ran to the room, and took up the baby to quiet it. I patted her little belly in such a way that the poor little thing stopped crying, and I walked up and down singing to her until she was fast asleep. I put her in bed and she stayed asleep until morning.

The same thing happened the next night. I got up and did what I'd done the night before. The third time mama held me back, "Don't you go! What kind of nonsense is this, spending your nights nursing a little nigger?" And she wouldn't let me go.

The little girl had already got used to me and she wouldn't stop crying. Mama was furious with the *coitadinha* because she wouldn't

* A "doctor" is any man—doctor, lawyer, engineer, etc.—with a university degree.

let my father sleep. Virginia was mad, too, because Seu João had to get up early and he couldn't rest. And the little black baby kept on screaming. Virginia said she didn't walk the floor with the baby because it would spoil her and afterwards she'd be the one who'd have to put up with it. The poor little thing never stopped crying, and Virginia gave her a slap that we heard in our room. I leaped out of bed and went to get her. To let her cry with pain, and then on top of that to beat her,—I couldn't stand it. I didn't even have to stay with her half an hour. The poor baby sobbed herself to sleep.

This kept up, with mama furious with both the baby and its parents. In the daytime, at the mine, she talked to papa about his finding some way of getting us away from there. Papa kept saying, "How? If I start to make a cabin now, I won't finish in time. Besides, we can't take the men away from the job. We have to make the most of the rains, and they may stop at any time. Let's endure it." Mama said, "But this girl, with this mania of hers of not being able to hear a baby cry without wanting to comfort it, she'll be the death of me. You don't know how mad it makes me to see her jumping out of bed these cold nights, staying in her bare feet taking care of somebody else's nigger baby!" Papa: "If we can't do anything about it we'll just have to be patient."

The little girl didn't stop crying nights, and mama, who is obstinate sometimes, brought us back here. I and Luizinha are with grandma in this disgusting city, and mama, papa, and my brothers are enjoying themselves there in that heaven.

I think mama was right to be angry with me. But what can I do if I can't change my nature? I think that if the little girl had been white, mama wouldn't have minded. But she always scolds if we nurse Negro babies. Is it their fault if the poor little things are black? I don't make any distinction, I like them all.

Grandma shuts me up in the parlor for hours and hours to study, and shuts Luizinha up in the bedroom. Luizinha sleeps like a log, but I can't possibly sleep in the daytime and I write to kill time, and keep dying of envy of mama and my brothers there in paradise, while we're here.

Just then Luizinha said, "Good for you! You're an idiot, and without doing anything wrong I get punished along with you."

Tuesday, February 13th

Our holiday is over this week. Thank God my suffering is coming to an end, envying mama and my brothers, who are still in Boa Vista.

When I wake up every morning and open my eyes and find myself in the city instead of being in Boa Vista, it makes me so sad that I offer it as a sacrifice to God. I spend the best part of the day thinking, "Oh! If I were in Boa Vista!" I don't tell my cousins because they like it when they know I'm unhappy. But Luizinha keeps saying, "Serves you right!"

I wasn't angry with mama for bringing me back because I saw how frantic she got with the little pickaninny in Boa Vista. Mama finally got up to quiet her herself. Virginia didn't want to let her, and only let her after a lot of fuss, but the little girl screamed louder than ever. She only wanted me. Then mama said that the little girl would only get used to being without me if she took me away from there.

Children seem to sense that I'm crazy about babies, because all those I know are so fond of me. Uncle Joãozinho told mama it's because she didn't give me any dolls when I was little, and now I'm making up for it.

Friday, February 16th

School opened yesterday and classes are going to begin Monday. We received the list of books but they haven't given out the class schedules yet. Everyone is excited.

I'm going to write down here something very sad that happened yesterday at grandma's. Since the days of slavery the Negro women at the *chácara* have all been black, and I don't know why one of them turned out to be white and pretty. Her name is Florisbela but we call her just Bela. She married a Negro who is so ugly it breaks your heart. On the day of the wedding there was a table of sweets and it was painful to see Bela, *coitada*, sitting there beside the bridegroom. Marciano is the most highly respected Negro at the *chácara*. He learned the trade of blacksmith and he comes into the parlor to pay his respects to grandma and my aunts. Even so I didn't want Bela to marry him. She is really so pretty! She looks like a rose camellia, light, rosy, and with beautiful teeth. On the wedding day, papa said, "It's throwing pearls before swine." Everybody was sorry. But she wanted to do it and grandma approved because Marciano is very good and a good worker.

Grandma is always complaining that the law of the 13th of May* set everybody free except her, because she was left with a houseful of Negro women, and babies, and old men. She's very pleased when any of them get married; she gives them a trousseau and a table of sweets. The old slave quarters have a room for weddings that opens onto the yard. Every once in a while the room has to be fixed up for a wedding. Grandma is delighted and quite a few of the Negroes have got married. Bela was the last one, and now she is so unlucky!

Today Marciano, with a friend helping him, carried her in in a hammock. When he started to lift Bela out of the hammock we were all horrified and started to scream, and he said, "No, she isn't dead. Something's been made."† Grandma had her laid on a hard table, with only a pillow on it, dressed as she was. She was half-dead, half-alive. They only knew she was alive because when they held a mirror in front of her mouth it clouded over. But

---

* At the time of the Emancipation many of the able-bodied male slaves left for the large cities.
† A veiled reference to witchcraft.

nothing had any effect on her, nothing at all. She looked more beautiful than ever that way, pale, with her mouth and eyes closed. I watched her a whole hour, hoping to see her wake up. I felt so sad to see her like that! Bela was like a daughter to grandma and we are all so fond of her!

Marciano told us what had happened. He said that a friend who shared his house and took his meals with him was jealous when he saw him married to Bela, so light and pretty, and he wanted to run away with her. Because she wouldn't do it he brought her a bottle of wine he'd prepared, and when she drank it she fell down as if she were dead. Marciano waited in Formação* for a day to see if she would come to, but then he lost hope and brought her here.

He stays sitting beside her, watching her and crying. The doctor has been here and says there's nothing to be done; we can only wait. What a strange thing! She's been like this for two days now.

Tomorrow I trust to God that when I get to the *chácara* I'll find Bella conscious.

Saturday, February 17th

It's impossible to say whether it's a sleep or not; it's more like death. I'm so unhappy about this sleep of Bela's that I went through the vegetable garden and climbed a tree so that I could think by myself. I thought that if she'd been black and homely this wouldn't have happened; that devil of a man wouldn't have done what he did. The only thing that consoles me is knowing that she isn't in pain. Since they brought Bela here the only thing I've been able to think of is seeing her wake up.

I asked Marciano if no one could do anything to make her wake up and he said that only the villain who did the deed could undo it. But that fiend has already told his friends that even in death he'll never tell what he did; and that he'd rather die and go

* Formation: a Negro district of Diamantina.

to the depths of hell than see Bela married to Marciano! Marciano is so good that he only keeps saying, "I didn't deserve such an angel. God gave her to me and God is taking her away."

At the *chácara* they're just waiting until the mirror doesn't show any more mist on it to bury her. She is as good as dead already to almost everybody else; but I begged grandma to let her stay the way she is a while longer, sleeping on the table.

I'm very sad because I kept holding up the mirror all day long and I didn't see the least little cloud on it. Dindinha said that she could see one and I pretended to, too, but all the others were positive they couldn't. The coffin is already ready; they're just waiting until the mirror doesn't cloud over any more.

Today at School they gave out the class schedules. They're better for the pupils who live a long way off than they were last year, because they give more time for lunch.

Sunday, February 18th

Today they held Bela's funeral. Everyone in the *chácara* was convinced she was dead except me. If I could have, I wouldn't have let them bury her yet. I said that to grandma, but she said that she couldn't do that. Bela was exactly the same as she was on the day they brought her from Formation, only a little thinner.

Everybody says that the pangs of death are the soul struggling to free itself from the body. I asked grandma, "Why did her soul leave her body without the slightest pang, without her even making a little face as it left?" Grandma said that all that is a mystery, that we never really know these things for sure. Some suffer a great deal when the soul leaves the body, others die quickly without suffering.

We all went to accompany Bela to the Church of the Rosário. I came back again in order not to see her fall into the grave, and see the earth put over her. Glorinha watched everything. She came and told me that she had heard Bela cry out when they pressed down the earth on top of her and swore that they had buried her alive. I think she said it just to upset me even more. But we have to go on living. Tomorrow I have classes at School. I'm going to see if I can really study this year.

It's lucky for us that they've adopted a uniform at School. It's of strong cloth, dark blue, that doesn't show the dirt and wears well. Mama can stop struggling to keep me in dresses to wear to School; it gave her an awful lot of work. Now with the uniform everything will be easier; I can wash it myself on Thursdays and iron it on Fridays. I'd like to know who had such a good idea; they should have had it a long time ago.

When someone is always lucky they say to him, "You must have been born with a caul." That's what they told me. I wanted to know what was the opposite of being born with a caul. Because that's what must have happened to me. Why should I be so unlucky in everything in my life? I attribute it all to Aunt Madge's affection for me; but she does help me sometimes and is always so kind that I realize she does everything for the best. She doesn't know how to sew the way Aunt Efigênia does, but she doesn't know it. Aunt Efigênia is Luizinha's godmother, and a dressmaker, and once in a while she takes a dress to make for her. Whenever she takes anything it is very well made. But if I want to have a dress made the way I want it I have to have it done without Aunt Madge's knowing.

Aunt Madge knew about the business of the uniforms and she immediately told papa that if he would buy the material she'd make them. Aunt Efigênia made Luizinha's and did it beautifully. Aunt Madge tried to make mine with a skirt like those they're wearing now, bell-shaped, and I thought she wouldn't know how to cut it. It turned out perfectly awful! The skirt was short in front and long behind, and to complete my misery, she only basted the sleeves, and that's the way I went to school. The basting was weak; if it'd been stronger what happened to me wouldn't have happened. Seeing that the sleeves were only basted, Elvira pulled on one side and Jeninha on the other, and left me with my bare arms out. I had to put the sleeves back with pins and go running to Aunt Madge's. There I was scolded and scolded and she said I should get rid of friends who are so mean and have such bad manners.

My bad luck, would be more like it!

Thursday, February 22nd

Today grandma had the idea of sending a present to Dr. Teles, her doctor. Dindinha called Rita and sent her to pick out the best fruit in the garden. She filled the big silver tray, covered it with a lace-trimmed cloth, and tried to find someone who could deliver a message well, and knew where the house was. At that point Chica arrived, and grandma thought she'd send her to take the present. Grandma taught her the message carefully; she knew the house, and she went. When she came back with the empty tray and the cloth, grandma wanted her to repeat what she'd said. She began to tell the story: "I went to Cavalhada and I stopped in front of the doctor's door. I clapped my hands* a long time before the servant came. I said I was bringing a present for the doctor. The maid went inside and came back saying that Siá Donana said to go up. I went up the stairs and into the hall, which is very long. Then I went into the dining-room and said to Siá Donana: 'Here is a present that Dona Teodora sent for the doctor and she hopes that he will enjoy it.' Siá Donana told me to put the tray on the table, and I did. Siá Donana uncovered it and said, 'What lovely fruit!' Then she told me to sit down on a bench, and I did. Then she began to ask for news of the Senhora and Dona Chiquinha. I told her that the Senhoras were well, by the grace of God. And then she took the fruit off the tray and put it on another one. And she told me, 'You tell Dona Teodora that I am very pleased with her

---

* Way of summoning servants; possibly Moorish.

remembrance and that I know the doctor is going to enjoy the present very much, too.' And she praised the fruit some more. She said, 'Her orchard has such lovely fruit! I never realized they grew so big and lovely!' Then I said good-bye and got up, and took the tray and the cloth and went down the stairs and came back. I am always at your disposal, Senhora, whenever you have need of me." Grandma said, "I know that, Chica; thank you very much."

I'd like to know if grandma enjoyed quite such a long-winded explanation!

Sunday, February 25th

My father hasn't any vices, he doesn't drink anything except water and coffee, he doesn't gamble and he doesn't smoke. Sometimes he takes his pinch of snuff, but I don't think that's a vice because all my aunts take it. But my father is very friendly with his brothers-in-law, and he enjoys being in their company, and mama thinks that that's his only fault.

Uncle Joãozinho came to get my father to go with him to that Civic Guard that Seu Cadete and some others are starting now in town.

Mama waited at the *chácara* for papa until ten o'clock, both she and grandma very uneasy because when Uncle Joãozinho drinks he's apt to get into fights. At ten o'clock Uncle Joãzinho and papa arrived, not even able to walk in a straight line. They were both all bent over. Mama ran and took hold of papa and put him on the sofa. He couldn't get out a word. Mama got cabbage tea, strong coffee, and ammonia for him to smell, and she did so many things that he got better. Mama said to him, "For shame! This isn't like you, Alexandre! How awful of you to behave like Joãozinho! It would have been better if we hadn't left the house today!"

Papa said, "Don't be upset, Carolina. What does it matter, my girl? I wasn't used to it and I got drunk. And then, a man can't have perfect judgment all the time."

Grandma and Dindinha laughed a lot at this answer, and we went home late.

Today papa was telling us that yesterday they went to Seu Cadete's and found the parlor full of men; he was elected a major in the Civic Guard and Uncle Joãozinho, too, and they had to pay for their commissions. The commission meant they had to provide wine and beer for the others. He said that there were Florianistas and Custodistas all mixed up,* and they were all officers and there weren't any soldiers, and that he thought Seu Cadete had thought up this idea of a Civic Guard just to sell the liquor he had left on his hands.†

Thursday, March 1st

Today papa came home from Boa Vista with Uncle Joãozinho to vote for the president of the Republic and for Dr. João de Mata‡ for representative. All our family are involved in politics because of Aunt Aurélia and Uncle Conrado, who are very influential. He's the brother of Dr. Mata's mother and is a great friend of his, and all the family took up this friendship, too. Even I think everyone is right in considering him an honor to Diamantina, because he's a very good man. Everyone was very angry when Floriano put him in jail. My father says he hopes he's going to be elected president of the State and afterwards the Republic.

What I think is funniest on election day is that everyone takes sides and nobody forgives anyone who votes the other way. There's so much excitement in town that one would think it really mattered to us. After the election nobody remembers it any more. Seu Cadete is so influential that he gives clothes and boots to the

* General Floriano Peixoto, President of Brazil, and Admiral Custódio José de Mello: the Custodistas were in rebellion against President Peixoto.
† He was a storekeeper.
‡ Note in M V de M: "Counsellor João de Mata Machado, who was Foreign Minister under the monarchy and president of the Chamber of Representatives at the time of the revolt of ´93, and was imprisoned by Floriano."

Negroes so that they'll vote. The Negroes of the *chácara* who know how to read, that is, Marciano, Roldão, and Nestor, were all dressed up early in clean clothes, for the election. Grandma advised them: "Don't you listen to what anyone says to you, and don't accept any piece of paper if anybody wants to give you one. You stay close to Joãozinho and when the time comes to vote you do what he tells you to." They left, very proud.

I like to see the excitement in town but I don't believe it can make things any better for us.

Sunday, March 24th

Everyone has the weakness of thinking anything that's foreign is better than what they have at home. The only doctor who is any good comes from someplace else. In order to make an impression on the girls, a boy has to come from out of town. What we have is worthless; only things from other places are any good. Even I used to think this way. But from now on I'm not going to.

Luizinha broke a front tooth and papa wanted to have the Diamantina dentist fix it. She didn't want him to, saying she didn't believe he could do a good job, with that lame hand. Papa kept letting it go, and besides, Luizinha didn't mind being without the tooth. Then a very conceited mulatto, who said he was a good dentist, arrived in Diamantina. He gave himself such airs. Luizinha immediately wanted him to fix her tooth. Papa had him come to the house and bargained with him to fill her teeth and to put in a front one. The dentist asked for two hundred *mil reis* and finally accepted one hundred and fifty. He filled her teeth, and when he got to putting in the front one he pulled a box of matches out of his pocket, took out a little piece of match-stick, sharpened it to a point, and stuck it in the tooth and put on some cement, too. I didn't think that was right and I asked him if the match-stick would hold the tooth firmly. He said, "It isn't the match that

holds the tooth, it's the cement." He stuck the tooth in and Luizinha was radiant. Papa came back from the mine and saw it and
paid that dreadful dentist.

Thursday we went to Jogo da Bola Street, where there was a
visitor who'd come from Curralinho to vote in the elections and
had brought his wife. Aunt Agostinha put preserved figs and a
cake on the coffee table. The woman put a fig in her mouth and
a big ant bit her lip and she kept trying and trying to brush it
off. I nudged the others and we kept swallowing our laughter until we almost choked. So everything was quiet. And in the silence
at the table we heard something hit a plate, *clink-clink!* Luizinha
looked around horrified and exclaimed, "My tooth!" We nearly
died laughing and Luizinha almost cried.

And now, after robbing a lot of other people, that awful dentist
has gone away someplace else. Poor Luizinha, when she wants
to look her best now, she sticks her tooth back in with wax.

Saturday, March 10th

There was great rejoicing in our house today.

Monday papa went to Bom Sucesso where he's mining. It was
the week for working and he had great hopes of the panning.
Papa is so unlucky that we don't expect the luck to change at our
house. But he keeps saying all the time: "Keep hoping. The unlucky can't cry forever. The day will come." But it never comes.

When he was getting off the mule today, mama said to him, "I
think you're looking pleased. Did you find something?" He didn't
answer. He unfolded a piece of paper on the table and smoothed
it out, and then, so slowly it was torture to me, he put his hand in
his vest pocket, pulled out the *picuá** and poured the diamonds
out on the paper. There were some big ones and some little ones.

I ran and hugged him. There was a great uproar and everyone

* Note in M V *de* M: "*Picuá:* a little tube of bamboo or cane, in which to
keep diamonds."

began to ask for things. Renato and Nhonhô asked for new clothes and new boots; I and Luizinha asked for dresses.

Papa estimated that the diamonds were worth sixteen *contos*, but Seu Antônio Eulálio only gave thirteen *contos* five hundred *mil reis* for them because they weren't of the best quality.

Papa says that the mine is very promising and the formation is good, but that there's very little water. But even so he hopes to make up for last year's losses and make a good profit this year. But mama says that she's used to a miner's life: taking something out of the ground one year and putting it in again the next. That it's better to spend more of it on the family.

Thursday, March 15th

I don't know why I have this weakness of not being able to bear being contradicted, having been brought up in our family with everybody so meek and mild; and being the child of my parents, too, who never argue and never want to get mixed up in anything. I always think that education isn't worth a thing. Each one is born the way God made him, and that's the way he'll have to be.

We are four brothers and sisters and mama always says that I don't seem like her child, nor like the child of anyone in the family, and she doesn't know whom I take after. Papa says I take after a married sister who lives in São Paulo, whom we don't know. Her name is Alice. She married a doctor like grandpa and came on a trip to Diamantina, then went to São Paulo and never came back. My brothers and sister are very different from me.

I pay attention to what the grown-ups say and I take sides, although I know very well it's none of my business. But what can I do if it's my nature?

Ever since this fight between Custódio and Floriano began, God only knows how many times I've been mad without needing to be. My father and my uncles are Custodistas and they talk about so many bad things Floriano has done that sometimes in

order to get to sleep I have to pray to God to take the hope that
he'll be killed out of my head. He put Dr. Mata in prison and lots
of other bad things. Papa says he thinks it's funny I get so mad,
because he takes sides but it doesn't worry him.

The day before yesterday I really suffered. Jeninha came to get
me to spend two days in Palha. I went and we were walking in
the countryside on a beautiful afternoon, perfectly happy, when
we saw several men on horseback coming, shooting off firecrackers
right from their horses. We ran to hear the news. It was Jeninha's
father and brothers-in-law and some other men, who were all
coming to Palha to celebrate Floriano's victory with the family.

I turned pale, I was so disappointed, and they all laughed. Then
Jeninha's father said, "So our little English friend is against us
and we didn't know it?" Jeninha said, "I knew it all along. She's
had fights over Custódio every day in School." And then she
said to me, "What difference does it make to you which one of
them wins? They don't have any idea who you are, do they?
Don't be foolish and be disappointed over nothing at all. If he
wins or loses, it's all the same to me. Stop being silly, let's go and
celebrate with them, too."

I pretended, but I could only think of how sad my family would
be. And then they set off more firecrackers, and drank a lot of
beer, and paid no attention to me.

Tuesday, March 20th

I had a pimple on my face that bothered grandma and Aunt
Madge a great deal, and even Dona Gabriela's family. Yesterday
Clélia decided to take it off in a way she'd learned. She took a red-
hot coal and threw it in a glass of water; the coal hissed, she
opened it up and put it on the pimple, hot. She did it three or
four times and the pimple got soft. Then she squeezed it and
enough tallow came out to make a candle. When I got home
mama called me an idiot because I let anyone do anything they
want to to me. I said to her, "I know if I'm an idiot or not. The

pimple was growing and it could have got as big as an orange and
the Senhora and papa just kept saying over and over that it wasn't
anything. I was the one who was getting homelier every day. I'll
let anybody do anything they want to if it's for my good."

Last night my face was very swollen and Clélia was very worried, but I told her that it wasn't anything and not to worry. Today it's almost gone already.

Saturday, March 24th

Papa thinks it's awfully funny the way the Negroes at the
chácara never leave the back yard except to see the Judases* hung.

Today was Hallelujah Saturday. We had just finished lunch at
Uncle Geraldo's when all the Negroes went by, in clean clothes,
saying to grandma, "Praise the Lord, old Senhora." There were
three couples, Bemfica and Generosa, Mainarte and Magna, and
Machadinho and Henriqueta, and two men without wives, Joaquim Angola† and Quintiliano.

Grandma asked, "What's this? Where's everybody going like
this?"

Bemfica was the one who answered: "Ginirosa never seen
trevas.‡ All right; Ginirosa never seen *treva*. Ginirosa never seen
footwashing.§ All right; Ginirosa never seen foot-washing. Ginirosa, and all of us, never seen them hang Judas who sold our Little
Lord; don't you see it can't go on like this?"

Grandma said, "No, it can't, you're perfectly right. You may
go."

And off they went, each of them with a stick to beat the Judas
with.

* Effigies of Judas are hung the Saturday before Easter, Hallelujah Saturday.
† Named for the part of Africa he came from.
‡ Referring to the church service held the Wednesday before Easter.
§ When the priests wash the feet of twelve poor men representing the twelve
apostles.

Monday, March 26th

Here I am today, Monday, feeling sorry that Holy Week is over, I enjoyed it so much! For me, Easter Sunday is the best day of the year. First because I'm tired of fasting and on that day I make up for it by eating lots of meat and chicken; then because it's the happiest day in the year. It's grandma's custom to spend Holy Week at Uncle Geraldo's. We all go to church to hear the Hallelujahs. What a feeling of joy when the Hallelujahs burst out! All the bells in the city, big and small, ring at the same time. Suddenly the city is gay. In the streets the man in the red cassock, swinging his watchman's rattle, is seen no longer. Everything is simply joy.

Since I was little I've never seen a sad Easter Sunday. Even the sun is different. On that day Dindinha brings grandma's silk damask bedspreads to Direita Street to hang them over the balconies with Uncle Geraldo's. The streets are beautiful with the balconies decorated with silk bedspreads of every color. Grandma's said that when I grow up and have a home of my own she's going to give me one of her rich damask bedspreads. I'm going to choose the prettiest one.

Thursday, March 29th

Grandma went to spend Holy Week in Direita Street, at Uncle Geraldo's, in front of the Cathedral, and she hasn't come back yet. She doesn't go to church any more, but she likes to watch the comings and goings of the bishops and priests, and the people in the streets, from my uncle's balcony.

Day before yesterday, after lunch, we all went for a walk to the *chácara*. Mama decided to have Césarina wash the clothes there because there's a big clothes-yard. When we got there we all went running to the garden. Mama stayed in the house with Uncle Joãozinho. He took a book, went to his room, and lay down on the bed to read. The Bishop, who was taking an afternoon walk with three other Bishops from out of town who had come to see the Holy Week celebrations, came to call on grandma. Since she wasn't at home, Rita called mama, who was very pleased, thinking it was just the Bishop alone. When she went into the parlor and saw so many Bishops all together she thought they were priests and shook hands with all of them and only kissed our Bishop's ring. She didn't pay any attention to their clothes, she was so confused. Then the Bishop introduced the others and mama, terribly embarrassed, couldn't correct her mistake; she just told them grandma wasn't at home. They said good-bye and left.

When I went into the dining-room mama turned on me and said, "Why were you so bad-mannered in that manner, leaving me all alone in the parlor full of Bishops? You should have come to help me so what happened to me wouldn't have happened. I only kissed our Bishop's ring and I shook hands with the others like priests."

Uncle Joãozinho, who was listening to the conversation in his bedroom, came out and asked mama, "Inhá, what does that mean, what you said, 'bad-mannered in that manner'?" Mama didn't know how to explain and he laughed a lot and afterwards he told the others. Now it's become a family saying, when anyone does something impolite someone is bound to say "bad-mannered in that manner."

Monday, April 9th

Mama went with my sister and brothers to spend three days in Boa Vista, and in order not to miss classes, I came to stay in Jogo da Bola Street. I already loved Aunt Agostinha, and now I admire her even more. I'd like to help her so much! So very little would help her, but I can't even do that. But I suffer sometimes seeing her struggle for even a penny, like today. The hens, famished, were picking at the lace-pillow, and she said to me, "I'm praying, child. In a little while there'll be money for corn."

There was a knock at the door; I went to answer it; it was a little boy with two hundred *reis* to buy herbs. I sent him away and came back. Aunt Agostinha asked who'd knocked. When I told her she said, "Run after that little boy and call to him that I'm getting the herbs. It's the money I asked for for the hens' corn."

The boy came back; Aunt Agostinha went to the garden, which was scraped bare, and got the herbs. Then she sent for two quarts of corn for the hens immediately and was happy.

I remember, too, an ordeal that I saw her go through when she couldn't even get five hundred *reis*.

Dona Vicentina was Glorinha's piano teacher, for six *mil reis* a month. One afternoon, Dona Vicentina came to give a lesson and she asked Aunt Agostinha if she'd advance her two *mil reis*. Aunt Agostinha said it was impossible. Dona Vicentina went down to one *mil reis*; impossible. Then she said, "Couldn't you possibly get me five hundred *reis*, Dona Agostinha? My girls asked me today if I'd make them a black bean *tutu*, they're so sick of cornmeal."

Aunt Agostinha said, "I'm in the same situation, Vicentina. Believe me."

Thursday, April 12th

The other day, when I told him a cousin had told me that man is descended from the monkey, Father Neves said that it's a great sin to listen to such things. Hadn't I read the story of Adam and Eve in Sacred History? I didn't say anything. But if Father Neves knew the monkey we have in our neighborhood, even he could believe it. This monkey's more intelligent than lots of the boys I know. He belongs to Siá Ritinha, the woman who steals her neighbors' hens.

She's very fond of my father and mother and the way we know she's the person who steals the hens is like this: she doesn't really like to steal ours, and when there's one missing when we go to

shut them up, we always know we can expect a visit from Siá
Ritinha soon. She catches the hen and puts it in a covered
basket and comes to call on us. Then she waits for mama to say,
in the middle of the conversation, "One of my hens was stolen
today, Siá Ritinha, such-and-such a hen."

She answers, "Really, Dona Carolina, the people in this neighborhood are disgraceful. They've already eaten up all of mine."

"Yours, too?" says mama.

Then Siá Ritinha hurries away and lets out our hen. If it were
anyone else's, she'd eat it.

I think she's trained the monkey to steal, too. He won't leave us
alone. Mama said that if she wasn't afraid that Siá Ritinha would
suspect her, she'd poison him. If mama is careless and leaves the
kitchen door open for a minute, he steals everything he can get.
He's stolen cheese, salt pork, beef, and even the coffee strainer.
A few days ago he even brought a piece of salt pork he'd stolen
somewhere else into our yard. I'm sure it couldn't have been Siá
Ritinha's.

Papa has a damascus peach tree in the yard that bears beautiful
peaches; but nobody's allowed to pick one of them. He waits
for them to get completely ripe and then he picks them himself
and gives them to us. We're crazy about those peaches. But now
we've discovered a trick and we've eaten a lot of them. The monkey, whose name is Chico, climbs the peach tree and we tell him,
"Chico, throw one here." He throws them down and we've been
eating the peaches from the top of the tree without papa's missing
them.

But the monkey's worst theft was my beautiful rosary that I got
the day of my first communion, and had had such a long time!
When it was raining and I couldn't go outdoors, I used to put the
rosary out in the rain, since I've been told that works even better
than praying to Santa Clara. One afternoon when it was raining
and papa had promised to take us to the circus, I put the rosary

out in the rain hoping that the weather would change and we could go. But the rain didn't stop after all, and I was left without my rosary.

Our teacher Dona Joaquininha's back yard joins onto our kitchen garden. She never cuts down her bunches of bananas until they're ripe. But we found out we could ask the monkey for bananas and he'd pull down lots for us. So now the teacher has the bunches cut while they're still green.

Chico annoys the whole neighborhood, and if he didn't belong to Siá Ritinha he'd surely have been killed before now.

Monday, April 23rd

Today when we came home from School, Renato threw down his books and ran out to look for eggs from his two hens. Before we went to School he'd felt them and seen that they were going to lay; when he didn't find the eggs he came back and asked mama. She hadn't gathered them. Then, without another question, he picked up the broom and started up, saying, "I'm going to kill that miserable animal this minute!" and rushed after the cat. Smarter than he is, she ran away, with him after her like a lunatic. Then mama asked, "Who said it was the cat?" "Then who was it? Didn't she eat Helena's chickens?" Mama said, "A chicken isn't an egg. It might perfectly well have been a big lizard that's been around, that Siá Ritinha said had been sucking her eggs. Are the shells there?" Renato said, "No. That's why I think it was the cat. A lizard would have sucked the eggs and left the shells." Mama said, "Then go see if the gate is open. I think it's the doing of some boy off the street who came in here under the house, while I was indoors, and stole the eggs."

Renato went to see. The gate was open and he was inconsolable for the theft of the eggs he'd counted on eating fried, for dinner. He's like a lizard for eggs himself.

Thursday, April 26th

When I was little I used to suffer from envy a great deal but now I don't any more.

I'm grateful to grandma for this. She got me over it.

I'm the poorest girl in my set. I see the differences between my life and theirs, but I don't envy them. If they knew all the work I do at home and at the *chácara*, they'd feel sorry for me, even though I really like doing it. I have to iron clothes, clean house, and every Thursday I have to scour half the floors with sand. Luizinha scours the other half. I have to wash and iron my uniform. I have to clean the kitchen every Thursday, too. I asked mama myself if I could do it.

At the *chácara* I help pick *jaboticabas* and press them to make vinegar, and I help pick coffee and fruit. I help tie up bunches of vegetables to sell, and to make candles, and other things, too. I like doing all these chores, but candle-making best of all; we do it in the yard with grandma looking on. We dip the wicks in the tallow and hang them up to dry. When they're dry we do the same thing over again until they're as thick as we want them. I'm the quickest of all and grandma is pleased to see how fast I do it. But grandma's the only person who doesn't like to see me work a lot, and the only one who likes to have me study.

I don't know why until today everybody says that they were sorry for the slaves. I don't feel that way. I don't think I'd be unhappy if I had to work all day long. To have to do nothing would be torture to me. Sometimes mama says she'd even like me to be lazy, my energy gets on her nerves. Then I tell her: "If I were lazy I don't know what would become of you or papa or my brothers and sister, without a servant in the house." I swear I'd like to let things go here at home and not do anything, just to see. But I can't.

I know why mama would like me to be lazy: so I'd stay at home with her all the time, like Luizinha. But it's impossible. The very thought of it appals me. Sometimes I wonder what it would be like if I got sick and had to spend a whole week indoors, like poor João Antonio, who got sick at the Seminary and has been in bed at the *chácara* for two weeks now. And the *chácara* is big, too, and much more cheerful than it is here at home.

Tuesday, May 1st

Naná is pretty. I remember until today something sad that happened to me once when Naná got sick. I was seven years old and I was sillier than I am now.

Naná got sick and Inhá sent for me to keep her company. Then Dr. Teles arrived. He was new here then and didn't know me. He saw Naná in bed all flushed with fever and he said, "What a pretty girl! What's her name?" Inhá replied, "Maria Orminda." Dr. Teles said, "She ought to be called Helena." Inhá said, "There's an Helena, right there." He looked at me and turned away, as much as to say, "She doesn't deserve the name." I'll admit I felt very disappointed.

Naná always comes to the *chácara* to spend the afternoons with me and grandma is very nice to anyone who likes me. She keeps telling me, "Take Naná to walk in the garden. Take her to see the flower garden." She never tires of giving her candy and fruit. I say to Naná, "Let's go play on the lawn so grandma will leave you in peace."

Iaiá dislikes me because grandma loves me so much and doesn't like Nico Boi Pintado* whom she brought up like a son. The same way that Iaiá says to grandma when she gives me things and does things to please me, grandma says to *her*, "That boy's going to be ruined. You're constantly spoiling him." Iaiá gets mad, but she can't take it out on grandma so she takes it out on me.

I know that Naná's pretty and I'm not; but I don't know why Iaiá thinks she's bothering me by constantly making comparisons. Today grandma noticed that what she says is on purpose to tor-

* Spotted Bull; because he has freckles.

ment me, and she asked, "Henriqueta, do you really think Naná
is beautiful, or do you just say it to make the other one envious?"
Iaiá said, "Gracious, mother, why? Can't anyone mention what a
pretty girl Naná is without the Senhora's getting angry?" Grandma
said, "No, I'm not angry; but you know Renato spends his days
telling this silly child she's homely and she believes it. Here I keep
trying to get it out of her head and you never miss an opportunity
of talking about how pretty the other girls are when she's around."
And then she said to me, "It's all a lie, daughter; you're the pretty
one. Nobody has your wit and intelligence and your good heart.
You're the leading girl of Diamantina. You can be sure of that."
I said, "Grandma, I don't like to hear the Senhora speak that way,
because I know that you think I'm envious. You can be sure,
grandma, that I was only envious of them when I was little; and
then only when they marched as virgins in the procession. Let
Iaiá talk. Don't worry, grandma."

What an annoying aunt Iaiá is!

Friday, May 4th

The days I spend in Palha I have the most fun. There are lots
of people at the diamond-cutting factory, the house is very agreeable and the country is pretty. How lovely and gay everything is
there!

On Wednesday I woke up very early, with everything ready, because Jeninha was going to come and ask mama if she could take
me, the way she usually does. Mama gave her permission and we
went and met her family, who were at Cruzeiro de Rosário, waiting for us. What fun Jeninha's family is! So different from mine!
Mine spend most of their time praying.

Sometimes I get to thinking that it's very hard for people to
get to heaven and I lose all hope of it. I see grandma doing so
much for Our Lady and Our Lord that I think it reaches the
point of idolatry. In the *chácara* the Negro women spend all their
time making lace, to decorate the altars; the ones who embroider

embroidering silk robes for Our Ladies. Grandma's ordered robes for Our Ladies of Luz, of Carmo, of Mercês, and even for Our Lady of Rosário, who belongs to the blacks. Every year for the Holy Spirit I have to carry a certain amount of wax in the procession. This year there was so much wax that my cousin Glorinha had to help me carry it. And Masses? If grandma would give me the money she spends on Masses, I'd be rich. I don't know if what I'm writing is a sin. I'll tell it all to the priest to be on the safe side.

I was talking about Palha and got off the track. This year the pole* and the Santa Cruz were simply heavenly. We do everything so well for the Santa Cruz! The cross† at Palha stands on the top of a hill, and the decorations, bamboos and banana leaves, and the light of all the little lanterns, and the flowers, were a sight to see! I helped a lot and enjoyed everything. We raised the pole with music and fireworks, we jumped through bonfires, and had fortune-telling.

In the evening I didn't want to dance. This made the girls from the factory say I was too proud to dance in their company. I wasn't too proud to dance with them. I wanted to get out of dancing with some of the men who were there.

Saturday, May 5th

Today I went to see Cecília and because I had to go home again to do my composition, the only compulsory thing at School, I said to her, "I can't stay with you because I still haven't done my composition, and early tomorrow I'm going to Palha for two days and I shan't have time."

She said, "Don't go home for that. I'll loan you my book and you can copy out a letter in a second, and take it."

* Decorated poles or masts, set up for religious festivals, with a picture of a saint at the top.
† See introduction.

I took the book and was amazed! I asked her where she'd bought it. "Such nice letters, so well-written! That's why you always have such nice exercises. Oh! If I'd only been able to buy this book, too!" Cecília said, "You don't have to. When you want it I'll loan it to you." I said, "Then I'm going to want it every day. You can bring it to School, because I can copy it there and get it done, and have the evenings for studying."

She agreed. I copied a letter I thought was a beauty, folded it up small and put it in the front of my dress. I came home well satisfied. I kept thinking of the moment when Seu Sebastião would read the compositions in class, the way he does when he finds one well-written, and would praise me. "How beautifully you're writing! Congratulations!"

I handed in the exercise yesterday. Today when I got to class he had a pile of exercises on top of the table and he was calling off the names, the way he does, to give them back. When it was my turn: "Helena Morley!" He looked at me and stopped for a minute. My heart was pounding, waiting for compliments. Then he yelled, "Where did you find the manual?" The pupils began to roar with laughter.

How mean of Seu Sebastião!

Monday, May 7th

Perhaps it was mean of me to enjoy what I saw yesterday. I suppose I should have felt sorry to see such a pretty girl as Quita fall down like that in the middle of church, in a faint. But I can't help saying here that I liked the excitement very much. I'd never seen anyone have an attack and I thought it was all very amusing. I liked seeing how fast Chiquinha rushed to the middle of the church, picked Quita up, put her over her shoulder, went down the steps of the Bomfim Church, carried her to Américo de Matos', and put her in their bed. The boys should have been the ones to carry her but they all stood around with foolish faces. I was surprised at all the excitement and I admired Chiquinha's strength; but she is big and fat, and Quita is small and thin. She put Quita on her shoulder as if she were a baby, and went out.

I thought Quita was lucky to have such pretty things to show when they began to undo her clothes. Petticoat, corset-cover, corset, chemise, all embroidered and very pretty. We were all envious of the pretty things she had hidden. I left wondering what would happen to me if I had an attack like hers, I, who don't have anything pretty for the others to see. I was telling this to mama and she said, "Joãozinho always says that we should always go prepared, in case of having an attack in the street, but I never thought about it. It's the first time I've thought he was right." I said to mama, "When they undid her clothes and so many pretty things appeared, I was envious of the attack and thought it was all very romantic. But finally I thanked God it wasn't me." Suddenly Luizinha had an idea. "When you do have a lot of pretty underwear, you can pretend to have an attack like hers. I think it would be easy." I answered, "It's easy, but not when one laughs the way we do. Could either of us pretend to have an attack for very long? Let the rest of them do it."

Thursday, May 10th

In the morning there was a knock on the door and because it's Thursday I was already ironing clothes. I opened the door and it was Juca Parrudo [Stocky]. I asked him in and took him out to the garden where papa was banking up plants. I stopped ironing because I never miss grown-up conversation, particularly men's. And it was a good idea, because I found out something I'd wanted to know very much.

Seu Juca brought up a very pretty little girl, named Maria da Conceição. She was in school with me at Mistress Joaquininha's and one day another girl had a fight with her and called her "Maria of the Gutter." The teacher punished the girl for not speaking charitably to her schoolmates, and said, "Is it Maria's

fault if she was thrown in the gutter?" Then they told me how
she'd been found, but I didn't believe it, I thought it was a story.

Seu Juca came in and said to papa, "How lucky to find you
here! I came after some parsley; they tell me it's very good for the
urine. Yesterday Sebastião Coruja said to me, 'If you don't find it
in Alexandre's garden, you won't find it anywhere. He's the only
one who has these things.' And how right he was! How nice
everything is! My dear man, you certainly come from another race.
We have a vegetable garden, too, but not like yours. But from
now on I'm going to follow your example."

Papa gave him the parsley and mama asked him, "How is
Maria da Conceição?" He answered, and from there he went on
to tell the story of Maria, that I shouldn't think he'd like to remember.

He said that he and his wife had had only one child, José. When
he grew up they were unhappy, the two of them, and they wanted
a little boy or girl, and so God remembered them, and sent them
Maria in a very strange way. They had gone to bed and the house
was all shut up, when his wife said she heard a baby crying under
the floor. He told her it was just her imagination. Then she said,
"Put your ear here and see if it's my imagination." He put his ear
down and heard a little baby crying. He rushed to the kitchen,
got the axe, and took up the floor-boards. Then he took a mattock,
pulled away the stones and opened the gutter that ran under the
house, and there was the poor little thing, who had rolled all the
way from Carmo Street as far as Bomfim Street. She was all cut
with splinters of glass and filthy dirty. He picked her up and his
wife gave her a bath in water with salt and arnica in it. The little
girl didn't die because she was a present from heaven, sent to
them by God.

Thursday, May 17th

Aunt Agostinha is the best human being I've ever seen. If she
can do anything nice for anybody, she's happy. So she always

has a house full of relatives and guests. I admire her more than any other aunt.

She received an invitation to the celebration of the Holy Spirit in Curralinho, from some friends there who often visit her. She asked me and Luizinha to go with her. The news got around, and when the day came all the cousins were all ready to go with us. My aunt said, "I can't take everybody to Júlio's house, *coitado.* I'm only going to take my girls and Helena and Luizinha." They said that the Emperor of the Divine, Seu Rodrigo Pimenta [Pepper], is very rich and lives there and they'd stay at his house.

Sunday, we walked there, as we usually do. When we got to Curralinho, Aunt Agostinha said to her friends, "These are your guests. The others are going to Rodrigo Pimenta's house."

There were lots of people, the place was full. Seu Rodrigo had prepared a big lunch for everyone at the celebration and my cousins made the most of it. We stayed at Seu Júlio's and had black beans, rice, and chicken. Then we went out to see the *festa* and came back for dinner: rice, black beans, and chicken.

That night when we were all in bed there was a knock at the door and it was the cousins, asking for a lodging, because they hadn't been able to find any place to sleep. We took two of our mattresses to give them and we were going to sleep together on the rest, when the girls of the house appeared and wouldn't let us, and gave up their own mattresses.

Monday, the same thing for lunch, only more of it: rice, black beans, and chicken. At dinner we thought the legs of the chicken seemed rather big. Aunt Agostinha said, "If the roosters don't crow tonight, we'll leave early tomorrow, before lunch."

The third day, before we got up, our aunt came into our room and said, "Just what I thought yesterday, girls. No more roosters."

We came back to Diamantina early and they didn't insist very much that we stay. *Coitados!* We ate them out of house and home.

When papa had that good luck at the Bom Successo mine two months ago, mama insisted that he put the money in a store, to get some return from it and so we could eat cheaper. At first papa was against it, and said that he didn't want to be a store-keeper. But mama convinced him that he could get an honest man to run it, and every week, when he came home from work, he could do the accounts.

Papa finished by giving in, as usual, and began looking for the honest man. He looked until he found a very slow old man, named Seu Zeca, who lives at the end of Luz Street, and makes his living by making straw cigarettes* to sell. Then he rented a shop for the store, behind Seu Cadete's house, that already had shelves, a counter, and everything, even scales. The shop is near the drovers' shed,—marvellous. Isaias stocked it. He bought a mule-load of cakes of brown sugar, a big bag of black beans, another of rice, of manioc flour, a hamper of salt pork, a barrel of very good raw castor-oil, and one of *cachaça,* very good salt, starch, corn, corn-meal, cheeses, and everything, even *palmito.* The store was ready in a jiffy and Seu Zeca went to take charge, getting twenty *mil reis* and lunch at our house, because he lives a long way off.

Uncle Joãozinho went to see the store and came back laughing at papa. "You went and took that foolish Zeca away from his little cigarette business to run your store! What you need is someone smart, who knows how to do business. I have my doubts about that one; we'll see what happens." Papa said to him, "The smart ones would cheat me. I can't be there in person."

Seu Zeca is an old man and full of notions. He doesn't eat dried meat, cabbage, fried pork, cucumbers and everything, like us. He only eats stewed meat with okra, rice, porridge, and things like that, all very well cooked, because he says he suffers from gas. We didn't understand what that complaint was until a few days ago.

---

* Cigarettes with corn straw wrappers, still used in the country.

One day we were at the table and Seu Zeca turned to mama. "Will you excuse me, Dona Carolina?" "Certainly, Seu Zeca," said mama. He went out in the hall and we began to hear things I can't write down. I and Luizinha held our mouths in order not to laugh, but it was impossible; we exploded. Mama was furious and scolded us, and Seu Zeca said, "I'm a sick man, girls; if I don't get rid of the gas it will rise up in my chest and suffocate me."

Mama forbade us to eat lunch at the table and we are eating in the kitchen. Even so, if we so much as see Seu Zeca through the crack of the door, we can't stop laughing.

Today he brought his wife, Siá Margarida, to talk to mama. Because it's Thursday and we're at home, we listened to her conversation and then came in my bedroom to laugh. She came to explain Seu Zeca's gas. She told mama that he was very much distressed that we'd been punished because of him. "He can't eat away from home, Dona Carolina. Onions, cabbage, sweet potatoes, spicy foods, anything like that turns to gas in his belly. If he holds out all day, the way he's done here, it's awful for both of us. He comes home suffocated, with his belly like a drum. I make him very strong aniseed tea, and that's the only way to get rid of the gas and give him relief. I came to ask the Senhora to give him ten *mil reis* more salary, and he can take his little pot of the kind of food he's used to to the store, and then we can get some rest."

Mama agreed. Siá Margarida stayed until five o'clock, made some cakes, had dinner, and went away. She invited us to go to her house, at the top of Luz Street, where she has lots of fruit.

Tuesday, May 29th

I swear it's the first time I ever saw one of my aunts do anything so rude. But I must confess that I enjoyed it, too. Aunt Clarinha lives in Montes Claros. She went there when she got married. Once in a while she comes to visit grandma. She writes when she's coming and Dindinha gets a bedroom ready for her. This time she wrote she was coming but she didn't set the date, and Dindinha neglected to get things ready. And besides, I thought that she could arrange it the day she came, because there are so many rooms at the *chácara*, full of beds, mattresses, and pillows, and so many Negro women in the house, what trouble would it be to tidy up a bedroom?

But this aunt wants to be treated like a queen. She arrived, and we all rushed to receive her. After the *abraços** she immediately started asking about her room. Dindinha said, "We waited for you to let us know what day you were coming. But don't worry, I can arrange it in a second. Go in Henriqueta's bedroom while we're doing it."

I think she was mad at finding her room being used by Aunt Henriqueta, who's been spending some time at the *chácara*. She said immediately, "I didn't come here to make work for you; I thought it would be a pleasure. Since it's so much work, I'm going to stay with Agostinha." And she went out the door, got on her mule again, and went with the whole troop to Aunt Agostinha's, in Jogo da Bola Street. She just gave grandma time enough to exclaim, "Well, I never!" as usual.

Grandma and my aunts say she was always like that, and that a crooked stick will never be straight.

It's only me whom people keep trying to straighten.

Saturday, June 2nd

One of the things I like best is to have supper in Dona Juliana's doorway at night. Raquel puts what's left over from dinner in a pan, mixes it with manioc flour, and in the evening I always go to get a tray with the pan on it, and take it to the doorway. We always eat it between seven and eight o'clock. When they play lotto, and keep playing until ten o'clock, Dona Juliana gives us *canjica*,† or cornmeal porridge with milk.

* *Abraço:* the Brazilian hand-shake which, with anyone met before, always includes an embrace.
† *Canjica:* hulled corn, cooked in milk.

Yesterday Laurinda brought the milk bowl to the table and said, "There isn't any *canjica* today. Have some cornmeal and milk." The bowls came, soup spoons, and cornmeal. Laurinda took the cover off the bowl and gave a shriek and a loud laugh. Then with two fingers she pulled out a mouse, full enough to burst, by the tail. She showed it to us and there was an Oh! Oh! of general dismay.

Laurinda and João César exclaimed, "What luck! Now we're going to profit from it." They took the bowl, that holds at least three quarts of milk, for themselves and drank it all, smacking their lips.

Horrors!

Wednesday, June 6th

Now I see that God was helping grandma when Aunt Clarinha didn't stay at the *chácara*. She brought a grandson, seven years old, named Arício, who's worse than Judas. Just at the sight of the little devil I shake. Now I understand why there are murderers in the world, after dealing with him.

Nobody has a minute's peace with him around, and nobody can say anything without making Aunt Clarinha furious. He only likes to do mean things. He's already pulled down all the humming birds' nests, and the sparrows' and the blackbirds', that were hidden in the orchard; but that's nothing to what he did to Naninha's chickens. He got mad at Naninha, ran to the yard and grabbed a chicken, squeezed with his hands and went to show it to Naninha with its little insides hanging out. He squeezed the chicken, laughing with pleasure. Won't he grow up to be a murderer?

Sometimes I hate him so much that I'd like to do to him what he did to the chicken. One of these times was at the table today. There was chicken on the table and first Aunt Clarinha had to pick out the parts he likes best, the parts I like too, the wing and liver. Then there was a big platter of fried eggs, one apiece. That little demon only wanted yolks and Aunt Clarinha took three yolks and put them on his plate. I got one white. How I hated him!

One of the things he likes best, too, is to lift up our skirts to see if we wear drawers, when there are men around.

What would it be like if he were at the *chácara?* We don't go to Jogo da Bola Street every day; but we almost live at grandma's *chácara.*

Grandma deserves to have had God deliver her from this pest that Aunt Clarinha brought, and that's why she did something thoughtless. God made her do it.

Monday, June 11th

Seu Manuel Matias invited my father to take some hands and start mining with him at Lomba, where he's found a very promising formation. Mama thinks that my grandfather already worked it and she sent papa to ask grandma. He came back mad at grandma and mama couldn't get the reason out of him; but he was right.

I was in the dining room at the *chácara,* peeling guavas to make paste, when papa came in, greeted grandma and sat down beside her. Then he said, "Mother-in-law, I've been asked to work a mine at Lomba, and I came to tell the Senhora about it."

Grandma said, "How's that, my son?"

He said, "It's at Lomba, on the side of the hill."

Grandma interrupted, "Reginalda! Take this hen out of the room!" Then she said to papa, "What were you saying just now, Alexandre?"

Papa began again, "It's that place over there by the river, where there's a big rock."

Grandma: "Rita! Look after this baby, she's going to fall!" And then she turned to my father. "What were you just saying, my son?"

Papa repeated it and Andreza came in with a basket of eggs. Grandma said, "Leave the basket here. How many eggs did the hens lay today?" Then she said to papa, "Where were we, Alexandre?"

Papa began again. And then grandma couldn't remember if the mine had been worked or not.

I know grandma's always like that. Even at prayers she interrupts to ask Dindinha anything at all.

Friday, June 15th

Since Aunt Clarinha's been at Jogo da Bola Street, I've been afraid to go there. With my quick temper, I'm afraid of losing patience some day and spanking Arício and Aunt Clarinha will be angry with me.

Naninha was saying to me at the *chácara*, "It's worth your while to go there now, to see how he's reformed. He's like wax." "Really?" I asked. "How did you do it?" She said, "Once when Aunt Clarinha wasn't there, I took the opportunity, settled myself in the bedroom with him with a whip in my hand, made a murderous face, and threatened to give him a whipping if he kept on annoying me. He was terrified and begged me not to, for the love of God. Then I said, 'All right, pest, don't forget! You've been warned! The first time you do anything to me I'll beat you with this whip! And don't you say anything to Aunt Clarinha, or I'll get even with you!' "

Today we spent the afternoon there and Arício, with a little switch in his hand, annoyed everybody except Naninha. Once Aunt Clarinha said, "See, everybody! I don't recognize this boy. He teases everybody except Naninha. I don't know what she did to make him like her like that." Naninha, looking at him, said, "He knows, don't you, Arício? I promised him something nice if he'd be good, because I can't stand bad boys."

He went on teasing us; he wouldn't leave anyone alone. But I'm hoping for a chance to do the same thing with him that Naninha did. I've seen that he's a coward and I'm glad of it. I don't know how anyone can bring a pest like that to other peo-

ple's houses. Aunt Agostinha is an angel of mercy, but we all live
in constant hatred. I keep planning to give him a good pinch, at
least, but I don't have the courage for fear of Aunt Clarinha. If
she were at the *chácara* with Arício, Nico would certainly teach
him a lesson. But at Jogo da Bola Street we have to be patient
until Aunt Clarinha goes away.

Sunday, June 17th

Yesterday was Aunt Aurélia's birthday and all the family went.

After dinner the grown-ups stayed in the parlor and we stayed
in the hall, where the oven is. Nobody enjoys parties in this house,
in the middle of town, because there isn't any good place to play.
When we get tired of playing forfeits we begin to tell stories. Each
one has to tell something he makes up or that happened to him.
All of a sudden I thought of mine and I kept quiet, waiting for
the others. Nobody made up anything; none of us have any ideas
in our heads. Glorinha told something that happened in Itaipava
when she was very little. A woman who didn't believe in God
cooked some sausages to eat on Good Friday and they turned to
snakes in the pan. Sinhá told the tale of a girl in Biribiri who disappeared at dinner time. Her father and mother almost went crazy
looking for her. Everybody was in despair, thinking she'd fallen in
the cistern and drowned. Finally, very late, they opened up the
factory and the little girl was sleeping peacefully behind a bale of
cotton. So everyone told his story and stretched it out as long as
possible if it was short. When my turn came I began:

"Once there was a man who was a miner and one day he found
a virgin *caldeirão* and he took out lots of diamonds and became
rich. He lived on a farm and had eight daughters, seven very obedient and one very naughty. This one, from the time she was
little, was full of whims and nobody could manage her, not even
her mother and father. If she didn't want to go to school she hid
in the woods and it was a struggle to catch her. When she was
locked up in her room alone she almost beat the door down.

Spanked? Who would spank her? So this girl grew up different from the rest. She was also more intelligent. When she reached the age to get married, her father told her about the suitors who came, and she said, 'I won't marry because I don't want to.' Her mother said, 'This one's going to give me trouble; nobody knows what she wants.' The father chose husbands for the others and they accepted them; but this one, no. After a while she began to change and grow sad. Her mother was worried to see her so quiet, always silent, without knowing why. At this time one of her brothers died of yellow fever in Rio de Janeiro, and she suffered so much that the mother thought she was going to lose two children at once. She closed herself up in her room with the window shut, just crying, without taking any sort of nourishment. On the *fazenda* they almost forgot the death of the other one, thinking about her. It was hard to make her cheer up and leave her room. After a certain time the father died. Everybody was very sorry and the girl went back to her dark room again, crying and not eating. The same thing happened as the other time. The mother and sisters had to stop mourning the death of the husband and father just to take care of her. She was like this for more than a month when a cousin appeared to ask for her in marriage. The mother went to tell her, just to tell her. She didn't think she'd accept, she was so unhappy, *coitada!* The mother went into the room and saw the girl turned toward the wall, so sad, and said to her, 'Daughter, I came to tell you just to salve my conscience. I don't want to force you, but So-and-So is here; he came to ask for you in marriage and he wants to hear the answer from you.' She jumped out of bed, asking, 'Is it true?' She got up, washed her face, went to the parlor and forgot to weep for the death of her father any longer. Her melancholy had been a secret passion for her cousin."

Everybody listened to me attentively and at this point Aunt Aurélia's children protested, "That isn't fair! That's the story of mama!"

Monday, June 25th

I can't go to bed without writing about the scare we had today. Everybody says it was a miracle, and it was.

Yesterday we went to celebrate St. João's and Uncle Joãozinho's day, in Boa Vista. There was a bonfire and fireworks, but very few people because the new cabin isn't finished yet, and there wasn't much excitement. Today we were sitting in front of the house, the whole family, on some boards that Uncle Joãozinho had put there for benches. We were praying. As there isn't any *oratório* here, Dindinha said that we could pray just sitting by the door. She told her rosary and when she'd finished she wound it around her arm. Then she took out the litany and we all gave the responses. We continued to talk and enjoy the moonlight. Dindinha, thinking that the rosary felt very cold, looked to see what it was. She gave a scream and shook her arm, throwing something off, saying, "It's a snake!" The moonlight was like day. We went to look; it really was a snake and Seu Manuel Camilo killed it.

How can you explain that the snake didn't bite Dindinha? It really was a miracle.

Thursday, June 28th

Never have we found so many snakes at Boa Vista as we're finding now.

This is already the second one. My uncle says it's because he didn't cut the grass around the house. We came here before the big cabin was finished, because it was my uncle's birthday which falls on St. João's day. He had two bedrooms covered over in a hurry, with thatch, to put us up. I like everything all mixed up the way it is very much, and think it's very funny.

The old cabin is very small. It only has one bedroom for my uncle and papa and a smaller one for Siá Etelvina, the cook. She does the cooking and we go there for breakfast, lunch, and dinner.

Siá Etelvina is a fury. She's furious when we're here because she has twice as much work. This time, besides the aunts, five cousins came, and Zulmira. She can never make enough food for us. To-day even Zulmira stole a can of sardines that my uncle keeps on the beams in his room.

The new house is all open and hasn't any doors. My uncle put some boards in the living room for the boys, and we sleep with the aunts, all together in the bedroom. It's awfully funny.* The only thing that bothers us is Siá Etelvina who, if Uncle Joãozinho didn't go into the kitchen to look into the pans, would starve us to death.

The new house is in the loveliest spot and near some *gabiroba*† bushes; you step out of the door and there are the *gabirobas*. To-day we were all in front of the house, sitting on the boards, with Ester sitting on an ant-hill. My father, who always has a stick in his hand, was sitting in front of Ester. Without calling any atten-tion to himself, he got up silently and suddenly hit the head of a *jararaca*‡ that was getting ready to strike at Ester's foot. If any-one else had seen it, he would have screamed, and Ester would have stepped on the *jararaca*. But because it was papa, who is the calmest man in the world, he struck it right on the head and killed it.

Thursday, July 5th

Mama and my aunts planned for us all to go to Pedra Grande and have a picnic there. It's such a pretty place! It's funny; I notice that every place we go I think is prettier than the last one. When mama discovers a nice walk, she sticks to it for the rest of her life. I don't know how she agreed to go to Pedra Grande to-day.

It made all the girls unhappy to see the awful thing our brothers did—washing their feet in the water of Pau de Frutas, which is

* Literally: "It's a pagoda."
† *Gabiroba:* a small, yellow, cherry-like fruit.
‡ *Jararaca:* a small deadly serpent.

the water we drink in Diamantina. Beatriz even cried to think her father was drinking it in town. My aunts consoled her by saying that by the time it gets there it's clean. Besides, we knew that a donkey died in the stream and stayed there until it rotted. I think that water is filthy. If I thought about it I'd never drink it. But we do everything without thinking, thank God.

We started back at five-something and it was almost night when we got home. My aunts walk so slowly it seems as if they were standing still.

Monday, July 9th

Today we went to Jogo da Bola Street for lunch. There were two guests there, friends of the family. The man is called Anselmo Coelho. He's good-looking and very nice, married to a terribly homely woman who speaks through her nose, called Toninha. I asked my cousins why such a handsome man had married such an ugly woman, and they said that he was the widower of a very pretty wife, and, living in Itaipava, he met this teacher, and because she wouldn't be any expense to him, he married her.

At the table I noticed how little feeling the man had for his wife and I felt sorry for her, *coitada*. After lunch we stayed at the table and he got the conversation onto his first wife. He praised her brains, her beauty, and her sympathy so much that I kept looking at the poor creature and feeling sorry for her. He said, "But she was so jealous that she made me suffer. When I miss her I always try to remember how jealous she was. If I had to go out alone on business, before I got to the door she'd fall down in a faint." He told all this and then added, "I even miss the faints."

After a while he looked at his watch and said, "It's time. I have to go." He got up to go and that fool of a homely wife ran and held onto his arm, trying to imitate the other wife. He kept going out, saying, "Stop it, Toninha. Stop this nonsense!" And the woman kept clinging to his arm and he kept on going. We stayed at the table pretending not to notice in order not to embarrass him. Suddenly we heard a noise, the sound of a body falling on the doorstep. We all ran and there was the poor homely woman stretched out on the ground, with a horrible face, and her husband prodding her with his foot and saying, "Get up, fool! Stop acting! Get up! Don't disgrace me!" He said this still prodding his wife with his foot, without leaning over. Naninha said, "*Coitada!* She's had an attack!" He said, "She wants to do what I said the other one did. But you can leave her here, it isn't anything. She'll get up in a little while." And off he went.

We waited a little for her to open her eyes. When she didn't open them, we carried her, two with her arms, two with her legs, almost dragging her, and put her on the bed and ran outside to laugh.

Aunt Agostinha said to us, "Now you see, while you're girls, that men don't care for silly women. He treats her well, but you see what she did today."

Thursday, July 12th

Siá Ritinha came in and, because I like to listen to gossip, I managed to stay nearby.

Mama was asking her how Inhá was.

"She gets along, Dona Carolina. Very busy, as always."

"Did your chickens hatch, Siá Ritinha?"

"They're a joy to behold. If anyone was sick, I could kill one already if I wanted to. But we're going to let them grow some more. And your vegetable garden, Dona Carolina, is it doing well?"

"Doing nicely. We can't plant green vegetables in this weather. Now I've got cucumbers, squash, and *xuxus*."

Siá Ritinha: "I got what the Senhora sent us and I was very grateful. The Senhora doesn't realize how much it means to us. Inhá kept saying, 'We're very fortunate to have people like Dona Carolina and Seu Alexandre for neighbors. They only give us pleasure.' And speaking of neighbors, Dona Carolina, the Senhora knows what happened to Siá Antoninha?"

Mama: "No. What was it?"

"Haven't you seen that the girls don't sing in the moonlight any more on the steps, and that the house is all closed up as if someone were dead?"

Mama: "No. I almost never go to the window, and when I do go I only look out the side where the cross is to see if it's going to rain. I never look out that side. But what was it?"

"The Senhora didn't know that Antoninha's daughter, Mariquinhas, was going to get married?"

"No. I only know the things you tell me, Siá Ritinha. You know I never go out of the house unless it's to go to Mass or to my mother's."

"Well then, I'm going to tell you everything, from the beginning. Mariquinhas was engaged to Seu João Sampaio's Sebastião. You should have seen the airs she put on. She used to go by our door with the boy, looking like a queen. All the neighborhood was surprised, because he's rich, as the Senhora knows, and to marry into Antoninha's family! Well, it was to be expected. She used to go by strutting so and so full of herself that we even left the window, we were so disgusted. And then didn't we just learn that the boy, I don't know why, threw her over and ran away to Conceição?"

Mama: "Poor Antoninha! She must be so unhappy!"

Poor Mariquinhas, such a disappointment! I'd already noticed in spite of the fact that she's in the fourth year that she hadn't been to School for a good many days.

Sunday, July 15th

Today, Sunday, I should have been able to study my lessons and do my exercise, but mama took us to grandma's early, and spent the day playing cards with my aunts, until late. And we spent it as always, playing, all the cousins.

Today something awful for all of us happened. Mama and my aunts thought they should send us, all the girls, to call on Seu

Carneiro, because of his mother's death. But before we went they told us we should behave respectfully and have sad faces. And Naninha, too, as the eldest, never stopped telling us, "Don't laugh! Remember it's a visit of condolence." That alone was enough to make the worst happen.

We got there, went up the steps, and clapped at the front door. Seu Carneiro came to open it, dressed in a long frock coat, and said through his nose, "Come in. Please do me the honor." I was already choking, trying not to laugh, and at that minute I put my hand over my mouth to contain myself, but I couldn't. I gave such a suffocated laugh that the others couldn't help themselves and we all went down the stairs in a gale of laughter. The man stood at the top of the steps, looking at us in astonishment, without knowing what was the matter. We went down the street laughing, with Naninha scolding me.

Now I think that when I meet his daughters, who are friends of mine, they'll want me to explain what was the matter. I'm going to try to make up some story or other to tell them.

Thursday, July 19th

Today I'm tired because it's one of the days I have the most work. But shouldn't I tell what happened to me yesterday, here in my dear diary? I imagine that today all Diamantina hasn't any other subject of conversation: "Did you see Helena and Luizinha dancing all night long last night, with their aunt lying in her coffin?" I'm only sorry that they won't say it to me personally, because I could explain. But what bad luck we have! Aunt Neném [Baby] spent the whole month dying and then had to draw her last breath yesterday.

I know very well that Aunt Neném is my father's oldest sister and that he esteems her highly. But I confess that I can't cry for the death of an English aunt whom I didn't know. She's been sick for many years at the *fazenda* and none of her nephews or nieces knew her. When my father learned that she was very low

he went there, a week ago. We'd already been invited to
Leontina's wedding here. It was the first dance I'd ever been to.
My rose-colored dress was the first pretty dress I'd ever had. How
could I miss all that?

Then, I don't know how, the news spread through town. Papa
only wrote to mama, who was all ready to go to the wedding, too,
and didn't go; but she herself thought it was a shame that we
couldn't go, after getting the news at the last minute. She planned
it with us: "You go with your cousins and I won't tell anyone
about Neném's death today. I'll keep the news until tomorrow."
But I'm so unlucky that I'd barely put my foot in the door of the
bride's house when I received condolences. It seemed like spite.
But I lied bravely, with a blank face. "Condolences for what?"
"The death of your aunt." "Who said that? It isn't true. My
father's at the *fazenda* and he hasn't sent word to mama." But
they wouldn't leave me alone until they convinced themselves that
I was more interested in amusing myself than in weeping for the
death of an unknown aunt.*

Oh! What a wonderful night! In spite of everybody's eagerness
to spoil my fun, they didn't succeed. It was the first time I'd gone
to a dance. How wonderful dancing is! And how quickly I learned
all the steps! If I hadn't gone to the wedding yesterday I could
never have been consoled for having missed it. There's a party
like that so seldom! And then I think nobody's going to remember the lack of feeling we showed for very long. It would have
been better if Aunt Neném had died after the wedding and we
could have shown more feeling. But it wasn't God's will. What
could we do?

* Mourning is still strictly observed in Brazil. In a recent personal interview
program on the radio, a girl was asked if she intended to vote in the election
being held the next day. She replied, "No." "Why aren't you going to vote?"
"Because I'm in mourning."

Saturday, July 21st

Just now we were all sitting around the stove, talking. It's one of my pleasures, when papa's home and it's cold, for us to sit around the stove listening to stories of bygone days and roasting peanuts. I like mama's stories better than papa's, even if she does repeat them a great deal, just the way he does.

Today the conversation got onto the subject of intelligence in the family. According to papa, nobody has my intelligence. He's sure that I'd be considered a genius if I weren't lazy and didn't have so many cousins to take up my time and keep me from studying. I think he's right. I'm not a genius, but I'd get better marks than I get at School, where I rarely get a good mark on an exercise. And also I must confess here, secretly, in my diary, that when I do it's more because some of the teachers are fond of me than because of my knowledge.

Those who are considered the most intelligent in the family are Uncle Conrado's children. None of them is more intelligent than we are, but their father is more methodical, and the house is well run, and they can study. Papa says that the most intelligent of them is Leontino. Then I told about one time when I thought too, that Leontino was more intelligent than the other cousins. It was at a family gathering at grandma's, and we smallest grandchildren went to ask Reginalda to tell us stories. Reginalda is the Negro who knows the most stories, and one of them, about a flea, has been useful to me to this day. The man flea left home to make his fortune and when he said good-bye to his wife, he said, "If they squeeze me with their fingers, good-bye for a little while; if they squeeze me with their nails, good-bye forever." Reginalda explained, "So you see you shouldn't squeeze a flea with your fingers and throw him out, because he won't die. You should kill him with your nail, good and dead." This is the truest story I ever heard.

Reginalda went on telling all the stories she knew, but we wouldn't let her alone; we wanted more. Then she told one about some buzzards who were up in a tree and made dirt on the heads of some drovers who were lying down underneath it. I saw that she was making it up as she went along and it was so silly that I got up and left, and Leontino went with me, but we didn't say anything to each other. The next day, very early, I opened my bedroom shutter and saw Leontino sitting by the door, waiting. I ran to open the door, thinking he wanted to come in, but he said, "No, I don't want to come in. I just came to find out if you discovered that last story Reginalda told yesterday was made up, too." I said, "Certainly. Didn't you see that I left?" He said, "Then this evening I'm going to grandma's with mama, and I want you to help me tell Reginalda that we could tell that the story was made up. Otherwise she's going to think we're dumbbells like the rest of them, and keep on making up stories to tell us, and I consider it an insult."

I settled it with him and that night we went to get even with Reginalda. But we were disappointed because she insisted she'd made up the story because she'd already told all she knew and we kept asking for more.

Thursday, July 26th

I was sitting, pen in hand, trying to think of something to write, because nothing's happened for days. It's rained all week; today's the first fine day. I went to the window to see if by looking at the sky and the stars something would come to me. Nothing. A funeral went by, coming up from Rio Grande. I thought: Will that give me a subject? No, because I don't know who it is.

I turned around, thinking I'd just copy the exercise from *Ornaments of Memory*, and tell the teacher tomorrow that I hadn't had time for the composition. When I turned around I saw mama, very annoyed with my brothers, who were sound asleep, struggling to get them on their feet while the corpse went by. I went through the same thing when I was little. I was pleased, because I'd found a subject.

Superstition in Diamantina. Since I was little, I've suffered from all sorts of superstitions. If there were thirteen people at the table, I was always the one who had to leave. Combing one's hair at night, under any circumstances, sends one's mother straight to hell. Sweeping the house at night blights one's life. Breaking a mirror is bad luck. Rubbing one foot against the other, walking backwards, and other things I don't remember now, are all unlucky. They can explain why some of them do harm, but not others. Such as, for example, if a visitor stays too long, stand the broom behind the door, or throw salt in the fire, and she'll go away. I believe that salt in the fire works if the visitor hears it crackle, because she know what it means.

The funny thing is that everybody knows that superstition is a sin, but they prefer to confess it rather than do something that somebody says brings bad luck.

Once I asked grandma, "The Senhora doesn't like to sin, and how is it that you know superstition is a sin and yet have so many superstitions?" She answered, "There are things that are born in us, daughter. Nobody can see proofs, the way I have, such as thirteen people at the table and within a year one of them dying, or a mirror that fell and broke in Henrique's house and he had such bad luck afterwards, without being afraid. The priests all say it's a sin, but I don't doubt but that they believe in it, too. It's something we're born knowing, the people's voice is the voice of God." I said, "I know for my part that I'm not going to believe these things, grandma. If it's a sin it's because God thinks it's absurd." And she said, "Yes, my child, I don't say that you should believe in a lot of them, I think that's nonsense. But some are true and you oughtn't to ignore them. Like thirteen people at the table, and a broken mirror, you can't make light of them."

I'm almost fourteen years old and already I think more than all the rest of the family. I think I began to draw conclusions from the age of ten years, or less. And I swear I never saw anybody from mama's family think about things. They hear something and believe it; and that's that for the rest of their lives.

They're all happy like that!

Saturday, July 28th

My aunts always get together at grandma's in the evenings and Dindinha always has something ready for them to eat. Either it's chicken and okra or chicken with black sauce, or a stew of pork and tomatoes. At grandma's they cook a great deal of *couve** for lunch and dinner because there are so many people in the kitchen. Then Generosa invented, out of her head, a way of cooking the *couve* stalks with bacon and it makes a dish we like very much, too.

Yesterday we were all in the dining-room having supper when a woman came into the house with a little girl after her. They came in without any greetings and without looking at anyone and went through into the kitchen. Mama and my aunts said, all together, "It's Maria Pequena!" [Little Mary] and ran to the kitchen with us after them.

When we went in, Maria Pequena burst out crying, and started telling us what she'd suffered in Mata do Rio, she and Aída, her daughter. She said that her owners there were very bad and that their daughters put pepper in Aída's eyes when she was sleepy and didn't want to work at night. She told us this crying, and other bad things we couldn't believe. Grandma said to her, "Don't cry. With the help of God you're back again, and now you are going to be happy; why cry over nothing?"

I already knew the story of this Maria Pequena before she ap-

* *Couve:* variety of cabbage that doesn't form heads but grows on long stalks; one of the commonest vegetables.

peared. Mama says at the time of grandpa's inventory* she wanted to keep her, but that she went to Uncle Geraldo, with her daughter. She is mulatto and mama says she used to be pretty. I don't know what happened, but Uncle Geraldo's wife, who lived at the *fazenda*, took a dislike to her and sent her to be sold at Mata do Rio. When mama heard of it, she sent papa after the man who'd bought her to ask him to sell her to her. Grandma was awfully sorry, too, and sent an offer to buy her back for more money. But the man said he'd already sent the slaves away several days before and they were already a long way off.

This was a sad event in the family. Nobody liked to mention it to grandma, who was very upset. Mama told us the story many times, and blamed Uncle Geraldo for letting his wife do a thing like that.

Maria Pequena said that she'd spent the years since the emancipation saving the money to come back, and that she'd never hoped to find grandma still alive.

Grandma said that now she can rest easy, knowing that Maria Pequena's safe.

Saturday, August 4th

Today we were talking about the lack of good luck in this house. Anyone else who starts a business is settled. Other people start stores and make money. But it's only by mining that papa makes anything.

When we went by our store we thought it was very strange; everything giving out, and Seu Zeca not buying any more supplies. Papa came home from the mine and I was the first to tell him about the store, that it was getting empty and that Seu Zeca wasn't buying anything, nor sending mama any money. Papa said that Seu Zeca is very honest and that he'd go to see what was the matter. He went, and Seu Zeca said that a lot of money would

* When the slaves were divided among the children at the time of the husband's death.

come in at the end of the month; that when he had it he'd buy supplies and make out the accounts. Papa was satisfied and went back to mining.

I went there this week and all I saw on the shelves were the bottles of *jaboticaba* vinegar that mama sent, the barrel of oil in a puddle on the floor, the sacks almost empty, and Seu Zeca smoothing out straws on top of the counter with a shell. I thought it was strange, since the end of the month went by several days ago, and the store was still empty.

Today papa came back and went to see the results. Seu Zeca had sold everything on credit and nobody paid him a cent. He even gave credit to Chico Guedes and Moisés de Paula, who hasn't a place to drop dead in. Papa saw that it was useless to go on. He sent back a few little things we can use, to the house, and sold the rest to Seu Sebastião Coruja for whatever he wanted to give, and even that without any cash; it's to be taken out of whatever mama buys from him.

And that's how the money from the store went. Papa and mama intend never to think about business again.

Friday, August 10th

This year the novena at the Mercês Church has been very popular; lots of people attended.

It was run by mama's cousin, Cristina Ferreira, whom we call Zizica, who has a tremendous nose. She lives at the Fabrica de Santa Bárbara with her niece, Virginia, who teaches school. The other niece, Zulmira, who's here studying at Normal School, is just like her daughter because she brought her up.

For a month before the *festa*, Zulmira talked about nothing except what Virginia wrote her, telling about the things she was saving up to bring: four suckling pigs, five turkeys, chickens, ducks, candy, cakes, everything in quantity, to give a supper to her friends and relations every night after the novena. We were all eagerly awaiting a *festa* with so many good things, and, since the beginning of the novena, every night we've gone to Zizica's house with the musicians, and stayed late, waiting for refreshments. If I should say that four days of the novena have gone by and we haven't had a cup of coffee there yet, I wouldn't be lying.

My cousin Lucas is very funny and naughty. Aunt Agostinha, his mother, brought up a cunning little boy, the son of one of her slaves who died. He is stunted and almost blind, but very intelligent. He recites verses and *corta jaca** very well and always has a funny answer to everything. This little boy is just like my aunt's handkerchief, she's never without him for an instant. Wherever she is, there's José sitting beside her. Lucas took him to his bedroom and made him memorize some verses to recite at Zizica's in the evening, and told him not to tell anybody or he'd beat him.

Last night almost all the relatives were at Zizica's. At a certain point Lucas clapped his hands and cried: "Silence! Zezinho† is going to recite, *cortando jaca*." Everyone stopped talking. The little boy came into the middle of the room, dancing and reciting:

> *"Everywhere I runs and goes*
> *I see Siá Cristina's nose.*
> *I have a belly-ache so big*
> *From eating four whole sucking pig."*

At this point my aunt got up and grabbed his hand, saying, "Idiot! Reciting such nonsense!" Everybody in the room burst out laughing and Zizica, I don't know if she was pretending or not, asked, "What was it the boy was saying, I didn't understand?" Everybody answered, "Oh, it's just boys' nonsense."

I was sorry Zulmira wasn't there then. She's scarcely shown herself since the beginning of the novena, ashamed of the lies she told.

---

* *Corta Jaca:* "A kind of dance, scraping the feet and reciting verses at the same time." The words mean "cuts the jack fruit," an enormous fruit of the breadfruit family.
† *José—Zezé—Zezinho:* Joseph, Joe, or, Little Joe.

Saturday, August 18th

At home mama and papa are always talking about the weakness grandma and Dindinha have for always having a pickaninny around to bring up and love, as if it were white. Each of them always has one. If that one grows up another one immediately comes to take his place.

Grandma always raises Negro girls and Dindinha Negro boys. When they're little I don't wonder, because I like little children so much, and I think the Joaquim that Dindinha is raising now is very cute. She sends him to say funny things to us and he is cunning. But to like big Negroes is something I find very strange.

Nestor is a very proud Negro and he makes himself much disliked at grandma's by the liberties he takes. He opens Dindinha's cupboards and takes whatever he wants. Dindinha's already put him to work at a shoemaker's but he won't stay in the shop, he's always at the house.

Once when grandma was alone I took the opportunity of asking her if the liberties Nestor takes don't make her angry. She said, "I don't like it, child, but I can't help seeing that she's right. He was born shortly after her little girl, Clarinha, died and he distracted her. Clarinha died, and a few months later the wet-nurse died, too, and left Nestor still nursing. Chiquinha had been staying in her room crying, and we were happy when she came out to take care of him, and now he's like her own son. But sooner or later he'll go away and leave us in peace. I've already heard that he wants to enlist as a police-soldier and I keep advising Chiquinha to let him. Leave things the way they are, child. Everything passes."

Thursday, August 23rd

Siá Ritinha came in and mama said to her, "You can sit right here, Siá Ritinha. Helena writes even with conversation going on, she's used to it."

"That's right, Siá Ritinha," I said, "you can stay here with mama, but don't mind if I turn my back so it won't distract me from my lessons."

But the conversation did distract me, because I was listening and just pretending to be writing.

Mama asked, "How is Inhá? I haven't seen her lately."

Siá Ritinha answered, "She's well, but she's always so busy sewing that she doesn't even have time to go to the window."

"And the monkey; he hasn't been around. Is he sick?"

"The Senhora doesn't know, Dona Carolina, what happened?"

Mama: "No. What was it?"

And Siá Ritinha went on: "Some brute, we haven't been able to find out yet who it was, took off all his skin with boiling water, *coitadinho*. The Senhora can't imagine how we've suffered. And it's put Inhá in a state, too, poor thing. The Senhora knows that Chico isn't an animal to her, he's a child. Just imagine if one of the Senhora's children was skinned by boiling water, and on top of that, not being able to find out who did it, to get revenge. If we knew, Dona Carolina, I swear to you that Inhá wouldn't suffer like this without getting even, you can be sure of that. I don't know how the poor little thing got home. He came in so silently and sadly it would stab you to the heart. Inhá, when she saw him, I can't tell you how she was. She was stammering; she couldn't get out a word. I was the one who had to rescue the poor thing, and I put a little lard on the burns. I don't know if he'll ever be what he was again. That intelligence, that liveliness!—all gone. Now he just looks at us with such a sad face, it would stab you to the heart . . ."

Mama said, "Poor Chico, so smart, so intelligent."

Siá Ritinha: "Just think of it, Dona Carolina. A little animal like that, meeting a wretch who had the heart to do what he did to him. Nobody has an easy lot in this world. We suffer in all kinds of ways. I was saying to Inhá, 'You had to have a little animal like that and get so fond of him, just to have him suffer so.' But we can't escape suffering. Perhaps God sent us this instead of something else."

Mama agreed. "That's the way it is, Siá Ritinha. God knows what He's doing. It's better not to grieve too much for the animal; God could have sent a greater affliction."

"He couldn't have sent a greater, Dona Carolina. He can only send us another one on top of this one."

I couldn't do my lessons, but I'd learned why poor little Chico had disappeared. He's amused us so much and thrown down so many peaches and bananas for us, that in spite of the times he's robbed us, we couldn't dislike him. It must have been the neighbors he stole the salt pork and meat from who did it.

Poor Chico! How he must be suffering, *coitadinho!*

Saturday, August 25th

I think it's funny, in our family, the way we all crave peace and quiet. Papa, grandma, and everyone only ask God for peace and quiet.

Today I went by Uncle Conrado's house and there were some poor people at the door. From behind the counter he gave me some money to divide among them: a penny apiece and two for Father Felipe. I asked him why only Father Felipe got two and the others one. He answered, "It's because the others say, 'May God make you prosper,' and Father Felipe always says, 'May God give you peace, master!'" So I saw once more that everyone in our family, that lives in the greatest peace anyway, doesn't want anything else.

When I see Father Felipe with a bag on his back begging alms, I remember how Mama Tina made me suffer when I was little. She used to say that Father Felipe went around with a bag on his back to catch children and that once she'd seen a little girl in it. And that Father Felipe went from door to door begging

alms, beating the bag, and saying, "Sing, sing, my bag, or I'll
stick my big knife in you!" And the little girl inside the bag would
sing:

> "Oh! Senhora of the house,
> Have pity, I beg,
> On the poor little wretch
> Inside this bag."

Then the lady of the house would take pity and give alms.
Mama Tina said that the little girl had been kidnapped.

I used to have such a horror of Father Felipe that I remember
the agony I went through on Saturdays, when he came to our
door, begging alms. I barred myself in the wardrobe and stayed
there, sweating with fright.

Tuesday, August 28th

Today was my birthday and grandma had told me that I could
bring my schoolmates to have something to eat with me after
School. Grandma had sweets on the table, biscuits, raisins and
port wine, and was so nice to my friends that they all went away
enchanted with her.

At the table she asked, "How old are you, child? Thirteen?" I
answered, "No, grandma, fourteen. Doesn't the Senhora know?"
She said, "I thought it was thirteen. You were born yesterday."
Grandma knew perfectly well, but she likes to make us out
younger than we are.

She told my friends they could go to the garden and pick what
they wanted to. We found some fruit ripe and a camellia tree full
of camellias. Everyone picked lots of camellias and enjoyed everything very much. They liked grandma and were envious of my
having such a nice kind grandmother.

When grandma, *coitada*, thinks that someone likes me, she just
can't do enough to be nice to him. Even if it's someone she doesn't
care for, if he makes a lot of me, he gets into her good graces,

the way it happened with Uncle Antônio Lemos, a son-in-law I'd
never heard her say a good word for. When he came to the *chácara*,
I ran to hug him and when grandma saw how he loved me she
immediately changed toward him. When he left she said to
Dindinha, "He's not a bad person, Chiquinha. He has feeling.
Did you see how he likes the child?"

That was three or fours years ago, before he moved away from
Diamantina. But it stayed in my head. I remember almost everything.

Thursday, August 30th

I'm convinced that here in Diamantina prayer is worth more
than work or influence. For me and all our family it never fails. If
only we pray a strong prayer and have faith, it's answered immediately. But today I saw it proved that in the house of very
good people, like Seu Juca Neves, it's only a matter of asking and
God listens, without even praying.

Today I got up and went to Seu Juca Neves' *chácara* to have
lunch with Catarina, so she could teach me a crochet stitch I didn't
know. Seu Neves' *chácara* is the pleasantest spot in Diamantina.
Any place you are there, it's nice. Catarina said, "Let's find a good
place to sit." We went out through the orchard and found a wonderful place where we sat on a stone, under a tree. In a little while
Júlia, a *cria** of the house, appeared and said, "Dindinha,† the
cook sent me to say that there isn't enough salt pork for lunch."
Catarina answered, "Ask daddy; he's over there."

Seu Neves was weeding the garden with a hoe. Júlia gave him
the message and came back to Catarina. "He says that he hasn't
any money, but it doesn't matter; God will provide." I said to
Catarina, "And if God takes too long, Catarina, then what will

---

* *Cria*: a child of slaves, born and raised in the house, or adopted as a baby,
a common custom in the days of slavery; in the country servants are still often
called *criadas*.
† *Dindinha*: apparently Catarina is godmother to the *cria*.

happen? Don't you think it would be better if I left?" "Why?" she said. "Can't you eat what we eat?" But I was afraid God wouldn't send the money for the salt pork, because to me He's only given ideas for how to make money.

We kept on crocheting and Catarina told me about God's kindness toward them. I really was envious. And it wasn't very long before Seu Neves arrived with money for the salt pork. Catarina asked him, "Where did it come from, daddy?" "From God," he answered. I was curious and wanted to know, "Where did the Senhor meet God, for Him to give him the money?" Seu Neves said, "God sent it by a crooked path. Pedro Moreira owed me some back rent for pasturage, and God made him pay me today."

Monday, September 3rd

Friday, Uncle Joãozinho was in town. He came to get money and other things he needed. As he had an extra horse, I suggested that I go back with him to see papa the next day. I went, and being obliged to keep silent for eight miles, since my uncle has no conversation, I began building castles in the air. I built a castle in the air about finding a big diamond and being rich, and the idea grew so much along the way that when I got to Boa Vista I was a millionaire. I didn't even know what to do with so much money.

When I got there, instead of going to the house with my uncle, I went to the mine to give papa a surprise. I got down and ran through the troughs; papa had such a shock, *coitado*. He was sitting in the shack, watching the men work, with his feet so swollen that right then I came back to reality. I began to laugh, and told papa about my castles in the air. He laughed, too, and said, "As long as they amuse you, go right on building them, they do no harm. But remember, daughter, never think of having a lot of money, it never brings happiness to anyone and sometimes it takes it away. Just ask God that we don't lack for the necessities. Aren't we happy? Would you change places with any of your rich friends or cousins?" I wanted papa to get on the horse and I'd go on foot, but he didn't want to. So we walked back to the house, he holding the horse's bridle.

In spite of papa's advice, I can't help thinking that if I really found a big diamond I wouldn't let him walk all that way every day with his feet so swollen, *coitado*. He's so good!

Saturday, September 8th

Today was the *festa* of Our Lady of Protection. As we hadn't gone to the novenas we decided to go to the *festa*; and it's too bad I went. I don't like to see sad things, and today, coming out of church, something so sad happened that I was upset all day.

The children always stay in the church doorways waiting for the skyrockets to go off, to pick up the sticks. I don't know why they fight and struggle so and run a long way after those sticks. What do they do with them?

There were some children in front of the church, and when the sung Mass was over and we were coming out, a Catherine wheel was set off. The fireworks were all going off at the same time. Instead of going up, one rocket turned and went right through a little boy's body, like a dagger. The poor little boy fell down. His mother was in the crowd, and when she saw him she ran and threw herself on top of him, screaming and shrieking to wring one's heart. Some men who were nearby carried the little boy up the street to Chico Lessa's pharmacy. The mother went along crying like a mad woman. I don't know what happened afterwards, nor if the poor little boy died. But I didn't enjoy anything the rest of the day.

Wednesday, September 12th

Why do my schoolmates worry so much about my life? I don't know why, since they've never given me anything and wouldn't if I needed it. How I'd like to tell them, "Don't interfere with me; mind your own business." Some friend is always coming with a message from a brother or a cousin or some other boy for me.

Fininha brought me a poem her brother had written for me. I keep telling them that I don't want to have a sweetheart, that I don't love anybody, and to leave me alone. Today they began to tease me and call me an old maid. Mariana said, "You're fourteen years old already. If you don't look for a man now, when you're older no one will want you and you'll be an aunt. You're going to be an old maid." I said, "But if I want to be an old maid, what do you care?" She said, "If you don't care, it's all right; but we care, because we like you. That's why." Biela said, "You don't understand Helena. She wants to get married just as much as we do, but she's proud, she wants something special. I bet that if a doctor* appeared she wouldn't send him away." The others said, "Then she can just keep sucking her finger. There aren't any doctors here, unless she's waiting for her cousins who are studying in Rio. Anyway, what's the difference between a doctor and the rest of them? They're all men, aren't they?" I listened to it all in silence. To cut the conversation short, I said, "Don't worry so much about me, my friends; remember the saying, 'Marriages and shrouds are made in Heaven.'"

Monday, September 17th

I'm going to unburden myself here of the disappointment, the rage, and the sorrow, that I suffered yesterday at my cousin Zinha's wedding. She's my rich uncle's daughter, and the wedding was an important occasion.

My uncle ordered dress-lengths of silk from Rio de Janeiro for his girls. All my other cousins were making themselves silk dresses, too. Mama bought two lengths of fine pink wool for me and Luizinha. Aunt Madge took mine to make and Luizinha's went to another dressmaker.

Aunt Madge came back from Rio recently and since then I haven't had any peace. I have to carry a parasol so I won't get sunburned, because the girls in Rio don't have freckles. I have to

* Doctor: see page 97.

wear my hair loose because the girls in Rio wear their hair loose. The same nagging all the time; the girls in Rio dress this way, the girls in Rio wear their hair that way. I didn't mind if the dress was made like those the girls in Rio wear. I just wanted it to be pink.

Aunt Madge took the material and never asked me to try it on. I went to her house every day as usual, and saw nothing of the dress. Once I got up my courage and asked for it. She said, "Don't worry. You're going to the wedding looking prettier than all the others."

The wedding was day before yesterday. I and Luizinha went to Dudu's house to have our hair arranged, and we left delighted, with hair-dos that made us look like young ladies. Luizinha dressed up in her dress and we went to Aunt Madge's; my dress was nowhere to be seen. Aunt Madge said, "There's no hurry, child. It's early yet." And taking a comb, she said, "Sit here. You're a little girl, why do you want to wear your hair like a young lady?" She wet my hair, pulled out the curls, and let it fall down on my shoulders. Then she went and brought in the dress: a simple dress of navy-blue wool with just a row of buttonholes down the back, bound with red ribbon.

Today I think it's a pretty dress; but at the moment I had one of my attacks of rage and I couldn't hold back my tears. Unable to say a word, I kissed my aunts' hands and ran out in the street. Luizinha followed me, in silence. I went up Burgalhau Street, into the Cavalhada Nova, and into Direita Street, running all the way, and blind with rage. I couldn't see a thing. Grandma's been at Uncle Geraldo's for several days, waiting for the wedding. I went into her room and fell on her bed in such a storm of tears it frightened her. But all she said was, "My God! What's happened!" Luizinha came in and grandma asked, "What's the matter?" Luizinha said, "It's because she was longing for a pink dress and Aunt Madge dressed her like that."

When I break down, it's always with grandma. I feel that she's the only one who understands me. Then grandma began with her usual remarks: "Another of Madge's and my trials with this girl! She doesn't understand that we're only trying to do what's right for her. She always wants to be just like all the plain girls!" Then I raised my head sobbing, and said, "I'm the most miserable, the skinniest, the stupidest of them all, grandma, and I always have to be inferior in everything. I'm so envious of Luizinha because Aunt Madge doesn't like her!" Grandma said, "Stop crying over nothing, silly child. Some day you'll see that your godmother, who's so good to you, and I were right. Go wash your face and let's go to the parlor. They're all there already." Then I showed her my hair and said, "Do I have to go into the parlor with my hair like a lunatic from the asylum, grandma?" She said, "It's pretty, child." I said, "Grandma, the Senhora just doesn't know what I'm going through. I was looking forward to my pink dress with such pleasure, and today, to dress like a widow, and to see all the rest of them in pink and pale blue and everything? No, grandma, it was too cruel of Aunt Madge. I don't want her to take any more interest in me, grandma. This is the end!"

I'm only sorry I can't quarrel with Aunt Madge so she'll leave me alone once and for all.

Thursday, September 20th

The Pitanga girls are the nicest and gayest in School and the other girls like them very much, because they have two brothers who are nice and intelligent, too, and who always get the best marks in exams.

Their life is different. Their father lives in Retiro, making butter and cheese, and when he comes to town he just embarrasses them, saying foolish things in front of company. Their mother is paralyzed and lives in the depths of her bed, and they have no servant. All the work is done by a little boy, the youngest brother. So they always go to dinner at other people's houses but never invite their schoolmates to dinner or to eat anything after school at their house.

They go to Aunt Agostinha's a lot. Lucas is Miloca's sweetheart, and Naninha is Joaquim Heitor's, one of their brothers.

Yesterday Naninha and Lucas asked me to go to the Pitangas'
house with them because Jacinta likes me very much, in spite of
being older. When we got there they all ran inside to tidy themselves up and Jacinta stayed to receive us. They receive visitors
in the dining room and the hens are everywhere. We sat on a
bench and on the table there were two hen-dirts and, in the
middle, the bowl of manioc flour. It didn't bother Jacinta. She
took a spoonful of the flour and covered up the piles, making two
little mountains. Then she sat down and began to talk. I already
wanted to laugh but by the grace of God I held it in. After a little
the others came in and Jacinta left to tidy things up better inside.
Seeing the two little mountains on the table, Miloca took the
spoon, spooned up the flour and put it back in the bowl again.
Then with the back of her hand she cleaned off the table thoroughly, saying, "How careless of Jacinta, to leave that here like
that!" Naninha looked at me with a stern face, afraid of one of my
fits of laughing. But at such moments, in order to contain myself,
I think about something sad: mama with a broken leg, Luizinha
stretched out in her coffin, and I manage not to laugh.

I swear never to go back there because I think it's bad for one
to hold in one's laughter. But when we left I got even. Naninha
said that she hadn't been able to talk straight, she'd been so
scared I'd explode.

Saturday, September 22nd

Raising the masts* in Diamantina are the best *festas*. I like to go
to all of them. But those at the Rosário and the Mercês I like best
of all.

There's a very funny Negro couple at the *chácara*. She's called
Henriqueta and he is Machadinho. The way they fight because
of jealousy is very funny. He's very small and hideously ugly, and

* See page xix

his wife beats him with a strap because she says he runs after other women. I die laughing to see how Machadinho runs around the stove, he's so afraid of Henriqueta's beating him.

Grandma hates my hanging around the kitchen. But I tell her that at her house the kitchen is more entertaining than the parlor.

Machadinho earns money by beating the drum to announce the mast-raisings. He beats the drum all day long, and every time he goes by the vegetable garden, Henriqueta, who may be at the far end, runs to see Machadinho beat the drum. When he sees his wife he sticks out his belly and beats with such fervor that she drools with joy. On those days she keeps a dish of food for him and doesn't fight with him. I can see that she thinks he's someone of the greatest importance.

The other day, Lucas, who is very bad, played a dirty trick on Henriqueta that made me feel sorry. Machadinho had to go out in the street on an errand and Lucas went up to her and said, "Don't be scared, Henriqueta, it wasn't anything."

She asked, "What wasn't anything, Seu Lucas?"

He said, "The mad bull."

Already very scared, she asked, "What mad bull?"

He: "The one that chased Machadinho."

Without waiting to hear another word she rushed out into the street, like mad.

Lucas began to laugh his wicked laugh and we saw that he was joking. We called Zé Pedro and sent him after her; she was a long way off already.

Thursday, October 4th

On rainy days our aunts amuse us by telling stories. Since we were little the Negro women have told us fairy tales, but now I like the stories about the old days better, particularly about my aunts' marriages, which were all different.

Today Iaiá was reading *Gil Blas* and telling us stories from it. Then I asked her to tell the story of her marriage and how she managed to love a husband she didn't know.

She said she was fifteen years old and saw him for the first time the day of the wedding.* At first she was angry and afraid of him. She spent her days hiding and only thinking of how to get rid of that man. She cried and was so unhappy that he decided to go away on a trip, to treat his patients. He was a doctor.

"While he was travelling," said Iaiá, "he wrote me some very nice letters, calling me 'my beauty,' and 'little angel fallen from heaven,' and he sent me a present from every place he stopped at. I began to like him and even to miss him. One day I was in the kitchen, mixing some cakes to fry for the priest who stayed with us every Saturday, for Sunday Mass. I was just that minute thinking of the doctor and how I'd like to get a letter from him, when he came into the kitchen. I ran and hugged him, hanging from his neck in my joy. I remember that my hands were covered with dough and I got it on his neck and his coat. That was the day our honeymoon began."

Iaiá always called her husband "doctor." Then he had a sick-ness of the head and died, leaving a son, Pedrinho Versiani. Iaiá is very proud of this son, who is an engineer and off somewhere building a railroad.

Monday, October 8th

I don't know how it's possible to acquire a vice. I don't see how people can drink till they're drunk; after one glass of wine I don't have any desire for another. I don't see how people can drink beer, it's so bitter; but at dinner I see everyone drink one glass after another. I can't stand *cachaça*, not even the smell. It's with disgust that I take the spoonful of *cachaça* and rhubarb that mama gives us sometimes when we grind our teeth in the

* Girls were sometimes married as young as twelve and thirteen. There are stories of little girls being given dolls as bribes to induce them to marry much older men.

night. Gambling,—I can't gamble very long at a time. If the game's for money and I win, I'm sorry to get it; if I lose and they get my pennies, I'm sorry, too. Also, I get sick of gambling very quickly. But in our family there's one vice that everyone has, and I like it, too, and I can hardly wait to grow up and take it up, in spite of papa's saying it's ugly. It's snuff. When I have a cold and my nose is stopped up and mama gives me a pinch, I like it very much. I think it's very nice, too, when one person meets another and opens his snuff-box and offers him a pinch. In our family only Dindinha and Uncle Geraldo have gold snuff-boxes. Uncle Conrado's is silver. The others are of something black that looks like horn.

I've noticed that Dindinha never misses a chance to offer a pinch to the others, just to show off her gold box; and that's the reason she almost lost it yesterday in church, at the benediction. She took it out to take a pinch. Then instead of putting it in her bag, she put it on the floor. At the moment of benediction, when Dindinha was beating her breast very contritely, a woman near her threw her handkerchief over it and pulled it towards her without Dindinha's noticing. When the benediction was over, we were just going into Uncle Geraldo's house when Juca Boi arrived with it in his hand and gave it back to Dindinha. He'd seen the woman doing it and took it away from her to bring back.

I've already asked Dindinha to leave me the snuff-box in her will, because I know I'm going to take snuff like my aunts. The other day mama and my aunts were surprised to see my weakness for these things to stuff up the nose. We were all at the *chácara*, I beside grandma on the stoop. Seu Procópio came by, and knowing that grandma always likes a pinch of dust, he took a horn out of his pocket, opened the cover with a snap, and offered her one. I asked for one, too, and sneezed hard, because his snuff is stronger than ours.

Papa always says that smoking is an ugly vice, and that my grandfather wouldn't even permit one cigarette. Because of this, my

English aunts don't take snuff, but he takes his pinch from time to time. I've already told papa that I'm going to take it when I grow up and that I don't think it does any harm. The vice I think is awful is to chew tobacco, like the Negroes at the *chácara*. Generosa chews tobacco while she cooks, and spits all around. It turns my stomach. I don't know why grandma allows it.

Wednesday, October 10th

Today Beatriz said to me, "Let's have lunch at my house, because Luizinha didn't come to School and you're alone." I like to have lunch there because it's so near School and we can take more time to eat.

I saw two funny things there today. In Uncle Conrado's sister's house there lives a decrepit old woman, with a black handkerchief tied around her head, greedy and gossipy like nobody you've ever seen. She only thinks about eating. Besides this, she has a way of talking about other people's affairs that we find very funny. She leaves Mass and goes running from house to house, taking coffee in all of them. At each house she comes to she says, "If I hadn't just left the communion table, I'd tell you what I saw at Seu So-and-so's house. Mouth! Shut up, mouth!" and she hits herself on the mouth first on one side, then the other, and then tells everything she saw.

She arrived while I was there and Aunt Aurélia asked her if she'd like some lunch. She said, "I accept, Dona Aurélia. I only took black coffee at Seu Assisi's house. Hum! What a fight was going on between him and his wife! Mouth! Shut up, mouth!" Aunt Aurélia filled a plate for her and sent her to eat in the kitchen. After lunch the dishes were taken out to the kitchen, and, seeing a big dish of tomato sauce, she thought it was a stew, and took a ladleful and poured it in her mouth. The sauce was full of pepper and she choked. You should have seen the face she made. She came back to the dining-room and said, "Dona Aurélia, give me a piece of cheese to *repair* my mouth after that pepper!" Aunt

Aurélia replied, "There isn't any more cheese, Siá Antoninha; the cat ate it all."

I thought it was so funny!

Saturday, October 13th

Can anyone understand how it is that a person who likes someone else very much can have such a knack of upsetting them? The case of Aunt Madge and me is the strangest I ever saw. She's my confirmation godmother,* and I know that she finds good qualities in me almost the way grandma does. If I tell her a story she laughs until she can't laugh any more. She tells everybody that I'm intelligent, witty, and good. Everything that one person can do for another, Aunt Madge does for me. And yet I must say that almost all the disappointments I've had in life have been her fault, because of this passion she has for being interested in everything concerning me. I'd be much happier if she were like the other aunts, who never notice what I'm doing. But, *coitada*, all the nice things she does only upset me and sometimes really make me suffer.

Aunt Madge couldn't bear to see me go by her door with my head bare in the sun, and she wanted me to carry a parasol, and talked about it to papa every day. When she saw that papa couldn't be bothered, she went to the old cupboard and found two parasol frames with ivory handles that my English grandmother had brought back from England, and gave them to my father to have covered. My father went to Siá Eufrásia Boaventura, who covers umbrellas, made a bargain with her, and when he came home, said to mama, "I ordered those frames Madge found covered. Now I'll have some peace as well as the girls."

The parasols came but we didn't like them and were very un-

* A child has two sets of godparents, one at baptism and one at confirmation. In small communities with large families this naturally leads to everyone's sooner or later being a godparent, often several times over. Godparents of the same child refer to each other as "co-godparent," and this title, *compadre* or *comadre*, gets into general use as a title of respect.

happy, because one was round like a bowl and the other was flat. We went to Aunt Madge's carrying them. She was radiant. "Now! That's it! Now you aren't going to be covered with freckles any more. Show your schoolmates that they have ivory handles, and say that they came from England."

We went on to School. The girls were at the door and Luizinha heard one of them say to another, "Just look at what the little Englishers have got now!" and they started giggling. We went in feeling very uncomfortable and I decided with Luizinha, "Let's hide them, hide them well, so the girls won't see; later on we'll get rid of them."

We went in and hid the parasols in the work cupboard. One girl found them, called another, and the two of them went through all the rooms with the parasols opened up. None of them carries a parasol to School, only umbrellas when it rains. When the girls saw those two strange objects, they burst out laughing and they all went along on the exhibition. Luizinha and I were terribly afraid that they'd discover they were ours and we tried to keep hidden until the game was over. Fortunately at School such things can't last very long because the intervals between classes are only fifteen minutes. I said to Luizinha, "You can miss a class better than I can. When the bell rings you run to Aunt Aurélia's, leave the parasols, and come back."

When we told this story to Aunt Madge and papa, they thought it wasn't reason enough for us not to keep on using the parasols. If they could think the way the grown-ups do, life would be much easier for the young.

Saturday, October 27th

If there were diviners of dreams today, the way there were in the time of Joseph of Egypt, what a fine thing it would be! I can never get that story of the seven fat cows and seven lean cows, that meant seven years of plenty and seven years of famine, out of my head.

When I was little my teachers on the subject of dreams were the little Negro girls at the *chácara*, but I lost confidence in them after they scared me by saying that it was a sin to think a priest was homely, and I told it at my first communion and suffered for a year afterwards because of it. From time to time in a catechism class Father Neves refers to it, and says, "This year there won't be any silly confessions like last year's. I confessed two little girls who disappointed me with their silliness. One of them confessed to me, horrified, that she thought I was homely. The other one, when I was giving her absolution and thinking she was contrite, was counting the buttons on my soutane. This year I'm going to put an end to that. I'm only going to let those who are well prepared receive their first communion." I was already shaking for fear that the others would find out I was one of the silly ones.

Even now I suffer from strange dreams and I don't believe the explanation Mama Tina gave me when I was little, even if it would be easier to. When I told her my dreams and asked her to explain them, she used to say, "Dreaming is when the soul doesn't go to sleep with the body and keeps on thinking. If a person is good and lives according to God's will, he has good dreams; if he's in mortal sin, he has bad dreams." I don't want any other girl to suffer what I suffered over my soul's being in mortal sin when I had a bad dream. I told them to Mama Tina, and she put me on my knees to pray. I had no idea what my mortal sin was, but then I remembered that I must have been envious or greedy and I calmed down a little and made resolutions to correct myself.

I don't want anyone else to go through what I went through as a child, for fear of hell and spirits from the other world, werewolves, and the headless mule* the Negroes told me about; but I can't get the explanation of dreams out of my head. I don't know why to dream of *jaboticabas* means death; I have my doubts. But to dream of lice means that you're going to receive money; this I know, because it's happened to me and other people.

* A woman who lived with a priest turned into a headless mule at midnight.

I suffer a great deal from dreams and one of the worst I had when I was little was the disillusionment I suffered when I died and went to heaven. How horrible heaven was that night! I remember until today the dismal life I led in heaven until I woke up. It was an enormous yard, clean and bare, filled with old women in cloaks, with shawls on their heads, holding their hands up in prayer, not paying any attention to each other. No St. Pedro, no angels, nothing. When they were tired of kneeling they walked around in that enormous yard with their heads bent, still praying. When I woke up and saw I wasn't in heaven, what a relief!

I told this dream to Mama Tina and she explained to me that it was because she'd told me that the road to heaven is full of thorns; but the road to hell is clean and bare, and in my dream I'd changed them around.

Dreaming that I'm at Mass at the Cathedral in the middle of the crowd in my underwear, is something horrible that's always happening to me. Lots of times I've dreamed I was at School in my bare feet, without knowing where to hide them. It's a constant martyrdom. But I've had marvellous dreams, too. I can't count the times I've flown, without wings, to Boa Vista or over the houses of the city. It's delightful! Or I was in a marvellous palace, like the little girl and the dwarfs. And I've dreamed of being in a field of peanuts, and I kept pulling up the plants and finding silver coins at the roots.

But last night's dream was horrible. I dreamed I'd turned into a monkey, and in spite of my grief I could have resigned myself to being a monkey if I hadn't had a tail, but my tail was enormous!

If Mama Tina were alive, I wouldn't have to ask her to explain this dream. I know quite well it was because we were speaking about Siá Ritinha's monkey at dinner yesterday.

Saturday, November 3rd

Renato is very shy. He doesn't associate with any girls except his cousins. He doesn't talk to any of the girls at School and he never goes to anybody's house outside the family. Aunt Madge is worried about him and she said to mama, "We've got to do something* about Renato. He's fifteen years old already and he behaves like something from the backwoods. All he wants to do is go fishing and trapping birds and he's never even learned how to enter a parlor. What will become of him if he grows up like that? We've got to get him into society, and I'm going to do something about it."

When my friends come to the house Renato stays in his room. He only comes out when Belinha comes. And I suspect he likes her because he feels perfectly free with us when she's here. He always keeps one of his drawers full of fruit: plums, *maracujás*, guavas, and more besides that he gets from friends of his who have an orchard, but he never gives us anything; he's stingy with us. But when Belinha comes he gives her fruit and we all make the most of it.

Yesterday Aunt Madge said to mama, "Compadre Francelino is going to give a party at his house today; it's Gegênia's birthday and he told me to bring your children. Don't forget to send Renato; it will do him good. It's going to be a very small party. I'll wait at home for the children, at eight o'clock, to take them."

When Aunt Madge left, Renato said he wouldn't go. Mama and all of us insisted; but he got stubborn about not going; he said his clothes weren't good enough and that he had holes in the soles of his boots. Mama answered that by saying that at night all cats are gray and that no one was going to see the soles of his boots, anyway. We insisted so much that finally he made up his mind to go.

We went. Luizinha made him dance with her, to get him used to it, and we had a pretty good time. Then they started playing forfeits. We all sat in a circle. When it was Renato's turn to pay a forfeit, Gegênia chose "Senhor São Roque."† They put a chair

---

* Literally: "un-donkey Renato."
† In this game of forfeits, a boy kneels before a girl (or vice versa) and re-

in the middle of the room and got a candle, but he didn't want to do it. Edmundo grabbed him by the arm and said, "Come on! You're a big boy and you can't act like that in front of the girls." And he pushed him toward the chair. Renato knelt down with his back to Luizinha and me, right under the Belgian lamp that lit up the room quite brightly. When we saw the two eyes in the soles of Renato's boots, we shut our mouths to keep from laughing, but we couldn't contain ourselves. The other girls who were near him started to laugh, too. Renato got up without needing to know anything more, and said to Luizinha and me furiously, "Idiots!" and went out the door.

When we got home we found Renato still furious and mama very sorry for him, but she had to laugh, too.

With such an unfortunate beginning it's going to be hard, now, for Renato to get to be more sociable.

Aren't these things mysterious?

Monday, November 12th

Joviano, who's already graduated from Normal School, came to arrange to take English lessons from my father. He comes every afternoon from five to six, and he's interfered with my studying a lot, as well as our life at home.

Our house is small and every sound can be heard in the parlor. Since Joviano's been coming, papa's ordered us not to laugh or talk in the next room, because the boy keeps his ears open to hear what we're saying and doesn't pay attention to the lesson.

We don't make any noise; but stopping laughing, since it's forbidden, is impossible. Papa reaches the point of yelling from the parlor at us to stop.

Today, talking to Maricas, Joviano's sister, I told her about it and how we suffer because we laugh for no reason at all, particu-

---

peats three times, "Senhor São Roque, I kneel at your feet, without crying, without laughing, without laughing, without crying," etc. If he laughs, the girl can impose a forfeit: have him crow like a rooster, kiss her, etc.

larly since her brother's been coming to take lessons. She said, "It's because Seu Alexandre hasn't suspected yet that Joviano really likes hearing you laugh better than taking the lessons. He told us at home that he'd like to have you laughing and talking near him all day long. Don't you remember how silly you were the day we came here in the rain? Your elastic-sided boots were cracked and full of water, and you came in the door shaking your legs and throwing the boots off in the hall. At the table Viano said he knows he's going to be a bachelor, because he'll only marry a girl who'll do things like that and he knows he won't find one."

Thursday, November 15th

Today my father, like everyone else in town, is very pleased about Prudente de Moraes' taking office. There was joy in town when the telegram came, and everybody rejoiced as if it had been something for us. But papa says it's because nobody here likes Floriano, and they didn't expect he'd give up his office to Prudente, because he has great influence with the army. With Prudente de Moraes, everybody expects things to improve. I always say to papa that I can't get through my head why a change in presidents has any effect on us here in Diamantina. My father says it has, because the government is a well-organized machine and that a good president and a good government benefits all Brazil and even us. I told him I'd only believe it if the president gave us water-pipes and repaired our streets. He said that those things aren't done by the president, in Rio de Janeiro, they're only done by a local man like Dr. Mata, who could even have a railroad built from here to Ouro Preto.* If there's something I have no hope for in Diamantina, it's a railroad. But we don't really need one. Horseback is good enough.

* *Ouro Preto:* black gold, name of the most famous gold-mining town, at this time capital of the state of Minas Gerais.

Sunday, November 18th

Mama never knows what to think of next in order to earn money, but she's so unlucky that everything she does comes out at a loss. She began by making *rosquinhas** and sweet bread to sell; the tray came back full and we had to eat them all ourselves. She planted a garden, to sell vegetables. When they were big enough she filled a tray and sent it out in the streets; in the afternoon it came back, with everything withered. She made rice cakes to sell at the church door at early Mass. Mama thought it would be easier for everybody to buy them there than to go all the way up to Siá Alexandrina's house. The tray came back full and she had to send them to her sisters in order not to waste them. Then she made carnival lemons to sell.† Emídio went out in the streets with the tray and came back with it empty. He'd sold them on credit.

Dindinha's Nestor enlisted, and because he wanted to eat meat cakes and manioc at night, he came to us with a fairy-tale about how there was a lot of money in that business. Mama made meat cakes the whole month. Nestor came and got the tray every night, and at the end of the month he didn't bring her a penny. She made turnovers, *carajés* and hotcakes, to sell at the door of the theatre, and nothing sold.

When papa realized that the money wasn't amounting to anything, he decided to do the accounts of mama's businesses. When he saw the loss he turned to her in his quiet way and said, "Carolina, my child, you're killing yourself for nothing. These businesses of yours are getting us into debt. It's better for you to go visiting your mother and sisters and not try to be a business woman."

* *Rosquinhas*: a sweet, dry biscuit with a hole in the middle.
† Lemons molded of wax and filled with perfumed water, thrown on the last day of carnival.

Thursday, November 22nd

A few days ago I met Father Neves at my English aunts' and I felt that he was as pleased to see me as I was to see him. We hadn't met for a long time.

I studied the catechism up through sacred history and I had it on the tip of my tongue. I began at six years and stopped at ten. But I stayed all that time because I was chosen, with other girls, to sing in the Church choir, accompanied on the organ by one of Father Neves' sisters. We sang at the benediction on Sundays, in the month of Maria, and at some Masses. I always liked Father Neves, considering him a saint put on earth to guide souls to heaven. He wasn't disgusted at my saying in confession that I thought he was homely and he kept on liking me just the same.

Today I went to my aunts' house and Aunt Madge said, "After you left the other day, Father Neves praised you so much that I was very happy. He said that you are one of the simplest, best, and most intelligent girls he's ever taught. You should be pleased to have someone like him speak that way, and try to make the same impression on everyone." I answered, "Impossible, Aunt Madge! It's very different when one stops associating with saints and enters hell to associate with devils. We have to be bad, in School, and I'm really horrified by so much wickedness. I don't understand how the Senhora is so good, having gone to that School. Although it's against my will, I'm going to come out of there a demon." Aunt Madge said, "I went there when I was older, and you're a child; it's very different. But you mustn't associate with the bad girls."

I came home with Aunt Madge's words in my head and pleased by Father Neves' praise. It's one of the good things in life, to like someone and have it returned.

When I was in the catechism class I liked and admired Father Neves so much that my best day was Saturday, the day we met at his house for choir rehearsals. We waited there until his sister called us to their father's, next door, where there was a piano. I remember until today how he liked to entertain us with cakes and candy, but could never give them to all of us because of the eagerness of the greedy ones. I remember how sorry I was about some raisins he had made at his father's house. He dried the grapes and made raisins. One Saturday he told us, "I'm going to get you some raisins I made. They aren't as good as those that come from Portugal, but they're good enough to eat." He went to get them and brought a tray to pass around, a bunch apiece. The girls rushed forward and he could barely hold onto the tray. The floor was spattered with raisins and they were stepping on them and picking them up. I couldn't get a single one and I was sorry, not only because I like raisins so much, but because I wanted to try them because he'd made them. There were all sorts of girls in the group, even soldiers' daughters and Negroes. But Father Neves enjoyed everything like that.

Sunday, November 25th

Since I've formed this habit of writing everything down, I have to do it, even if I don't prepare my lessons. Today I'm going to tell something here that I don't want to write for Seu Sebastião. I can keep it a secret for a few days and then mama will have to know. It's just before examinations and I've said to mama over and over again that I can't present myself for the exams with my uniform all faded, and mended at the elbows, and she hasn't paid any attention. Mama's very good, of course I know that. I swear I wouldn't exchange her for any other mother in the world. But the life she leads, never going out of the house except to go to grandma's, does me a great deal of harm and embarrasses me. I know that if she compared me with the other girls and saw how different my uniform is, she'd do something about it. But she never sees anyone except grandma, the aunts, and the Negroes at the *chácara*. I have absolute faith in my prayers to Our Lady. Whenever I'm in trouble I say the rosary and some powerful prayers

I've just learned and I can be sure that she will certainly help me. I'm convinced that the idea that came into my head yesterday was from Our Lady. She didn't have any other way of helping me and so she gave me this inspiration. How could I have thought of such a thing myself? Particularly since the idea came to me after I'd begged her very contritely yesterday, to find me some way of getting a dress for the examinations.

In her drawer mama has a gold brooch that papa always says is going to be mine. I don't think much of this brooch since papa sold the diamond out of it. I don't like false stones and it doesn't even have a false one. I've already told him that he can give it to Luizinha. How can you explain that yesterday, just as I finished praying, such an idea came into my head? Mama says that this month there isn't any money to give me for a new uniform for the exams. Next month will be vacation and I won't need it any more. If I should speak to her about selling the brooch to a goldsmith I know she wouldn't agree and would hide it from me. I've pondered over this a lot since yesterday and I see that the only way to get a dress is to sell the brooch. I'm going to sleep on it tonight and I'm going to talk about it to Our Lady quite frankly. If she doesn't take the idea out of my head, it's certain that I should have the dress for the exams. Everyone in the house is asleep and I'm the only one awake now, at eleven o'clock.

Since my father's advice about only talking to my notebook, my life has grown worse and I think I'm getting even thinner. The girls at School all talk about my thinness and I wish they had all the chores I have, to see if they wouldn't be thin, too. If I could only sleep well, and eat peacefully, I know I'd get fatter. But for a long time I haven't even had half an hour for lunch.

Now I'm going to stop here, kneel, and speak to Our Lady again about my life. Only she can help me. Tomorrow I'll tell here, in my dear diary, what I've decided to do about the brooch with a hole, without any diamond in it.

Tuesday, November 27th

I finally carried out my plan of taking the brooch and selling it. Could it be called stealing? I don't think so, since the idea was given to me by Our Lady.

But I must admit that I was very brave. The idea stuck fast in my head for two days in a row. Today I got up early and the first thought that came to me was that wretched brooch. And everything conspired to help me. Papa has a drawer with a bell where he keeps everything and it was in the drawer. I took the opportunity of their all being in the kitchen and turned the key very slowly, so as not to make a noise, and took the brooch. I took it to Seu Mendes. He weighed it and gave me thirty *mil reis*. I think he cheated me, I'm sure it's worth more, but I was so pleased at the sight of the money that I didn't complain. From the shop I went to the dressmaker and handed over the money for her to make me the dress.

I'm overjoyed with my idea; I'm going to make a blue wool dress with a jacket and a white vest; which will look like a uniform but also be good enough to go out in. I'm already dreaming of how elegant I'm going to be! Mama will only learn about my selling the brooch when the dress comes. I'm so happy that I even know what I'm going to say. When the dress comes I'll show it to mama and say, "This was bought with the money from the brooch that papa said was for me when I grew up. When I'm grown up I'll have my teacher's job or a husband, and I won't need a brooch with a hole in it. Now is when it can be useful to me." I know that mama's going to ask me why I didn't speak to her before taking this step. I'll answer, "Because I knew that the Senhora wouldn't let me, and I had to have the dress for the examinations."

Saturday, December 1st

My dress came today. I like it so much and I'm so happy!

Everything turned out the way I'd hoped. When mama and my sister and brothers saw it arrive, they rushed to see it, without understanding anything. I immediately told mama what I'd done and I was surprised at her not saying anything to me, and even more amazed when she went to her room, got thirty *mil reis*, gave them to my brother, and told him, "Go to the goldsmith's shop and tell him I'm sorry I sent the brooch to be sold and that I want it back." Renato went and came back saying that the goldsmith said he'd already melted it down and couldn't return it. I know Seu Mendes is lying. He wouldn't be so foolish as to melt down such a well-made piece of jewelry as that. I know he put a diamond in it and sold it, or he's going to sell it. But I don't care what happened to it. I'm so pleased with my dress and the success I'm going to have at School. Sooner or later things come true. My father is perfectly right when he says, "The unlucky don't cry forever." The remorse I might have felt disappeared when mama produced the thirty *mil reis* to get the brooch back. I'm very pleased with myself. I know I'm going to manage my life better. I'm smarter.

Monday, December 3rd

Today I wore my dress to School. I know that it's pretty because of the envy it aroused. The girls all said immediately, "There never was such a uniform, here or in China. The principal ought to see it and forbid it. After this they're going to have silk uniforms at School. Haven't you already made one of wool with a piqué vest?" I swear I was afraid they were going to complain to the principal and he'd even forbid me to wear it.

Sometimes I'm amazed to see how intelligent I am about certain things. But it was all Our Lady. She saw I needed a dress and a uniform at the same time and inspired it directly. The dress was made up entirely out of my head, without seeing a fashion plate. How could I have had such a good idea! When the examinations are over, I'm all ready. One day I can wear the dress with a vest and a tie; and when I want to vary it, the skirt with a white blouse or a colored one, and nobody will get ahead of me.

I enjoyed the envy I caused my schoolmates when I went by

Mota's store, going home to lunch and coming back, and they came to the door to look at me. Tião came out to compliment me on my dress. The principal passed me twice and saw it and didn't say anything. It was a success!

Wednesday, December 5th

I'm sorry for the boys growing up around here. Nobody can think up a way to earn money but what the others are envious immediately. My brothers are victims.

Renato had a business that brought him a few pennies. He's not at all stupid, he always thinks of some trick or other. He used to get money looking for gold in the gutters,* or hunting for it in the ground under the house. But his best business was always *lambaris*. And I never saw anyone as lucky as he is at fishing. Sometimes he made two *mil reis* a day. He caught birds and sold them, too. But in all these things he had his customers stolen from him. He began to make straw cigarettes to sell, better than João Quati's [small rodent], and the others copied him. This was the business we liked best and we even helped him smooth out the straws with a shell. He went to the market, brought back a lot of straw, and on holidays I used to amuse myself smoothing them out and tying up the bundles of cigarettes, which turned out very well.

So that he wouldn't be idle, and in hopes that he'd learn to do business, mama rented a shop and put some things in it: black beans, rice, flour, brown sugar, cheeses, and everything else necessary to start a little shop from the beginning. Instead of being satisfied, Renato immediately wanted to fill the shop with bottles, for the sake of appearances. He asked mama to make *jaboticaba* vinegar, and pineapple champagne, and send them to the shop. Mama did. She sent a lot of bottles, without thinking what might happen.

* Note in *M V de M:* "In the road-bed between the paving stones, after heavy rains."

My uncles liked to meet there in the evenings, to play cards. A few days ago, with the hot weather, the bottles fermented, and the corks began to pop with such loud reports that they startled the card-players. The pineapple wine and the vinegar spattered all over the shop and my uncles got it all over their heads and clothes. Renato just managed to rescue the white and brown sugars, so they wouldn't get wet. And that was the end of the shop. Then, too, we're about to go to Boa Vista for the holidays.

In our family the men only know how to earn money by mining. They have no gift for business.

Sunday, December 9th

Yesterday was Joaquim Angola's party. This Negro ran away from a very bad master in Serro and hid himself in a *quilombo** near Lomba. The Negroes from the *fazenda* took him food at night. When soldiers went there hunting for run-away slaves he ran and fell on his knees at grandma's feet, begging her to buy him. She got my grandfather to buy him and he stayed in Lomba, married, and had a lot of daughters. This was many years ago, on the day of Our Lady of Conceição, and Joaquim Angola's daughters always celebrate that day. One of them, Júlia, just married Roldão, and they took the opportunity of having an even bigger *festa*.

They invited everyone they know and the party was in the old *senzala*. They decorated the big room, where the slave women used to spin and make lace, with bamboos, banana-trees, and leaves. They had a decorated suckling pig, meat pies, hens, and all kinds of sweets. Grandma gave wine and they bought *cachaça*. There was a table for us inside and for the Negroes outside.

I gobbled up my dinner quickly and went to the *senzala*. I swear I never saw such a wonderful party. There are only three Negroes at the *chácara* now who came from Africa: Bemfica, Quintiliano, and Mainarte. They sang songs from their own country, turning round and round and clapping their hands and then bumping

* *Quilombo:* a place of refuge of run-away slaves.

bellies with the women. The Negroes from here are jealous of the old ones who know the African songs and who dance with more spirit. Then they sat down at the table like us and drank toasts. They all had on white trousers and shirts. Joaquim Angola was bursting with joy.

I like to see how happy the *chácara* Negroes are. Mama says that when grandpa died each of the children (there were twelve) kept his favorite slaves and grandma brought the rest of them, some ten or twelve, with her when she moved to Diamantina. Since there wasn't anything for them to do, and grandma never sold anybody, she put the men to work in the vegetable garden and the women made lace and wandered around the house. I still remember when the news of the law of the 13th of May came. The Negroes all stopped working and got together in front of the house, dancing and singing that they were free and didn't want to work any more. Grandma, angry at all the shouting, went to the door and threatened them with her cane, and said, "Away from my house, you good-for-nothings! Freedom came, but not for you, no; for me! Get out!" The Negroes shut up and went to the *senzala*. In a little while Joaquim Angola came in the name of the others to ask her pardon, and to say that they all wanted to stay.

Grandma let them, and those that haven't died or got married are at the *chácara* until today. Naturally, with the life they lead . . .

Thursday, December 13th

Today mama and Aunt Agostinha decided we'd go to visit Dona Elvira. We all went. Dona Elvira seems to be an extremely clean woman. She makes many mistakes when she talks because she's lived in the country all her life, but her house is very nicely arranged. The benches and tables are clean like new. The floor hurts your eyes, it's so bright. She was at home, wearing a very clean dress, and you should have seen how clean the children were, all ready for school. How is it that with all this cleanliness, she's so lacking in feelings of disgust?

When we got there she was very happy to see us and asked us into the dining-room and then showed us the vegetable garden, the flower-beds, and everything. In the kitchen, which was so clean it was like a jewel, she showed us a pot boiling on the stove and said, "I must have foreseen the Senhoras' visit. God gave me the idea of putting this kettle of *canjica* and peanuts on the fire to entertain you with." When I heard these words I thought of nothing except the *canjica*.

Lunchtime came, she opened the cupboard and took out a deep crockery dish with only one handle that I found very strange. But as it happened quickly, nobody noticed. When she brought the *canjica* from the kitchen and put it on the table, we looked at one another in bewilderment. Never in my life have I seen a dish of *that* sort in the dining-room. Everybody ate the *canjica* except me. I excused myself by saying I didn't like it.

When we left, Naninha said to me, "Silly, it was your loss. Didn't you see that she thinks that's a dish for food? If she thought it was for anything else, she wouldn't put it on the table. She's very clean."

Sunday, December 16th

Today Aunt Madge came by the house after dinner to take me to the Amarantes', in Romana Street. There they were talking about a sister of theirs named Biela Neto, who came to Diamantina five or six years ago and stayed at Dona Nazaré's *chácara*, Gupiara, where I went that time with Aunt Madge. Remembering that visit, she was telling me today about how rich Dona Nazaré was and the big parties she used to give. When Aunt Madge was a young girl she went to one of them with my grandfather, who took an Englishman who had come to Diamantina at the time. The party was a wedding, and it went on for three days, day and night. When one band got tired, another began to play. There was no counting the things to eat and drink. In the dining-room there was a big basin where the men emptied the dregs of their glasses, and when it was full it was thrown out and another was brought in. Aunt Madge says that the Englishman was amazed by the richness of the clothes, the abundance of food and drink, and the gayety, and he said that he never would have expected to find such a civilized place so far from Rio de Janeiro. When he went back to England he wrote a book in which he told the story of the party and spoke about grandma and grandpa and my aunts and uncles.*

Today the *chácara* of Gupiara is abandoned and the house is falling to ruin. Only one man, named Pedro Neto, lives there, and he stays in his room for years without going out, and doesn't speak. He isn't dumb, he hears everything that's said, but he answers only by signs. They say that every year or so he speaks a few words and then falls silent again. How strange!

I remember going with Aunt Madge to Gupiara when I was small, to visit this Biela Neto. She told me to call her aunt right away, saying that she and Aunt Madge were just like sisters. Then she called her daughter, Nazinha, a very pretty little girl of my own age, for us to be introduced and play together. Nazinha took me by the hand very nicely and said, "Let's play." She took me to the front of the house and began asking questions: "What are those spots you have on your face?" I answered, "They're freckles." "What makes them on people?" "They say it's the sun." "Do you like to be spotted like that?" I couldn't answer that. She looked at my boots and said, "Why are your boots holey like that?" I said, "Because the varnish fell off." "Do you think they're pretty like that?" "No." "Why don't you change to other ones?" And I, who'd never been ashamed of anything before, was ashamed to say,

* This was Sir Richard Burton, who wrote: "The toilettes were remarkably good . . . Every neck sparkled with diamonds; the other ornaments were the solid and honest, if not tasteful, jewelry of Diamantina . . . The ball seemed to be a family party, infinite in merriment . . . the dancing was chiefly quadrilles." Vol. II, p. 103.

"Because I don't have any others." With a charm such as I'd never seen in a little girl of that age, she said, "*Coitadinha!*" I didn't like the *coitadinha* but she was so pretty that I couldn't help being pleased at having made her feel sorry for me.

Then she asked me, "What games do you know?" I told her, and she said, "They aren't any fun for only two to play. Make up another one." I looked at the ground and saw some round white pebbles, and said, "Let's pretend to be hens and lay eggs." She said, "Wonderful! Let's." Then I ran, picked up some of the pebbles, hid them in the long grass and began to cackle like a hen. She came and got the eggs. Then she said, "Make up another!" I suggested that we play at cooking. She said, "What's that?" I said that it was a cooking game; we cooked, and made dishes, and put them on the steps for a table, and sometimes, if they were real, we ate them. She said that was a good idea, what did we need? I said, "If it's going to be real we need rice and meat and everything to do it. If it's just a lie, we have to pretend." She went to ask her mother for some food and saucepans. Her mother wouldn't let us, saying that we'd get our hands dirty, and burn them. So then we played pretend cooking. We picked some sweet-smelling plants that have a white bud that looks like rice, and some leaves to pretend they were greens, and amused ourselves that way for a long time. Then she said, "Let's go see my dumb uncle." We went into a bedroom and there was a man who didn't speak and carried on a conversation with her by signs, asking questions about me. I answered everything and he pointed to me and then to his head, meaning that I was intelligent. That was the only time I ever saw Seu Pedro Neto. He was sitting up in bed, with a table with some books on it beside him, and after a while he made a sign with his hand for us to go.

We spent the day there and I was enchanted by the little girl's prettiness and charm. When we were leaving she said to her mother, "Ask Aunt Madge to bring her here all the time, mama. She's so nice and knows so many games." Then, turning to me,

"You're coming, aren't you?" And she added, "Even if the varnish is all off your boots it doesn't matter; come anyway."

Today her aunt told Aunt Madge that she's at school in Rio, and has grown to be a very pretty girl, and I was thinking about what she must be like now and how much I'd like to see her again!

Thursday, December 20th

My music examination yesterday was a surprise to everyone. Who would have imagined I'd do so well? My schoolmates don't see anything in me. Sometimes I wish I had will power, and studied a little, just to show them all what I'm capable of. But it's better this way. Nobody likes to see that other people are more intelligent. I see how they are with Clélia and Mercedes. Perhaps they all like me because they think I'm different from what I really am.

To return to the music examination. Naninha, who is mama's cousin and advisor, told her a month ago, "Helena can do well in the other exams, because she has a good memory and can memorize the questions beforehand; but she won't pass in music. She simply can't stay in key. If I were you, I'd hire Modesto Rabequista [Fiddler] to give her lessons until the examination." Grandma immediately said, "Carolina! Send for Modesto tomorrow."

I studied all last month with Seu Modesto. The examination came. I got *Tantum Ergo*; I opened my mouth and got an *excellent*. I'm even convinced that I could be a singer.

The sad thing is that I don't care a thing about getting *excellent* in some exams, like music and gymnastics. I'd like a small *excellent* in Portuguese or arithmetic. But even now I can't even succeed in making a copy from *Ornaments of Memory* in Portuguese without making a mistake. And let's not speak of composition, analysis, and the rest. But I got *good* in geography and *fair* in the others, thank goodness. Now I'm through with the first year.

The *excellent* in music is just enough to mention casually to my English aunts, who are the only ones who ask. "I got an *excellent* at School." And now we're going to Boa Vista. Hurrah!

1 8 9 5

Thursday, January 2nd

I don't believe there's another woman in the world like my mother for work.

She doesn't call on anyone in Diamantina outside the family, but besides all the housework, that she does by herself when we can't help her, she never misses going to grandma's or to Jogo da Bola Street every night.

She's so hard-working that she won't leave my brothers in peace. When we're in Diamantina I think it's so funny the way mama sharpens a knife, picks up a stick of fire-wood, hands them to my brothers when they're walking around digesting lunch, and says, "Here; make some toothpicks out of this, it won't interfere with your digestion."

Now that we're here in Boa Vista my brothers don't get any

rest. Early in the morning they fill up the kitchen with fire-wood and at the same time bring in palm branches and switches. They leave the wood in the kitchen and go out to build a fire and clean the switches. Nhonhô, who's smaller and clumsier, has the job of taking the bark off. Renato is making brooms that he sells in Diamantina for two hundred *reis*, and bird cages and bird-traps, all to sell. He sells the cages with a bird already in them and there isn't any fixed price; it depends on the customer. The same for canes.

Renato's incredibly slow but he does everything very well. I envy the way he gets up and asks us, "Want anything from Diamantina? I'm going there today to take some things to sell." He makes up a bundle of brooms, puts it on his shoulder, takes a cage full of birds in his hand and starts off down the road early. By afternoon he's already back with the money.

If he liked to study the way he likes to work he might amount to something.

Tuesday, February 5th

When mama heard that Luizinha hadn't passed this year, she decided to put us both in the College of the Sisters of Charity. I was quite satisfied because I like anything new. Mama got our clothes ready and yesterday was the day we were supposed to enter. I know this scheme was Aunt Aurélia's idea, so that her daughters, who are entering there, too, would have company. I don't know why she wants to put those two girls in the College, they're so quiet. They just live to study and they never go out of the house. Of course if my uncle wanted them to become Sisters of Charity I could understand it. But he doesn't.

Since yesterday was the day we were supposed to enter, I decided beforehand to go around saying good-bye to my friends. I went from one house to the other, leaving them all dumbfounded at mama's decision. I left Ester's and Ramalho's house to the last. There I had to change my mind completely, because Ester and

Ramalho just wouldn't hear of my being shut up in the College. I was overjoyed to see how the two of them consider me so different from what my relatives do, even mama. Ester said to me, "Don't think of it! With all the Sisters' rules and regulations you'll lose your gaiety and sociability; you won't have any charm, you'll turn into someone else. Don't be silly; put your foot down and don't go." When I told her that I had no hope of ever being able to study here outside, she said, "Do you think that any studious girl is worth as much as you are, even if you do waste your time? Don't change your nature or your ways a bit. Stay the way you are, don't go to the College." She kept me there for lunch and kept repeating the same advice, she and Ramalho, too.

When I left their house I went along the street thinking: "Ester is a good friend of mine and she studied at the Sisters' College. I know that my nature and my ways wouldn't change. Everybody is the way he's born. But perhaps I might lose all the joy in living I have and just mope like Luizinha and my cousins."

I resolved not to go but I didn't say anything to mama. We all went to the College and I left my clothes at home to get them later. The Sisters received us in the parlor. I let Luizinha and my cousins go in and then, without anyone's noticing, I went out the door and down Glória Street and waited for them away down the street. I could see by Uncle Conrado's face that he was furious with me, but he swallowed his wrath. Aunt Aurélia asked me how I could do such a thing! Mama only said, "It'll be your loss, daughter, when you see how studious your sister's going to be, with good manners and like a little saint, while you just fritter away your time outside."

But I'm going to follow Ester's advice. I'm going to begin the second year of Normal School and study. I shan't have to repeat it the way I did the first year.

Thursday, February 7th

Today we went to the College to visit Luizinha. We all came back so upset that we couldn't enjoy anything the rest of the day.

I never suspected that Luizinha, Beatriz, and Hortência, who are always so obedient, were capable of behaving the way they did. They wept and wailed all the time we were in the parlor. When the time came for them to go back to the convent the three of them made a spectacle of themselves. They didn't want to go and they had to be dragged off by force. Luizinha, usually so good and proper, yelled loud enough for the Sisters to hear her, "Helena, you were smart not to want to come here! It's like hell here!"

Uncle Conrado and Aunt Aurélia went home so sad at the sight they'd seen that they took mama to their house, to keep them company and distract them a little.

I've talked to mama about taking Luizinha out, because she's not going to get any happier no matter how long she stays. They told us about the life they lead at College and I felt sorry for them, *coitadinhas*. They have to get up at dawn to go to Mass, in all this cold, and spend an hour on their knees on the hard floor. When they come back from Mass they get some watery coffee and *couscous* and begin studying. They say they can't endure the food. Cold baths and those nagging, unbearable Sisters . . . How wonderful I didn't go!

Thursday, February 14th

Thursday used to be the good day in our week, we got up happy and gay to go to the country. Now it's our saddest day.

I and mama came back from visiting Luizinha at the College so upset that we didn't talk to each other for fear of bursting into tears. I'm trying to persuade mama to take Luizinha out. Today I told her she doesn't have to go along with Aunt Aurélia in the education she's giving our cousins; that if they're there without Luizinha they'll finally get used to it, since they've always led very retired lives. But Luizinha, who was always at liberty, going back and forth between our house and grandma's, going to Boa Vista and on an excursion in the country—she can't get used to prison. The change is too great.

Mama made some meat turn-overs and sent them to Luizinha, who complains she can't stand the food at the College. Today mama asked her if she'd got the turn-overs and she said, "The Senhora sent me some? Now I see how they cheated me. The Sister put them in front of another girl and she and the girls near her ate them. I even thought: 'Those turn-overs look like the ones mama makes.'"

I can see clearly that mama isn't going to let Luizinha suffer like that. It's not just she; we're suffering too.

Sunday, February 17th

Classes begin at Normal School tomorrow. I'm sure I'm going to fail the second year the way I did the first. It makes me sad to have them think I'm stupid when I'm not, but what can I do? I won't complain any more. When mama buys a school book it's always for the two of us, me and Renato. He doesn't like to study and he won't let me study, either, and we keep fighting until I give in. The minute I take a book he says, "That's the one I was going to study." It's no use not giving him the book, because he torments me all day long until I'm tired and give it to him, anyway. Besides this, I have to go to grandma's every day and have to do my chores at home, and there isn't much time left over for study.

Papa says if I'd pay attention in class I'd learn. I know it perfectly well, but I had the misfortune to fall in with the worst group of girls at School. They won't let any of us sit in the front seats or pay attention to the lessons. We've been considered lazy since the first year and we shall be until the end. But what do I care? School is such fun and I spend my days there so happily that it doesn't matter.

Tomorrow I have to begin to write the letter or composition

every day and to copy out the exercise from *Ornaments of Memory*. We may be able to leave School without knowing Geometry, French, History, and everything else, but I doubt we'll leave without knowing how to write a letter. I love to write; it's the only thing in which I really fulfill my obligations at School. And Seu Sebastião waits in the door after class and as we go out we have to give him the exercise and the composition. No one has the courage to face him without the assignment, because we see that he's doing everything he can for our good.

Thursday, February 21st

Aunt Carlota's the aunt who makes us laugh, not because of her sense of humor, because she hasn't any, but because she's so different from the other sisters.

No one in the family bothers about themselves. All my aunts are wrapped up in their husbands and children. They never think of themselves. I never saw mama or any of my aunts touch a bite before their husbands and children had eaten. If there's a very little of something on the table, they never even know what it tastes like.

I think mama's even more self-sacrificing than the others because besides caring for her children she's the one who's most devoted to her husband. It's even talked about in the family. When I complain about how little she thinks of herself and how wrapped up she is in us and papa, she says, "You'll see, when you're a mother. Don't you know the saying, 'Those who have children never have full bellies'? It's the simple truth. You and your father are my life. If you eat, I'm more satisfied than if I'd eaten."

Dindinha lost both her husband and her little girl early, but she's the same way about grandma and everyone; she doesn't think of herself.

Grandma isn't like her daughters, but that's because the daughters live only to take care of her, to think about her food and to spare her anything unpleasant. Her cares are all for me.

Aunt Carlota's very different. She's the homeliest one and she married a teacher from Serro, a man old enough to have been her father, and until today she still talks about how much her husband liked to see her in a low-necked dress, with her arms bare. She's fat and loves to eat, and she says she never goes to bed without a bar of chocolate on the bedside table, to eat if she wakes up during the night. She says that every day before she goes to bed she eats a dish of scrambled eggs with dried beef or fried pork, so she "won't get weak." She has false teeth and when corn or anything like that is served she takes them out to eat.

She can hardly see a thing and I had to copy out the whole mass for her in letters as big as kernels of corn. She memorizes everything, and I had to sit with the book open in my hand while she recited it by heart, and she was letter-perfect.

Saturday, February 23rd

Everybody at School says that Zinha is crazy. She looks thirty years old, all twisted and homely, with skin like fish scales, coarse hair like a horse's tail, and teeth like big cloves of garlic. I used to think that the girls said she was foolish because she was so ugly. But today there I was in the second year class, sitting very peacefully beside Luiza, when she had the unfortunate idea of advising Zinha to comb her hair and not to go around with it so tangled. That was all it took to make Zinha start insulting her, on and on. It was funny the way she yelled, "Do you think you're my equal? Do you know who my father is, to have the audacity to advise me? I, with my hair, am worth all of you here, you cats! I'm Diniz Verejão's daughter!" I listened to it all and fell to thinking of the poor children she's going to teach. Isn't there any way of preventing such lunatics from becoming teachers? There are so many other things they could do.

When I went to grandma's I told the story and Uncle Joãozinho said, "Here in Diamantina you can't separate the idiots from the rest. Just build a wall around the town. The place is a regular asylum." And at home papa said, "He'd be one of the ones inside the wall; he's not so well-balanced himself."

Ash Wednesday, February 27th

How wonderful carnival was this year!

I suppose that carnival's always the same, but every year it seems better than the year before.

Luiz de Rezende made the carnival much more exciting this year. He brought lots of decorations and pretty costumes from Rio that we'd never had here before.

When carnival is over I always remember how rough we got, and think about how lucky we were not to have got hurt, and I decide to change my ways. But the next year I'm one of the ringleaders and do the same thing all over again. Could there be anything stupider than throwing a man in the basin of the fountain with his clothes on? It must be awful, because they get hurt and their clothes shrink. And that's why they always end up fighting.

We have to stop such rough jokes. The carnival lemons are really fun, and we don't have to give them up, unless it's for something more civilized. I only get upset at night during carnival, when all my cousins go to see the dancing at the theatre and I don't go. I don't know when mama and papa will let me go to the masquerade ball. If it weren't that grandma won't give her permission either, I swear I'd find a way to go. But grandma is so fond of me, and talks to me so lovingly, that I haven't the courage to disobey her. Two years ago I wanted to go and she gave me two slaps with her slipper, but I could tell she didn't want to hurt me, she was just pretending; and I was already more than twelve. It was the first and only time she raised a slipper against me. But even yesterday I was so envious when I saw all my cousins going to the theatre, all lit up and with the music playing, that I cried and stamped my foot and she really had to be angry with me.

But every time grandma gets angry I can count on some present or other.

Friday, March 1st

I finished translating La Fontaine's fable about the frog that wanted to be as big as an ox, and I didn't have time for the other lessons. I got to wondering why they require things like that of us at School if we're all just studying with the intention of being teachers. Why would I ever need La Fontaine's fables to be a teacher at Bom Sucesso, or Curralinha, or even here in Diamantina?

I spent four years at Mistress Joaquininha's school, which is one of the best, and there I don't remember ever hearing any of the things we drive ourselves to learn at Normal School. That is, the others are driving themselves. I can't say that I'm being driven; it would be unfair to Iaiá Leite [Milk], Mercedes, Clélia,* and some more.

It comforts me to think that when we get our diplomas it will all be the same whether we've studied or not and I'll be the lucky one, because I'm not killing myself the way they are.

Mercedes was telling me that she never had time to tidy up her room or even to make her bed. When I told her what I do at home she said, "No wonder you don't study."

Sunday, March 3rd

A few days ago a very nice boy whom Iaiá knows arrived at the *chácara*, coming from Bocaiuva on his way to Teófilo Otoni. Going through here, he looked up Iaiá, to stay with her.

The state he was in when he arrived horrified everyone. He was very thin and yellow as saffron. He said he'd caught a fever called the shaking fever,† which just wouldn't leave him. He was going to try a change of climate for his health because he'd been told that the fever could only be cured that way, by leaving the place where he caught it.

* The good students.
† Malaria.

Iaiá lived in those parts and she knows everyone there. She invited the boy into the parlor and began to ask him for news of everybody and everything. Suddenly the poor boy began to shake; I ran and got a pillow and he lay down on the sofa. He had a high fever, we put a blanket over him and he shook until he sweated. We were all worried, but Iaiá, who was a doctor's wife and who'd lived there, knew how to treat him. She sent out for some sulfate of quinine pills and kept giving them to him. He stayed right at the *chácara*, in the back bedroom, taking only milk and broth.

Today was the first day that Iaiá had a chicken killed for the poor boy. She was very much afraid it would make him worse, but she sent him a plate of chicken and some well-cooked rice for lunch. Rita went to get the plate and found it absolutely clean, without even a bone on it. Iaiá told her, "Go back; go pick up the bones. He's a country-boy and he probably threw them on the floor." Rita went and came back laughing at the poor boy and said that he'd eaten the bones, too.

Grandma said, "See how hungry he is, Henriqueta. You'd better stop being nervous about him and give him more to eat. If those bones don't make him sick, you don't have to worry. We'll see."

Tuesday, March 5th

A little black girl from Boa Vista, my goddaughter, came here today.

Her mother had to come to town and brought her to call on me. She must be five years old, but she looks three, she's so skinny and shy. She didn't say a word and wouldn't even answer questions. Her mother said she's always that way, very quiet. But I think it's either because they beat her or don't give her enough to eat.

I must have been ten years old when I was godmother at this little girl's baptism and on that occasion mama was so pleased with me that I remember it to this day. She said to papa, "I don't know whom this girl takes after. I never saw anyone so smart in my family, and I never heard of anyone in yours, either." Papa said, "She's something like my sister Alicinha, when she was small."

The two of them admired me like that because before the little girl was born, when I'd already been asked to be the godmother, I discovered that there wasn't any layette ready for her. Because I didn't have as much as a penny, I remember I collected old clothes from the family and ripped them apart and made a layette, copying things from a neighbor baby's. I spent hours sitting indoors, although school was finished, making everything by hand because we had no sewing-machine. For the baptism dress grandma went to the bottom of her tin trunk to get out some old silk, and I made it up with so much fancy-work that she was delighted and said she was well-paid for the trouble she'd gone to to find it. She showed it to everybody and talked to the family about my fancy-work and my will-power for a long time.

I'll never forget Renato's joy that day. The man who was going to be godfather with me had a big boy, older than we were. He and Renato went off together and a little later Renato came in giggling, as pleased as could be. "Know what? So-and-so [I've forgotten the boy's name] told me that he feels sorry for his father, having to go to church arm-in-arm with such a homely girl."

I didn't mind a bit because I was used to Renato's talking about how homely I was. It was mean of him to be pleased, but now I can't help seeing the boy was right. I had more freckles then than I have now, and I wore my hair slicked back with chicken fat, with a long braid hanging down my back.

Thursday, March 7th

Today was the day to visit Luizinha at the College. Mama was up early making *rosquinhas* to take her. After lunch we went to Aunt Aurélia's, to go with her and Uncle Conrado.

The cousins have got used to it already, but Luizinha is complaining of a stomach-ache and we think she's thinner. So I insisted that mama bring her home, to consult Dr. Teles. The Mother

Superior objected and said we didn't have to take Luizinha home because the doctor could go to the College the way he always goes to see the other girls. But mama brought her just the same. Mama hopes papa will come home to decide what ought to be done. I'm going to tell him to let Luizinha leave and I know he'll agree. She's very quiet, she doesn't go out all the time the way I do, and she shouldn't be shut up against her will. The College is for girls from out of town who don't have families here. Luizinha says that she won't go back unless she's tied and that she's going to ask papa to go back to Normal School just as a listener, if it's too late to enroll as a student.

Monday, March 11th

I've been the lady of the house for two days and for the first time I realize how easy it is if you know how.

Papa is in Sopa;* he went to start a new mine. He wrote mama that Dr. Vincent, the engineer who's working the mine, works even on Sundays and so he couldn't come this week. Mama's face fell immediately, and I suggested that she go to see him. "What?" she said. "How could I leave you three all alone?" I answered, "Why not, mama? We have to learn how to manage. You can go and leave the house in my care and I promise to make Renato toe the line." Mama agreed: "You are all so good, really, I'm going to trust you. And I know that God will watch over you, too."

She sent Renato to rent two horses from Seu Antonico Caixeiro, for one day only, so papa could send them back with a friend of his the same day. She went with Nhonhô and I became the lady of the house.

We divided up the work fairly. I told them: "The business of lighting the fire for cooking is up to you, if you want one. I have

* *Sopa:* soup. Refers here to a rock-formation of the region, for which the village is named. Small, hard stones are imbedded in a softer, more porous base.

lots of friends who'll give me breakfast with pleasure. And lunch and dinner, too,—I won't have to go without. When I don't want to go out for dinner, I'm going to eat bread and butter, bananas and cheese, and that's all." Renato answered back, "That's just so I'll have to do the cooking, because you know perfectly well that I'm not going to eat bananas for dinner." I said, "Then do it."

When I wake up in the morning Renato's splitting wood to make coffee. Luizinha, who doesn't complain of the stomach-ache any more, tidies up the house. I do my chores in half an hour and life is wonderful. I've studied and written as never before. When mama comes back I'm going to teach her to do as I've been doing, and she'll have a rest.

Now I've had an idea: it's to make mama go on these little trips every once in a while; instead of papa coming back, she can go to see him. I hate to see her work so hard!

Tuesday, March 12th

Everybody in our house has the same nickname all his life except me. I think mine change every month, at School as well as at home. When I was little at home I was "Sparrow's Egg" because of my freckles. When I started growing I was tall and thin and I became "Frutuosa Greased Pole," after a woman named that who's tall and yellow. Then I learned to fight Renato and not let him order me around the way he wanted to and my name changed to "Brassy Aninha," after a very quarrelsome woman here.

In School it was the same way. The skirt of my first uniform was short in front and long behind and I got named "The Droopy-Bottomed Hen." One day I went racing through the rain, so I wouldn't get wet, and the girls started calling me "Lightning." I fought with Seu Emídio in arithmetic class and they changed it to "Stormy" and papa thought that one was very appropriate.

My brothers and sister always have the same nicknames. Renato is "Cat," Nhonhô is "Turkey," and Luizinha is "Lazy." I think names like that are only used in our family. At Uncle Conrado's the children are even punished for using nicknames, but I think that's worse. In our house we don't have to fight to get even. We invent a new nickname on the spur of the moment and that's revenge enough.

Thursday, March 14th

Mama sent a woman who's the best thing that could have happened, from Sopa, to help us. Her name is Maria da Quitéria; she's worked in other houses in town and she knows almost everybody. She only wants to wait on us and to help us out of our difficulties; she seems like a gift from heaven. We're leading a wonderful life because she won't let us work.

Today João Felício came and said he was going to take dinner with us to keep us company because papa and mama are away. I was horrified. Mama left us just barely enough for the days she'll be gone, and not a penny of money. Without realizing what I was saying I told him, "Let me ask Maria if I can invite you." I went to the kitchen and said, "Maria, just imagine! João Felício wants to stay to dinner. I don't know what on earth to say to him." She said, "You can invite him and leave it up to me." But I kept saying, "Don't be silly, Maria; what can you make?" She said, "Go and invite the boy and leave it up to me, I'll manage. Go and sit down." I went back to the parlor and said, "I spoke to Maria and she said for you to stay to dinner. But I'm not responsible, because mama thought she was coming back right away and she didn't leave us anything good." Just then I saw Maria go through the hall and out into the street. I cheered up, thinking, "She's going to buy something on credit." At dinner time she came to the door and said, "Dinner is ready." We went in. My heart stopped beating.* Until then nobody'd ever cooked anything for me if I invited anyone to dinner, unless I provided everything and saw to it that it was ready. She brought in a soup of rice and cabbage. Then she put stewed chicken on the table, with macaroni, roast pork

* Literally: "I had a heart as small as a nut."

with fried potatoes, rice and black beans. For dessert, my aunts' guava paste, the best sweet in Diamantina, that they call "the English ladies' guava paste," with cheese. Besides this there was a bottle of Seu Sebastião Rabelo's wine. I was so bewildered I couldn't understand a thing. The four of us had dinner, I, Renato, Luizinha, and João Felício. I was so happy that it seemed like a great banquet to me.

At eight o'clock João Felício left to give me time to study my lessons. Instead of studying I came here to write what had happened. When he left I ran to the kitchen to kiss Maria. I said to her, "Thank you so much, Maria! Tell me how you gave us such a good dinner." She said, "If one is resourceful there's always a way out, and God made me very resourceful. I hustled over to Dona Madge's and told her about our predicament. She gave me three *mil reis* and the guava paste. I bought the wine, the pork, and the macaroni. The other things were in the house." "And the chicken?" I asked. "Where did you find that?" She said, "Oh, since there were so many neighbors' hens in the yard, annoying us, I caught one and cooked it." "Maria, that's a sin!" I said. "How could you do such a thing?" She replied, "Sin? I was born knowing that it's a sin to steal and not to get away with it."

Friday, March 15th

There was a great *festa* today in our beautiful Diamantina. They inaugurated the Post Office, with lots of fireworks and employees, in Seu Antoninho Marcelo's big house. Bonfim Street was full.

If they gave me Diamantina to run the last thing I'd start here would be a Post Office. Seu Cláudio, who's lame and has to be lifted by a black and put on his horse, delivered the mail so well, carrying the letters and newspapers in a sack on behind, that I can't understand why they have to have such an expensive Post Office now, with so many men. Papa says it's all politics, just to give people jobs. But wouldn't it be better if instead of a Post

Office they put in streetlamps for us, so that on dark nights we wouldn't have to walk slowly for fear of falling over a cow? And put in water-pipes? Wouldn't they be more useful, too? Nobody's going to die without a letter, but the water from Pau de Fruta, which runs uncovered, has killed lots of people who might be alive today. They say that typhoid fever comes from water. These things would help the city much more than a Post Office. But for myself I confess that I'd a thousand times rather live in any of the other places I know, like Boa Vista, Bom Sucesso, Curralinho, Biribiri, or Sopa. I'd rather be living in any of them more than in the city. I was born for the country!

Monday, March 18th

I hardly ever come home without mama's saying:

> *A woman and a hen*
> *Shouldn't go out walking;*
> *A hen gets eaten,*
> *A woman sets folks talking.*

And then she says, "Mother always recited that to us and that's the reason we were such modest girls. Boys came from far away to ask for us in marriage because we had the reputation for being homebodies."

I always answer, "You were homebodies because you lived in Lomba. And besides, the reputation was the pot of diamonds that grandpa found. Homebody—doesn't the Senhora see that nobody could have that reputation? How? If nobody saw you?"

But yesterday was one of the times I suffered the consequences of going so much to other people's houses.

We were all at Seu Antônio Eulálio's door and we had the idea of getting some meat-cakes from Aunt Plácida. The meat-cakes came, with manioc flour under them, and they were marvellous. We were eating them right in the doorway, on the street. Just

then Thiers and João César de Oliveira* came by and they exclaimed, "What? Are you eating meat-cakes from Aunt Plácida's?"
And João César said, "We're not going to eat them any more.
Imagine—a few days ago we got some other boys and went there
to have supper. She was taking away the plates and knives and
forks and bringing in others. I happened to look out into the hall
and I saw Aunt Plácida raise her skirt and wipe the knives and
forks on her petticoat and bring them back to the table. I'm not
the kind that gets sick easily, but I couldn't eat any more."
  When I heard this story I immediately felt sick to my stomach
and very sad, because Aunt Placida's meat-cakes are a godsend
to us evenings when we get hungry in the street or at other people's houses.

Thursday, March 21st

  The dentist, Seu Guilherme, is the most disgusting man in the
world. If one has the misfortune to have to have a tooth filled one
has to endure the face he makes; it's more nauseating than finding
a toad in one's bed. He can't say a thing without a diminutive.
"Will you do me the favor of opening your little mouth so I can
see the little tooth?" It's little mouth, little ache, little tooth,
without stopping. I went to him only once for him to look at a
"little tooth" and I didn't go back and I won't go back any more,
although I have a tooth with a hole in it, because I almost fainted
in the chair, I disliked him so much.
  But his wife and his daughters are nice. Yesterday Dona Rosa
went to Uncle Geraldo's house to tell about Angelina's engage-
ment. The people in the parlor had such a hard time trying to
think of something to talk about that it was embarrassing. Usually
in these moments of silence I come in with my own remarks when
I see they haven't anything to say. But yesterday I let everything
stop dead and just waited to see what would come out to break
the silence. Fortunately Bibiana had an idea and said, "What

* Father of Juscelino Kubitschek de Oliveira, at present President of Brazil.

good luck for Angelina!" Dona Rosa said, "Luck? Do you believe in luck in marriage? I used to think like that, too; but I see now that marriage is nothing but pursuit."

I thought Dona Rosa's reply very good.

Friday, March 29th

Seu Facadinha's* wife is crazy. If anyone who doesn't know about it goes by their house he gets a terrible fright, because she shouts from behind the lattice in an incomprehensible language. Once when I went by there at night she shouted from inside, "Cherréco, teméco, fréco!" and I ran up the street as far as Aunt Agostinha's. There they told me that ever since those foreigners came here to buy mines she's thought that she's a foreigner and that that's a foreign language.

Today I learned that her daughter had died and I went there. The poor little girl lay on the bed covered with a sheet and the mother with her foreign language lay on the floor. Seu Facadinha, already an old man, *coitado,* took the covers off the milk pans and showed them to everyone that came in, saying, "Don't think she died of want. Look here at the milk I bought. If she didn't drink it it was because she didn't want it." I asked what she had died of, since I'd seen her fat and rosy just a few days ago. He said, "Nobody knows what it was. The only thing she had was a cut on her hand that got bad and spread up her arm until she died. But she couldn't have died because of a little thing like that. God Himself wanted to take her away, poor little thing." Perhaps it was because of knowing about the mother's madness and the father's foolishness and old age, but I thought to myself that God did well to take her away to a better place.

Wednesday, April 3rd

There's no one in Diamantina who doesn't know Zé Lotério's Amélia. But they'd be happier if they didn't. She comes into the

* *Facadinha:* little cut or stab.

house, very agreeable and obliging, and then she goes out telling everything that she saw, from house to house, always saying, "If I were gossipy I'd tell this here and there, but I'm only going to tell you." She never leaves the *chácara* without offering to take a message, or buy something that grandma needs, or without taking in everything.

The other day when I was at Malita's house she asked me, "What was that fight between So-and-so and What-d'you-call-him in your grandmother's house?" I said, "I don't know anything about it. It's all a lie. Who tells you these things?" She said, "My little finger tells me."

At Uncle Geraldo's, Bibiana asked me, "You go to Marcelo's house a lot; don't you know about the fight Lauro had with Agostinho that started over a cow?" I asked her the same question and Bibiana replied, "I guessed."

You don't have to be very clever to discover who carries tales from our houses. Why grandma lets this woman in the house and is kind to her, is something I can't understand. I told her about Amélia's mischief-making and she said, "What could she pick up here to tell about us?"

Saturday, April 6th

I came home today dying of hunger and saw the parlor door open and the parlor full of people. I looked in and saw something on the table covered with a sheet. Mama said, "It's Zézinho, poor little thing!"

I had a horrible shock because it was only two weeks ago I saw Zézinho playing. That is, not playing, because he was a very quiet child. He watched the others play and just smiled.

This little boy was the son of Mama Tina, who was mama's slave and who nursed us all. She and mama always had children at the same time. Mama had no milk, but Mama Tina had, and nursed two. Mama stopped having children but Mama Tina kept on and had twins, and because of that she got weak and died of phthisic.

Dindinha took one of the twins to raise. She lost the little girl she had, at a year and a half, and now she likes to raise little Negroes; she's already brought up four.

Mama Tina's sister Júlia took this Zézinho to raise. She said that she brought him here after he died because when he was sick he kept asking to see me and she was remorseful because she hadn't brought him sooner.

I was very fond of this little boy and went to see him when I could and took him whatever I could get. He had a disease the Negroes at the *chácara* call the "dog hunger."* He was either eating or crying all the time.

Júlia came by here with him a few days ago. They'd told her to give him water from seven fountains to see if he'd get over the hunger, and she was going to begin with the Rosário fountain. But it didn't help at all, because he died!

It was a shock seeing him dead and I was awfully sorry. But he was so sad and his belly was so big it looked like a drum.

Mama and Júlia say that Mama Tina took him away because he suffered so much, *coitadinho,* she thought it was better to take him to heaven.

Tuesday, April 9th

The boys at School call the second and third year girls by nicknames. I think they're all funny and some of them are very apt. Maria Antônia's suits her very well. I was surprised that they remarked on the way her head is twisted to one side. Her nickname is "Torture." Elvira's is "Pie-Face." They still use the one for me that they gave me in the first year and that I know I deserve because of my outspoken manners, "Stormy." Papa thought it was very appropriate. The girls are envious of Sinhá Silica's, because it's "Pretty Girl."

* "Dog hunger": bulimia.

I know the reason for that. Sinhá isn't homely, but she isn't that pretty; there are other girls prettier than she is. But I think its Ângelo who chooses the names. He likes Sinhá very much.

I know all this through Leontino. He said it was a third year student who made it up. He finds out everyone's nickname immediately, and tells me.

I didn't mind keeping the name of "Stormy." It could be worse; there are some that are: "Greased Pole," "Ugly," and lots of others.

I keep thinking how lucky I've been they didn't change mine to "Greased Pole." I look much more like a greased pole than Iaiá Leite does; but they made up mine after my fight with Seu Emídio and it stuck.

Monday, April 15th

Mama says that one shouldn't be joyful in Holy Week because it's the week of Jesus' sufferings. I believe firmly in other religious things but I don't believe that anyone should feel sad about Jesus' sufferings after so many years, and since He's already in heaven, resurrected and happy.

I adore Holy Week! I never miss a thing, from the first day to the last. When I was smaller I once walked in the Passion procession, I and Glorinha, behind the bier of Our Dead Lord, carrying the nails and the sponge that was used to give Him vinegar to drink on the cross, on a silver tray; and I was horrified that the men in the procession could even pretend to be the Jews.

I think mama gets more satisfaction out of it than I do. She brings home the candles, bread, and palm branches that have been blessed. And when Our Dead Lord is shown we all have to go and worship. All the family take ten-penny pieces to change them for penny pieces from the salver at Our Lord's feet. I always believed in the palm, the candles, and the holy bread; but I never could believe it when they said that whoever took home a penny would always have money in the house. I pestered mama with questions she couldn't answer: "Mama, how is it that you take a penny change from the salver at Our Dead Lord's feet, every year, and yet we're always so poor?"

But I believe as much as she does in the holy bread, the candles, and the palm. We never have a doctor or medicine from the apothecary's shop in the house. When someone has a belly-ache if there isn't any mugwort tea in the house, a swallow of water and a piece of holy bread will cure it. And the holy palm and the candles? They can't prevent death, but they're infallible for everything else. If there's a thunderstorm, light a holy candle, burn a frond of holy palm, and you can be perfectly easy. If I'm going to take an examination I light a candle, burn a palm, and get at least one of the questions I want.

I never go to an exam without leaving mama on her knees in front of the *oratório*, with the holy candle lit.

This year, now that I'm bigger, I thought Holy Week was wonderful. I could appreciate Maria Beú's* singing. I liked seeing Maria Madalena, who was really Sinhá Mota, wiping Jesus' feet with her beautiful long hair. I could understand why the Senhor Bishop washed the student's feet in Holy Week.

And Hallelujah Saturday! What a marvelous day!

This year, besides the hanging of Judas, which I always like to see, we also had a greased pole. Seu Luiz de Rezende had a greased pole made and put some new paper money on top like a flag. I thought I'd die laughing when I saw, from Luiza Guerra's balcony, a very clean little woman in a red calico skirt and a white jacket come out of the crowd, carelessly pin up her skirt with a safety-pin to make pantaloons, push away the people in front of her, and begin to climb. Some smart men helped push her up. One got up on the other's shoulders and boosted her. Others helped her with a cane. She cleaned off the greased pole with her skirt all the way to the top, which was just what they wanted. Just as

* *Maria Beú: Maria B.U.*, that is, Maria *bene vixit*, to distinguish her from Maria Madalena, or Maria *male vixit*.

she could reach the money they let go and the silly woman slid straight to the ground.

After some other tries that entertained the crowd very much, a man finally climbed up and got the bills.

A very useful lesson!

Thursday, April 18th

Mama, who's never sick, seemed to have a fever day before yesterday, and aches and pains, and a bad cough. When Siá Ritinha sent her some *xuxús*, she learned that she was sick and immediately came to see her. Papa is in Boa Vista and I was going to stay home from School to take care of mama, but Siá Ritinha wouldn't let me, saying she'd take care of her herself. She made mama sweat. Then she had a chicken killed and took it to her house to cook and came back with some for mama. She did her own housework and kept coming here all the time to see if mama needed anything while we were at School. She only stopped coming after we got home.

I never thought I'd grow fond of Siá Ritinha; I used to marvel at the kind way my father and mother treated her when she came here. Nobody in the neighborhood likes her because she's only nice to my parents and hates everyone else; she spends all her time gossiping and stealing everyone's hens. And they hated her monkey, too, that used to be the pest of this part of town.

Papa always says that no one seems either entirely good or bad to everyone. Some like him, some don't. I'm beginning to realize it's true. Now I like the way she takes care of mama so much that I don't see her faults the way I used to. And when I see her coming to our house I'm pleased instead of being annoyed the way I was before.

Anything can happen in this life. I'm really convinced of it.

Friday, April 19th

It's the first time grandma's been to our house in a long time, although we almost live at her house. She only goes to Uncle Geraldo's, and just to her daughters' when they're sick or have babies. But mama's been in bed these days and so she came to see her.

I'm sorry for my brothers and sister about grandma. Since mama's been sick they've been so good that even I had to admire them. They usually leave all the housework to mama and me, but they've been helping with everything. But when grandma came in I was beside mama's bed with a bowl of broth. She came in and started saying, "Poor thing! She has to do everything! Studying isn't enough; now she has to do the cooking and everything else all by herself. The very idea!" I said, "No, grandma. They're all helping. You can't imagine how good they've been since mama's been sick. We've done all the housework without leaving a thing for mama to do, and when we go to School Siá Ritinha comes in to help." Grandma only said, "I should hope so!" and didn't say anything nice to Luizinha or my brothers; but they didn't mind because they're used to it.

Grandma thought that mama isn't doing well and spoke of taking us all to the *chácara* tomorrow. Mama said she could only go when papa came back from Boa Vista. She doesn't want him to come home and find the door locked and be frightened.

I don't like the idea of going to the *chácara*. I'd rather stay here and go to the *chácara* whenever I want to. Here, even if we have to do all the work there's still some time left over to study and write my exercises. But at the *chácara*, with everyone gathering there every evening, I don't know how it would be.

I'm sure that when papa comes he won't agree to our going to the *chácara*. And besides, I hope that by tomorrow mama's going to be better. Papa learned something about medicine from grandpa and he's always been right about any sicknesses we've had. Who knows but what he'll cure mama quickly. God willing.

Tuesday, April 23rd

I and Luizinha were saying that mama had to get sick for us to realize how mean we'd been to Siá Ritinha. We all hated her so that when we saw her coming we rushed to the kitchen to stand the broom behind the door upside down and to put salt on the fire, too, so she wouldn't stay.

She made us mad because she always came to carry tales and to tell mama not to let us run and play with our Negro schoolmates. Since we sit with the blacks in School, why couldn't we play with them in the street?

It was nice of mama to be kind to her. Now she's been so kind to mama that I look at her and wonder how I ever could have thought she was so awful. Today I saw her feeding mama a cup of broth so patiently that I realized how good she is and that she isn't even homely.

Papa's going to love her when he comes home from the mine. Siá Ritinha cooks at her house and gives meals to the soldiers from the barracks, and still she finds time to come here and take care of mama so we can go to School; isn't that doing a lot? Grandma sent a Negro woman from the *chácara* here to help, and Siá Ritinha sent her back, telling mama that she was just adding to the confusion.

I'm not going to believe the tale the neighbors tell about her being the chicken-thief of Cavalhada any more, and I'm not going to let them talk that way any more, either. A woman as kind and useful as she is couldn't be a thief. I'm sure someone who steals from other people couldn't be kind to them.

Mama says that one sin she never has to confess is speaking evil of others. I always have to confess it because if I don't speak evil myself sometimes I like to hear it spoken. From now on I'm going to correct this fault.

Papa came from Boa Vista and since he couldn't stay with mama because he's very busy at the mine, he brought her here. He listened to mama's chest and said it was an influenza that attacks the chest and that she'll be up and around in a week.

I don't like being here because I feel guilty doing nothing day and night. Besides the cousins, there are the little neighbors who won't leave me in peace. Mama's never let us waste a minute since we were little. Even when we have callers we always have some crocheting to pick up. I only do nothing when I go out; at home I either study or work. Here not even the Negro women work. They all have lace-pillows and make lace as an excuse and only know how to answer the door, or go to the garden after vegetables and fruit. And I hate to see a great big Negro like Nestor, who's wearing a soldier's uniform now, meddling in Dindinha's cupboard and taking whatever he wants. Papa always says that this soft spot Dindinha has for Nestor isn't kindness, it's just being weak and foolish.

Grandma never forgets to look after mama for a minute. But I am worried about her cough; it gets worse at night and she can't sleep well. I suspect that everybody's thinking that mama has Mama Tina's phthisic, because I saw her dishes put on the table in her room, separately, and Dindinha won't let us drink water from her glass, saying that her sickness is very catching. But since I only believe what papa says I don't care what they think. If papa'd thought that mama was seriously sick, nothing could keep him from leaving the mine and being here right beside her. But he went back to Boa Vista and told mama not to worry, he knows she'll be better by Saturday.

God willing. I'm dying to go home.

João de Assis is a funny boy. He's Uncle Conrado's clerk and he's well thought of by everyone because he's a very good person. We make fun of him because he suffers from a strange complaint: he's sorry for everyone, no matter who. If a pregnant woman passes by the door of the shop with a pitcher of water on her head, he almost dies of grief and turns his face away so as not to see her. Or if another goes by, with a bundle of firewood on her head, he's in agony and keeps saying, "*Coitada! Coitada!*" I told him he shouldn't feel so sorry because they're used to it and even like it.

He has a very strange nature and he can't make up his mind about anything. He likes a widow and an unmarried girl. One day he goes to one's house and the next day to the other's, and when he thinks about asking one of them to marry him he grows doubtful as to which one he likes better and afraid that he'll have regrets, whichever one he decides on. We think the state of indecision he lives in is awfully funny. I advised him to write down the two names and put them in a hat and draw one. He said he'd already done it and even so he couldn't make up his mind.

Today we laughed at him until we couldn't laugh any longer. He was invited to the dance last night at the Workmen's Society and the widow went, too. He got a dictionary, looked up the words, made up a sentence and went to Sérgio to see if it was nice enough for him to say to the widow. The sentence was: "I feel great compunction at not having been able to invite you to a waltz up until now." Sérgio pointed out to him that if the widow was a woman he had the gender wrong. He corrected the sentence, memorized it, and put the piece of paper in his pocket.

Today Sérgio asked him if he'd said the sentence without any trouble and he answered, "Oh dear! When I went over to speak to her, before I could begin she got up, took my arm, and we started dancing. I was completely dumb because she didn't give me a chance to say the only words I had in my head."

Saturday, May 4th

Papa always says he likes my nature better than Luizinha's; I'm frank, I say what I'm thinking and doing, and Luizinha is secretive and that's more dangerous.

Luizinha is so quiet that I never thought papa was really right to prefer my nature, but today she did something so bad that I couldn't help thinking he's right. I'd never have done what she did.

Anita took some red carnations to School and put them on the teacher's desk. Then it spread around that Anita had missed one carnation and had a razor and was saying that she was going to cut the hand of the thief who'd robbed her. We all ran and saw Anita with the razor in her hand. Raging mad, she said she'd found out who it was and she'd cut her arm or her hand if she didn't hand over the carnation. Without dreaming who it was, I said, "You haven't the courage to cut someone with a razor because of a filthy old carnation." She said, "If it's filthy, why did your sister steal it?"

I had a dreadful shock and couldn't answer. I ran to the first year classroom to find out if it was true that my foolish sister had really taken the carnation. There she was with the other girls, as calm as you please, with the carnation right in the front of her dress to show it off. I snatched it away and asked her why she'd done such a thing. She answered perfectly naturally, "I found some carnations on the desk; I thought they were pretty and took this one. What's wrong with that?"

I took the carnation back to Anita, ran to the Secretary and told the story of the razor. The Principal came down and took away that idiot's razor. But nothing more happened because she's a teacher's daughter.

Anita almost hit me, out of sheer hatred.

Sunday, May 12th

Today mama went out for the first time since getting up, and we went to visit some old neighbors who have moved to Macau Street, Siá Germana and Seu Ferreira. I was pleased to see how well they're doing, and even more pleased to see their little blind boy whom I helped take care of, who's already growing big and cheerful. If I were his mother I don't see how I could be happy the way Siá Germana is, after she and Seu Ferreira were responsible for his going blind.

I'll never forget the agony I went through when I realized that the poor little boy was blind.

Seu Ferreira repairs watches and he lived next door to us in the Cavalhada. We were very friendly; mama was friends with Siá Germana and I and Luizinha with Clementina and Brígida. We, the girls, were never separated; we were always together either in our house or theirs.

When Pedrinho was born, I and Luizinha were overjoyed, because at that time our greatest pleasure was to have a baby to nurse, and Siá Germana promised to let us take care of him. We took care of him from the minute he was born. While Siá Germana was in bed, we used to go help Clementina and Brígida wash his diapers, tidy up the house and everything, before School. Even after she got up he still belonged to us, and I think that no mother ever could have been fonder of her child than I was of that poor little boy.

When Siá Germana was up and about, papa went to call, and seeing that the little boy's eyes were running, he said, "Ferreira, that's something serious and if you don't take him to the doctor that baby's going to be blind." Seu Ferreira said, "Oh no! I know what it is, the others had it, too. It's just a little discharge that rose-water will cure." Papa kept insisting, "It's nothing so simple, Ferreira. Take the child to the doctor, right now, if you don't want to see your son blind."

Seu Ferreira didn't like my father's interfering and he changed the subject. I'd already looked after babies and I thought papa was right. But if the others had been cured with that rose-water . . . I spent hours washing the poor baby's eyes with rose-water. But what papa had said was never out of my mind and I thought about the baby's eyes constantly. I could see they were getting worse instead of better and I called his mother's attention to them. "Siá Germana, I think the baby's eyes are much worse." She showed Seu Ferreira and he said, "Keep bathing them with rose-water."

One day I could only go to their house late. When I looked at the baby I saw his eyes were completely covered with a white film. I picked him up and took him to our house to show papa. He looked at him and exclaimed, "Poor child! It's too late now!"

I couldn't bear to hear papa say that; I handed the baby to mama and went and fell on my bed, crying. I cried inconsolably and I felt as though it were my fault. I thought to myself, "Why didn't I kidnap the baby and go and ask Dr. Teles to treat him? How could I be happy when I saw that that poor baby was blind?" Mama and papa came in to comfort me. Mama said, "Don't grieve like that, child. God knows what He's doing. Who knows —perhaps God wants to make a saint of that little boy, for His Glory? God never errs, child. He always knows what He's doing."

These words helped a little, even if I couldn't understand why God would want a blind saint. He could make him a saint, but at least one that could see a little. We all went to Seu Ferreira's and papa said to him, "Look what you've done, Ferreira. Now the child's blind and nobody can make him see. Poor boy!" And he walked out.

Seu Ferreira took up his coat which was on a chair, put it on, and said to Siá Germana, "Wrap the baby up in a shawl and give him to me." He took Pedrinho to Dr. Teles. Dr. Teles said, "Why didn't you bring this baby here at the beginning? Now it's too late, there's nothing to be done."

He came back and repeated what the doctor had said. Siá Germana took the baby, gave him a kiss, and put him in his cradle. Seu Ferreira took off his coat, hung it on the back of the chair, sat down, picked up his tools and went back to work.

I'd hoped that Siá Germana would burst out crying the way I had, so that I could say the same things to her that mama'd said to me. But she didn't cry; she was resigned.

I ran out of the house and said to papa, "It's your fault, papa. If you were so sure, why didn't you get Dr. Teles or take the baby there?" Mama said, "A doctor's prescription costs twenty *mil reis*, child. Do you think your father makes steady money, the way Seu Ferreira does repairing watches?"

Wednesday, May 15th

After School I went to Jogo da Bola Street to see Naninha and Glorinha.

Aunt Agostinha said they'd gone to have lunch with their relatives Leocádia and Juvência, and hadn't come back. I said goodbye, went down the Palace hill and went to Leocádia's house and Naninha was there making a dress with them.

I admire Leocádia's will-power. She suffers from St. Vitus's dance and spends her life with her head shaking from side to side all day long, and even like that she sews from morning till night, to earn money. Juvência, the older sister, helps with the housework and repeats everything that Leocádia says. She's like an echo.

I sat down and we began to talk. I looked at the yard and said, "How pretty the garden is." Leocádia said, "It was prettier. We've sold a lot." Juvência repeated. "It was prettier. We've sold a lot."

After a little I asked, "Leocádia, are those papayas sweet?" She answered, "Very sweet. Would you like to try one?" Juvência repeated, "Very sweet. Would you like to try one?"

We kept on talking and in the middle of the conversation I asked, "Have you been doing much sewing, Leocádia?" She answered, "A great deal. I even had to refuse some customers." Juvência repeated, "A great deal. We even had to refuse some customers."

It was like that the whole time. Then Leocádia said, "Vência, go and get coffee for Helena." Juvência got up: "I'm going to get coffee for Helena." She was already on her way to the kitchen when she said it.

She returned with the coffee and put it on the table. Leocádia said, "Vência, serve Helena." Juvência said to Naninha, "Pass the sugar here to serve Helena." Leocádia turned to her and said, "Vência, that's wrong. I've already told you that *sugar* is a *man*."*

Naninha looked at me, but we didn't laugh. They're so nice, poor things. And then, where could they ever learn anything, raised the way they were in Itaipava?

Thursday, May 23rd

When I compare mama's family with papa's I see what a difference there is between them. In papa's family they're all alike. The brothers differ only in looks. As far as manners go, if you've seen one, you've seen them all. And the sisters, too, are the same way, almost. In mama's family there are such differences between one and the other it makes you wonder. In papa's, there aren't many relatives. There are only my uncles and aunts, Uncle Mortimer's children, and us. In mama's family there are so many relatives and she has so many cousins that we don't know them all. One of these distant relatives is intelligent and well-educated, and he used to be a book-keeper. But lately he's taken to drink, stopped working, and does nothing at all. He spends the whole day sitting on the stoop of his house with his chin on his hand, in silence. Since the foreigners came here to buy mines he's had the notion that he's French. When anyone tells him, "Abílio, stop being so lazy. Get to work," he replies, "I can't. I'm a French citizen."

* Vência makes sugar feminine instead of masculine.

Papa says that drink's always been the ruin of many intelligent boys in Diamantina.

Saturday, May 25th

I was so sorry for Siá Ritinha today. After all, what do I care if she steals the neighbors' hens as long as she doesn't steal ours? And then she likes my mother and father and never misses a chance to come here. It's Inhá who never comes.

Siá Ritinha came to pour out her troubles to mama. Since the monkey died, Inhá hasn't had anything to distract her. Ciríaco, a little mulatto they took to bring up, has turned out so badly he even steals money when the soldiers pay their bills. They've punished him, spanked him, made him go without dinner, but nothing helps. That little boy is so lost to shame that she and Inhá don't know what to do with him any more.

"If he were old enough," said Siá Ritinha, "I'd know, all right; I'd put him in the army; but he isn't old enough. Dona Carolina, what should we do? What would the Senhora advise me to do?"

Mama said, "I don't know, Siá Ritinha; it's hard to say. I felt the same way about Emídio and I sent him to mother's house."

Then Siá Ritinha told us how the soldiers act with her and I felt so sorry. "Hardly a week goes by that they don't send back the black beans and say they're full of weevils. But you know that the black beans one gets at the store these days are more weevils than black beans. You should see the work we go to, getting out even half of the weevils, so they won't complain; but it's no use. See how stuck-up soldiers are these days, expecting black beans without weevils! Where are they going to find them here? If I waited until I found black beans without weevils I'd never eat; and now soldiers are wanting the impossible!"

Mama agreed, "It's true, Siá Ritinha. The black beans have been coming very wormy."

Siá Ritinha went on: "This saying that 'From day to day God

smooths the way' must be for other people. For us He's been making it rougher ever since Neco died and left Inhá a widow. I'm tired of struggling! I come here, Dona Carolina, because you're always so kind and patient. I always say to Inhá that the only time I ever get my mind off my troubles is here with you."

She left and I felt sorry for her and angry with Ciríaco and the soldiers who don't want to eat black beans with weevils in them. Who would ever have said that I'd finish by liking Siá Ritinha?

Tuesday, May 28th

A very funny drunken relative came here today. He is Américo, Abílio's brother, a distant relative, who lives by panning gold all by himself in the streams near town. When he finds a little more gold than usual or a diamond, he comes to town and spends his time drinking until the money's gone. When he drinks a lot he always remembers our house and we get very upset because he comes in looking like a beggar, goes to sleep in the parlor sometimes, and stays the whole day until the fit has worn off. Today he came to see us and we were uncomfortable because we knew he was drunk. He came in without knocking and went into the dining room. Papa was at home, something he hadn't expected, and João Felício was with us. Papa began to give him good advice, and João Felício said, "Américo, you're a hard-working boy and you live just like a beggar. Use some will-power, stop drinking, put on some decent clothes and ask Seu Antônio Eulálio* to look after you, lend you some money, and let you work at his mine." He replied, "If I had enough will-power not to drink, and some good clothes, I wouldn't need Seu Antônio Eulálio's help! I'd look after you and him and everyone else."

Saturday, June 1st

Grandma moved to Direita Street, to the house she bought from Seu Dominguinhos. I don't know why grandma did it. I
_____
* A rich diamond-dealer and money-lender.

heard mama and my aunts saying that when old people decide to move it means they're going to die. I don't want to believe it. Grandma's eighty-four; but she's so strong!

She rented the *chácara* to Dr. Viana and his wife, Iaiá, who arranged everything very nicely and are very happy there. Because I can't forget the *chácara*, I go there every time Aunt Madge goes. She's very friendly with Iaiá Viana.

I know that grandma went to Direita Street just to be near Uncle Geraldo. I don't understand why she likes that uncle so much. Her children all say he's her favorite. I think it's because grandma has eight daughters and only two sons living. And then, Uncle Geraldo's never given her any trouble.

Every year for grandma's birthday he orders silk dress-lengths from Rio de Janeiro for his daughters, has new clothes made for all the children, and on that day the whole family goes from Direita Street down to grandma's, with everyone watching them. It looks just like the reign of the king and queen at the Rosário Church. Those girls think they can't go out in the street without being dressed in silk.

It's the only way those cousins are different from us. I don't think that we're much happier poor than they are rich any more. Only it's really sad the way they think themselves superior to us! Their brother Chiquinho told Rafaela, in front of me, that she shouldn't think we were equals; that their father is a potentate, and very rich, and that Rafaela is the most important girl in Diamantina.

Tuesday, June 4th

What a pity that Lucas is so funny but so bad. One can't enjoy his jokes because they're always mean.

Yesterday I came home from School up to my nose in lessons to do and mama said, "I was just waiting for you so we could go to have dinner at Zinha's. Look, here's a note from Lucas." The note said, "Inhá, all of you come to eat a *paca** that I got today from Retiro." Immediately I said, "Wonderful! For me, *paca* is the best game there is."

We went to Lucas's dinner. He received us with a face that already I know only too well, and that means he's going to do something bad. But I wasn't suspicious. We had soup, beans, rice, meat and vegetable stew, then the *paca* was supposed to come. Like a fool I even said, "This is what should have come first." The cook came in and put the supposed *paca* on the table. Everybody said, "What's that? It looks like a roasted baby!" Lucas didn't say anything because he'd burst out laughing. We looked again and saw that it was a monkey. No one could finish dinner, because it looked like a little roasted creole baby and made us all sick.

Mama said, "Zinha, how could you let him play this mean trick and do something so disgusting, roasting a monkey in your kitchen?" Aunt Agostinha replied, "Would that the only bad thing he'd ever done was to roast a monkey, Inhá."

Saturday, June 8th

I shouldn't write down what happened today in my notebook. But all the teachers saw it and it's a good idea to write down exactly what happened from the beginning.

Lalá Rosa's family moved to a house near ours. They began to exchange greetings with us and talk to us when we came to the door. Lalá sat on their stoop when we were on ours. Just as if she could see the future, mama began to order us to come in, saying, "You don't want to know those people." They understood, and from then on began provoking us. One day Lalá went by and saw me put a flat iron at the top of the stairs, to heat.† She took a huge rock and threw it at the iron and it fell down the steps and landed with the cover broken. I pretended I didn't see.

---

* *Paca:* South American rodent; a cavy.
† After the charcoal is lit, the iron is set in the open air until it burns without smoking.

Renato has a little cart pulled by a ram that his godmother gave him. One day he saw Lalá's brother Euzebio giving cornmeal with hemlock in it to the ram and he just had time to save the poor animal. But once when he left the cart in front of the door for a minute, Euzebio smashed it all to pieces.

And that wasn't all. One day Nhonhô, who's seven years old, was sitting quietly in the doorway. Lalá took his hand, pulled him behind the house, and hit him with a bunch of nettles. When we went by their house she ran to the window with a whip in her hand and she and Euzebio yelled, "You little white imps,* this is what you need!" And they threatened us with the whip.

But in spite of all this, mama wouldn't let us answer a peep. She kept saying, "They're the ones who want to fight. They're low people; there are two men at their house and here there aren't any. It's good your father isn't here to see these things. Let's avoid them as much as possible. When they see we don't want to fight they'll tire of it and leave us in peace."

Everything in life must have an end, so this had to, too. I was crazy to meet that sallow girl when mama wasn't around, and to-day was the day.

I went through the first year classroom and Lalá said, so that I could hear her, "I shan't rest until I've smashed that freckled cat-face." I went on my way to the second year room and told the girls. They got angry and said, "Let's get her!" When we got to the first year classroom I said to her, "Here I am. Hit me!" Then she said, "You have to come with all this troop? Coward!" and she flew at my face. The others fell on her with blows but she wouldn't let go of me, and I didn't see anything more. If the Principal hadn't arrived just then she would have scratched my face all up with her fingernails. Who had the idea of calling Seu Leivas?

* *"Branquinhas de uma figa."* *Figa*: English, *fig*; the immemorial gesture of contempt with the thumb between the first two fingers. Small amulets or charms, of jet or other materials, called *figas*, in the form of a hand making this gesture, are commonly worn in Brazil.

We went to the Office and all talked at the same time. But Seu Leivas didn't want to hear the rights and wrongs of the case; after a little good advice he sent us away. I admit I expected more of a reprimand.

I had a red face, but the others said that she really got a beating.

Thursday, June 13th

A family from out of town has been living for a while in Jogo da Bola Street, Aunt Agostinha's street. No one knows them well yet. We learned that the old man is a farmer in Serro and is called Botelho, and the girls, there are four of them, go by the name of "the Botelhos." They pass the time in the window or sitting on chairs on the sidewalk in the afternoons. They don't seem to do anything. When we go by we speak to them and they always answer pleasantly. We haven't seen the father yet. We found out that one of them is a widow and rich and the other three are unmarried and poor and live at the rich one's expense. We also discovered that the rich one is the oldest and fattest one. As time went on we used to go by their door more slowly and say a few words to them and they invited us in, but we never accepted.

Going by there recently one afternoon we saw on their house the hangings for someone who's died, the doors covered with black cloth trimmed with gold galloon. My aunt thought we should go in, so we did. It was the rich, oldest one lying in the coffin, looking just like someone sleeping without snoring. She really seemed to be sleeping peacefully. Her sisters told us that her death had begun with a heavy sleep. Then, when she didn't wake up, they saw she was dead. The sisters had such cheerful expressions that it didn't seem as if there were a death in the house. We left commenting on the sisters' cheerfulness and my aunt said, "It's because the other one was rich. It's money that destroys family feeling."

The funeral didn't take place that day. When we went by the

door the next day the black hangings were gone. We were intrigued, and couldn't understand what they'd done with the remains. I said to myself, "This mystery has to be cleared up. I have to go by that door until I find out, even if I wear out a boot." We had our eyes glued on the house and we saw the cook go out to go to the store. I ran, said good-day to her, and asked her why the funeral hadn't taken place.

"Then the Senhora doesn't know yet?"

"No!" I answered. "What happened?"

"Siá Donana came back to life."

"What? Then she wasn't dead?"

"Dead she was, that is, she wasn't, but she looked as if she was. I think somebody made something,* but we shouldn't speak of that. The Senhora's seen a dead person listening to what the living are saying? Doesn't it look like something to you? Siá Donana said that she lay in her coffin in a rage, hearing her sisters fighting over her things. They fought over the cows, the silver, everything. But it was a strange thing. The men picked up the coffin; it was very heavy and they let it fall on the floor to get a better hold on it. The coffin hit the floor hard and the defunct woke up. The Senhora can't imagine what it was like! The shock of her coming to life was worse than the shock of her death. She woke up and started fighting with her sisters and ordering them out of the house because she said that instead of crying for her death they'd just fought over her things. She's already sent for their father to come and take them back to the *fazenda* and she's going to live here alone. The girls have barred themselves in the bedroom and they don't even come out to eat. We expect their father any minute, to take them away. And that's what happened when Siá Donana died."

* Witchcraft.

Since grandma moved to Direita Street she's insisted that I eat lunch there every day, to be near School. I don't enjoy it, first because I don't get along well with Aunt Carlota, who's there now; second, because Glorinha eats lunch there, too, and I don't like to be with grandma when she's there. She always leaves saying, "Did you notice this or that that grandma did?" Sometimes it's the better piece of chicken grandma put on my plate, sometimes the bigger piece of cheese or the better fruit she gave me, and Glorinha's always asking the same question: "What do you do to make grandma treat you so differently? It shows in everything. She thinks you're the only one who needs to eat, that you're more intelligent, that you're smarter."

I say, "I know about the food; it's because my thinness worries her and she thinks it's because I don't eat enough. She doesn't say I'm more intelligent than you are; but smarter,—how could she help but say that? I do everything grandma likes me to do. I wash and chop up her lettuce so Generosa won't let it go to the table full of sand and chopped-up slugs, the way I've seen it. I peel and slice the onions and cucumbers very thin for the salad. I do it for my own sake, too. I'm very easily nauseated and I don't like to have Generosa doing those things; but grandma thinks that it's just because of her. You all think it's just to flatter grandma, but it isn't."

Glorinha said, "Grandma thinks you and João Antônio are the only grandchildren she has." I said, "You all complain about grandma's educating João Antônio and spending her money to send him to college in Rio de Janeiro. What would you want her to do, after she raised him from the time he was a little boy? Haven't you heard what she went through because of João Antônio? Uncle Joãozinho took him to Lomba with his wet-nurse and left him there for grandma and Dindinha to wean, and went away taking the wet-nurse with him. João Antônio cried so much that grandma had to set all the slaves to making a novena, for him to stop crying. And Dindinha had to spend the nights walking up and down with him in her arms, with grandma walking behind, holding the banner of the Holy Ghost over them. And grandma says that even that couldn't stop the poor little thing's crying. And you all think that grandma should let him grow up ignorant, and that she shouldn't be so fond of him. I wouldn't want to be the grandmother of a family like ours, I swear!"

Friday, June 21st

Glorinha's still having lunch in Direita Street. I don't mind, but I don't like to see the difference grandma makes between us, particularly since Glorinha complained. She never stops saying, "I don't know why it is that grandma's so much more partial to you than to me and the other granddaughters. What do you do, or what have you got, better than us?"

I don't know, either. I notice it myself. I won't say anything about the cousins. But Luizinha's her goddaughter too, and she's so good, much better than I, and grandma doesn't bother about her. It really is the way they say, there's no accounting for taste.

It's the same way with my aunts on my father's side. Mama always says that for them I'm the only niece. Only Aunt Efigênia, who was her confirmation godmother, is nice to Luizinha. The others, only to me. Luizinha doesn't mind, she even likes it. I think it's because I'm older and also perhaps because they like my outspokenness more. When we go to their house together they even think it's funny the way Luizinha never opens her mouth because I do all the talking, all the time. Glorinha was saying to me, "It's different with aunts. They can like whomever they want to because they're aunts and your ways are more to their liking. But I don't think it's fair of grandma. I think that a grandmother ought to be a second mother and like all her grandchildren equally and grandma makes a big difference between you and the rest of us."

Because I don't have the courage to tell grandma about these constant complaints I'm going to look for an excuse not to eat lunch there when Glorinha's there.

Tuesday, July 2nd

One of the girls from School, the same age as I am, hasn't any mother and lives with an aunt. Her father lived at a *chácara* in Rio Grande which has lots of fruit trees and Finoca used to invite me there to suck *jaboticabas*.* Once we met a very pretty girl we knew there, named Madalena, and Finoca told me, "That's daddy's sweetheart. He's foolish enough to want to marry a young girl, at his age." I asked, "Does she want to marry him too, Finoca?" She said, "Don't you see the languishing airs she puts on with him?"

When I heard of their wedding I went to call on Madalena. She was living at the *chácara* very happily, taking care of the garden and selling everything she raised. When she was about to have a baby they moved to a house in town, near grandma's, and we go to see her and she goes to grandma's a lot, too.

She had a son and they say it was born dead; but then the report went around that there had been time to baptize it and it was to be buried in the Church. The neighbors sent flowers and appeared for the funeral. Of course I never miss anything, so I went with my cousins. When they took the little coffin to Madalena's bedside for her to kiss the baby goodbye, she opened her mouth and cried:† "Oh! My son! My pretty little boy! Oh what a tragedy, for God to take away my son! Ah! My God, what will become of me!" The older people said to her, "Don't scream like that, Madalena, you're not strong enough. Your baby was baptized and went straight to Heaven." But still screaming, she went on,

* See page 64. Going to "suck" *jaboticabas* when they're in season is a ritual. Those who have no *jaboticaba* trees of their own sometimes get up parties and pay so much a head to go to a *fazenda* or *chácara* and eat as many as they want.
† Literally: "opened her mouth to the world."

"I know! But I'm crying this way because I don't think it's nice for a mother not to cry for the death of her son!" And she kept right on screaming.

Death is sad, but even so we couldn't help being amused by Madalena's play-acting.

Wednesday, July 10th

Papa is much beloved in my family. Everybody likes him and says he's a very good man and a very good husband. I like hearing it but I'm always surprised at their just saying that papa's a good husband and never saying that mama's a good wife. Nevertheless, from the bottom of my heart I believe that only Our Lady could be better than mama.

I don't think anyone could be a better wife to papa or a better mother to us than she is. With papa leading a miner's life, most of the money he gets goes back into mining; there's not much left over for the house. We complain about things sometimes, but never a peep from mama. She never says a word that might upset my father; she just keeps telling him: "Don't be discouraged; to live is to suffer. God will help us." But I, being less patient, build castles in the air before I go to sleep, about being invisible and taking money from the rich and bringing it home. I've discovered it's a good way to get to sleep.

When I see mama getting up at five in the morning, going out in the yard in all this cold, struggling with wet, green wood to start the kitchen fire to have our coffee and porridge ready by six, I feel so sorry I could die. She begins then and goes without stopping until evening, when we sit on the sofa in the parlor. I sit holding mama's arm on one side and Luizinha's on the other, to keep warm. Renato and Nhonhô sit on the floor beside the stove, and mama tells stories of bygone days.

More than once she's told us the story of how I was born. She said she was already used to having babies because I was the third, and she didn't have the midwife and didn't want to call my father away from the mine. At that time they lived in Santo Antônio, in a little thatch-roofed house near the mine where papa was working. When she realized that I was about to be born, she went to her bedroom, prayed, and I was born. Then she called Mama Tina, the slave who raised us, and sent her to the mine to get papa, who was just stopping work for the day. Papa came running, cut my navel-string, gave me a bath and put me in bed. When my navel-string fell off, he buried it in the gravel at the mine, according to mama's orders, to bring me luck. Mama always tells me: "Don't you see you're the only one in the family who's lucky?"

But this pleasant time never lasts very long. At half-past eight mama goes back to the kitchen to struggle with green fire-wood and get our porridge.

And yet nobody ever says mama's a good wife.

Sunday, July 14th

Today I went to Mass with Catarina. It was early so we sat down and were praying. Two women whom we didn't know came in and sat down behind us.

The priest hadn't come yet so the two of them began to talk about sickness and the conversation happened to fall on a certain herb for making tea that only grows at Catarina's father's place. I think one of them's the wife of the new telegraphist, or an official who came here just a little while ago, because she didn't know where Seu Neves' *chácara* is and the other one was telling her.

When Catarina and I heard them mention her father's *chácara* we kept our ears open listening to the conversation. The other one said, "If you don't find it there you might as well give up because you won't find it anywhere. When you want to go, come by my house and we'll go together. But I warn you, Seu Neves is stingy. Nobody takes a dry leaf away from that *chácara* without paying for it." I looked at Catarina and laughed. She turned around and said, "The men, their provisions, everything that goes into that garden has to be paid for. Nothing comes free; money makes the mare go."

The two of them were so embarrassed that they changed seats.

Monday, July 15th

In Diamantina a long sickness is more like a *festa* than anything else.* We, that is all the cousins, like to make sick-calls as much as making novenas. Seu Vieira's sickness has been a great distraction. One of my friends has already got engaged making sick-calls there. He's been sick for a month now, but dying for only a week.

If I miss going there for one evening I can count on my cousins' trying to make me envious the next day: "Last night such and such happened." When I do go, it's extremely interesting. He always has a sinking-spell or two, and there's rushing to and fro after an axe to put on Vieira's sister's leg when she gets a cramp in it, or a quilt to throw over another sister who's fainted and whose clothes are disarranged; and everybody's all ready to help.

The worst is that there aren't any refreshments or supper the way there are at richer people's houses. I shock the others when I go there because I'm always hiding my face on the table, and smothering my laughter. How can it be helped, with such goings on?

Yesterday it was Naninha's turn. She picked up a simply hopeless admirer, and I love to watch him courting her, she gets so mad at me, as if it were my fault! Joaquim Melo kept looking at her with the greatest tenderness, then he went out. Naninha cheered up because she thought he wouldn't come back any more. Inside half an hour he was back with a package in his hand.

* Burton: "Such an apparatus would injure the most robust; surely it would be humane to publish a Portuguese version of *Notes on Nursing* [Florence Nightingale]. The vile henbroth, which it is indispensable to swallow every two hours, is an infliction to be compared only with the 'beef-tea' in Great Britain."

I thought it was bananas and said to Naninha, "He's come back with a hundred *reis*' worth of bananas for you." She put her head down on the table with her face covered up and said to me, "Tell him I'm asleep." He went over to her; it was a penny loaf of bread. He kept standing holding out the bread to Naninha, hoping that she'd raise her head and take it. I was choking with laughter but with the help of God I managed to say to her, "Naninha, it's Joaquim Melo and he's brought you a loaf of bread." When he saw that she wasn't going to raise her head he handed me the bread to give her and left. We had to leave the dining room running, to laugh out in the yard.

But there was something else even better. A drunken friend of the family named Eloy went into the bedroom and they told him that Vieira was sleeping. He said, "Sleeping? The sleep from which there is no waking! Give me a candle."* They brought him a candle and he dripped wax in Seu Vieira's eyes and he gave a start. Eloy exclaimed, "What! Then you aren't dead?"

Tuesday, July 23rd

Whenever I have any free time at school I run to Aunt Aurélia's for coffee. She makes lots of things to sell and there are always lots of good things to go with coffee there. Recently I've felt awfully sorry for Aunt Aurélia because of the trouble she's been having with a servant who's making her life unbearable; she's rude, dirty, stubborn, stupid, and bad, and my aunt's been miserable all because of her. During coffee we always had to listen to Isabel's latest misdeeds. Uncle Conrado said, "Send her away," and Aunt Aurélia answered, "I do send her away; I shoo her out of the house every day and she answers back that she'll only go when she wants to." I kept feeling sorry for my aunt and she kept on not being able to find a way to get rid of Isabel.

My uncle lives on the main street and he was afraid if he threw her out on the street she'd make a scandal; so Aunt Aurélia re-

* When someone dies a candle is immediately lit and set by his head.

lieved her mind by talking about her all day long. Today I skipped drawing class and ran to take coffee at my aunt's. As soon as we sat down Aunt Aurélia started saying, "I have some wonderful news. I got rid of Isabel." We all asked, "How did you manage to do that?" She said, "I gave her a beating. She took fright and packed up and left, God be thanked." All my cousins said, at the same time, "What an idiotic thing to do, mama! She's strong and crazy, that Negro, and the Senhora is so small and thin. She could have beaten you and hurt you badly." "And even killed you," said my uncle. Aunt Aurélia said, "Do you think I'm an idiot? First I experimented with a little slap. When I saw that she didn't react, I gave her another one. Nothing happened. So then I took the chance, snatched up the broom, and really went for her."

We all laughed and thought my aunt's solution was very funny.

Friday, July 26th

I'm so sorry for Seu Domingos' sons, *coitados*. They're such good boys, but not a single girl at school will pay any attention to them.

Seu Sebastião's struggled with the two of them, trying to teach them some Portuguese, but I don't think he'll succeed.

Yesterday we were playing games at Seu Augusto Mata's house and they were there. We were playing *I Saw a Ship*. To make it easy they gave Estevam the letter F: farinha, fruit, flowers,—an infinity of words. When his turn came, "I saw a ship, loaded with . . ." he answered "roses." Everybody laughed but because it was the first time we didn't make him pay a forfeit. We explained again that he had to give a word beginning with F. The second time he answered "camellias."

Seeing that they didn't know the game and weren't going to learn, we decided to dance. One person played waltzes or polkas on the piano by turns and we danced. Estevam came up to ask me to dance and said, "Will you give me the pleasure of this polka? But excuse me if I don't know the step very well, because it's at least six months since I've danced *myself*."* Aren't those boys hopeless?

Friday, August 2nd

Everyone in Diamantina knows Parentinho [Little Relative]. Ever since I've known him he's been skinny, with such an old, greenish frock-coat, his head lost under a hard hat much too big for him, enormous shoes that would each hold two feet, walking twirling his cane down the *capistrana*† in the afternoons. He's a strange little old man, he calls everyone "my relative" and goes to everybody's house when they give dinners. Everyone receives him because he's very polite and clean.

I'd never spoken to him. Yesterday I was pleased when I saw him at an anniversary *festa* at Seu Guerra's. They asked him to dance the English solo.‡ He asked for a rose or a carnation. I loaned him a carnation I'd worn on my dress and he danced as gracefully as you could imagine, with the carnation in his hand.

Afterwards those who know the story of his life told me about his eccentricities. He has a sister whom no one's ever seen, who never leaves the house, and the two of them are very devoted. If you invite him to eat a sweet he always asks for a piece "for my little sister," to take to her. Yesterday as he was leaving he reminded Maria Emília of "sister's sweet" and she gave him a package of candy and cream-tarts.

They also say that they have a silver two-*mil-reis* piece that they never spend; on every birthday one gives it to the other with the same little verse:

Accept the little
Love can offer.

---

* Estevam makes the verb reflexive when he shouldn't.
† Note in M V d M: "Large paving stones laid down the middle of the streets so that pedestrians can avoid the steps that break up the sidewalks throughout the city." See introduction.
‡ Note in M V d M: "A kind of minuet, but with one performer."

If I had more,
More I'd proffer.

He and his sister have invented a very economical way of drinking coffee. They make it without any sweetening, put a piece of brown sugar in a corner of their mouths and then drink the coffee very slowly. If the lump of brown sugar lasts, they save it for another time. How queer!

Thursday, August 8th

Now we have a little family newspaper, thought up by my cousin Lucas, and called *The Peeler*. It's meant to tell the truth and to "peel" people. I don't know why Lucas didn't go on studying because he's funny, and seems intelligent.

Everyone in the family has to write for it. At first I didn't want to write anything because I was afraid I'd annoy my cousins and then they'd "peel" me. But Lucas has teased and provoked me so much in his newspaper that I made up my mind to send him an article. Leontino's the one who copies out the paper because he can print so well. I wrote an article with the title, "Horseshoes for Mosquitoes." That was all it took to get even with him for everything I've suffered because of this newspaper. The reason for the title is as follows:

When he came from Ouro Preto my poor aunt's money was almost gone. He didn't want to study so he started working at their place in Lomba. He made butter to sell and cheeses, from the skimmed milk, that were like rubber when they were fresh and turned to stone when they were old. Everyone stopped buying cheeses from Lomba. Since the dairy didn't bring in anything, my aunt sold the last securities she had and put the money into a store for him, near Seu Assis's and the others'. They were annoyed at having a rival taking away their customers and they gave pennies to the boys in the street to annoy him. One would ask, "Do you sell horseshoes for mosquitoes here?" Others would come look ing for "rubber cheese," or "black beans with weevils." Instead of just waiting until the boys got tired of it, he lost his temper and chased them with a broomstick.

It went on until he was forced to close the store and with it went my aunt's last cent.

Are there as many lunatics in other towns as there are in Diamantina? I and Glorinha were counting up the lunatics at large, besides those in the Asylum. What a lot!

But a town without lunatics would be very dull. At least I wouldn't like not to have Duraque here, and Crazy Tereza, Chichi Bombom, Zé Lotério's Maria, João Saint-maker, Crazy Antônio, and Domingos de Acenzo. They're all much funnier because of their crazy notions. But Domingos, who's a hairdresser and is mad about getting rich, has the craziest ideas of all.

Papa always has him come to the house to cut his hair, and I stay nearby, dying of laughter. He always tells papa his plans for getting rich, with such a serious face, and I run to laugh in my bedroom in order not to burst out in front of him.

He says he's saving money to go to Lomba and kill jaguars, skin them, and bring back the skins to sell. Papa asked him, "How are you going to manage to catch the jaguars? Aren't you afraid?" He answered, "I've studied all about it already. Doesn't the Senhor know a deadly poison for insects, called Persian Powder? I'm going to Lomba with some tins of that powder and find the place where the jaguars live. I've been told that they usually stay under the trees. I climb a tree with a gun and a tin of powder. From up above, I cough, to attract the jaguar's attention. She looks up, I throw the powder in her eyes, and then I shoot and kill her." Papa said, "It's a wonderful plan." Then Domingos told how besides the plan for catching jaguars he has another one for breeding sardines. He'll send to Rio de Janeiro for a kerosene tin full of live sardines, turn them loose in the pool in Silver Creek to breed; and he knows they'll bring him a fortune. But for this one he'll have to marry a rich girl who'll loan him some money.

It was because of this plan that he did something idiotic yesterday. Just to be mean, Seu Chico Lessa told him that Nhanhá was the richest girl in Diamantina and that if he caught her in the street and gave her a kiss, he'd have to marry her. That was all it took. Early yesterday Domingos put on his frock-coat, got himself ready, and posted himself in front of his barber-shop, next door to my uncle's house. When we went by there on the way to School, completely oblivious, he ran and grabbed Nhanhá and gave her the kiss. I couldn't imagine what was going on. Nhanhá gave a horrible shriek and fell to the ground. My uncle had her carried inside, sat her in a chair, and gave her water.

After the scene, Nhanhá was furious with me because of the fit of laughing I'd had. But how could I help thinking it was funny when I saw Domingos, very serious, go into my uncle's parlor and stay there waiting for the priest to marry them as soon as Nhanhá was better?

I didn't think they should have put him in jail, *coitado!* Doesn't everybody know he's crazy?

Thursday, August 15th

Now that I've just finished ironing it beautifully and hanging it on the hanger, I can't help writing down how fond I am of that white piqué dress of mine.

I think it's because it's the first I've had, choosing the material and the pattern by myself.

When I went with mama to buy the outfit to go to the College (and finally I wouldn't go), the Sisters required a white dress. I immediately picked out a piqué, of the best quality. Mama had it made but I chose the pattern.

No one would believe what this dress has meant to me. It's already more than six months old but it doesn't show it. I have only this one, but since I've had it I can say that I haven't missed a *festa* or the sending up of one fire-balloon in Diamantina. And not only here; it's already been in Curralinho and Boa Vista and

I can say with pride that this year nobody's got ahead of me. If it were any other color I might be named after it, like the telegraphist's wife, whom everyone calls "the girl with the green blouse." Because it's white they may even think I have two.

Sunday, August 18th

It seems like a dream that I escaped from Aunt Madge's school in just two days. Thank God the promise I made worked. Papa says Aunt Madge agreed to get a substitute, without being angry with me. Since the rain isn't going to let up, I'm going to take the occasion to write down this tragedy in every detail, in order not to forget what I went through and never again be tempted to be a schoolteacher. Never again in my life!

Thursday I went to Aunt Madge's and she told me, "I've decided to take a month's holiday and you're going to take my place at the school. Since I'd have to pay someone else, I'll give you the money, which will come in very handy for you. And then, you'll be getting in practice, because I intend to retire and leave you my place."

"But don't you know that if I miss a month at Normal School I'll fail the year?"

She said, "Ask one of the girls to answer to the roll call for you."

"That isn't it, Aunt Madge; it's that afterwards I won't be able to catch up with the others."

"I'm not worried about that. With your intelligence in a week you can do what the others do in a month."

"Yes, Aunt Madge. If it were for two weeks it might be possible, but a month is a long time. It would be better if you asked Zinha."

"But Zinha's sick. All right. I'll be thinking if two weeks will be enough and then I'll let you know."

I left the house cursing my luck and thinking to myself, "When will my sufferings, all because of Aunt Madge's love for me, come to an end? What will become of me if I have to leave school and my schoolmates and stop studying and everything to go to teach stupid little black children in Rio Grande?" To console myself I reflected: "Who knows but what this may be the turning point in my life? I'm restless and impatient. Will I be able to endure being stuck in a school for six hours every day, and then taking copy books home to correct? I'm a long way from getting my diploma and I've already thought about it a great deal. I'm going to try Aunt Madge's school and see if I'd make a teacher."

I got up early Friday, sad because I had to leave Normal School and go to Rio Grande. I went down the hill and went into the school. I asked one of the bigger boys how we should begin. They all stood up at the same time and said that first they had to sing the national anthem. I told them to sing. They sang off-key and all at different times. In the middle I hit the desk with the ruler and told them to stop.

"Stop! That will do."

Already the children were beginning to see what kind of a teacher they had. Again I asked, "And now what do we do?"

Each one said what he wanted to do and I didn't know what to do or where I ought to begin. Then I remembered that when I went to Mistress Joaquininha's school she always began by correcting the exercises, and I asked for their copybooks. I set them all to writing. Those moments were the first rest I had. They handed back the copybooks; I told them to put them on the desk and to take out their books. They got out their books and started showing me where they were in them.

One said, "I'm here, teacher."

"Then study up to here; study it well."

I marked off all the lessons, sent them all back to their places and told them to study while I corrected the exercises. I sat down, took up my pen, and began to go over what they'd written.

"Teacher, look at what Joaquim's doing! He's sticking a pin in me!"

"No he isn't. He's a good boy. It isn't true, is it, Joaquim? You wouldn't do a thing like that?"

"Yes he would, teacher! He's bad! The Senhora doesn't know!"
I gave back the copy books.

"Teacher, Joãozinho's pinching me!"

Then another, "Teacher, Chico cheated. He had another lesson."

"Teacher! Elivira lied! She's further on!"

One little boy: "Ugh! Go away, pig! Look what they're doing, teacher!"

I was dizzy trying to manage so many at the same time.

"Teacher! Amélia says that school's like Adam's and Eve's Paradise now. It will be nice if Teacher Madge is sick a long time."

So I said, to bribe them, "Then be good and I'll stay with you."

But another was yelling: "Teacher! Pedrinho put his finger in his nose and then poked it in my mouth!"

"Teacher!" "Teacher!" "Teacher!" "Look at this!" "Look at that!"

I got completely confused and didn't know what to do. Just then one of the bigger boys stood up and asked, "May I have permission, Teacher?"

"Permission for what?"

They all shouted together, "For the taboinha,* Teacher!"

They got up, came and rummaged in the drawer and gave me a very dirty taboinha, explaining, "The Senhora can only let him go outside with this taboinha, see, Teacher?"

I gave it to the boy. He went out to the yard, all grown over with high grass, and gave a yell: "Snake!" They all ran to the yard with me after them, and kept shouting, "See the snake here!" "No, it went there!"

With great difficulty I managed to get them back in again and in their places. I went on correcting the copybooks but the hubbub began again immediately. I thought to myself, "I'll make cakes to sell, like Siá Generosa; I'll wash clothes; I'll do any other kind

* *Taboinha*: "little board." Given to the pupil who has permission to go to the privy; an ancient device to prevent more than one child's going at the same time.

of work! I can see I'm not cut out for this. God Himself sent me here. I can't endure this; and besides, I'm ruining Aunt Madge's school. I'm going to let them go and find out what to do from Aunt Madge." I looked up at the children and said, "Didn't anybody study today's lesson?"

"No, Teacher. Almost all of us were cheating the Senhora."

"Not me!"

"Yes, you cheated! You were further along!"

"He's lying!"

I hit the desk with a ruler.

"That's enough! Today's wasted. I'm going to tell Aunt Madge what you did."

They said to each other: "Oh! Oh! She's scolding us! She's scolding us!"

I asked how they finished school for the day.

"We pray."

They prayed.

"Very well. You may go."

"Oh! Wonderful! What a nice teacher!" and out they went with all their hubbub.

I put my head in my hands and thought: "That's settled! Anything in the world except a schoolteacher! If I had to spend another day like this, I'd go mad." I closed up the school and went racing to Aunt Madge's to ask her to make some other arrangement, because I'd never go back. I went up the hill and into my aunt's house gasping for breath. Before I'd told her anything, Aunt Madge exclaimed:

"Why have you left school so early? It's over at four."

"I closed it to come to tell you that it's impossible for me to go on. The children don't respect me and I'm making them even worse for you to put up with afterwards. I'm not going back tomorrow."

"What? You're not going back? Then you want to disappoint

me and have me believe that a mulatto like Zinha is more capable than you are?"

"Than me! A lot more! I'm good for nothing!"

"But you can't be! Do you mean that I must let my dream of leaving you my school vanish in thin air? Never! You have to be somebody. You're very intelligent and very quick. But now you're just thinking about getting back to Normal School and wasting your time with the others."

"No, I'm not, Aunt Madge. It's that I wasn't meant to be a teacher. God brought this about so I could find it out and look for another way to earn a living. I've already been thinking; I'm going to make things to sell, I'm going to be like Siá Generosa."

"Generosa? You're going to be a teacher, and a good teacher. Look at what we did, Quequeta and I, we started studying when we'd already reached a certain age [they were close to forty] and today we're independent. You should follow our example."

"I don't think I can, Aunt Madge. I'm not good and long-suffering the way you both are. I like to work, to do any kind of work, but the job of teaching rude, stupid children and being a constant slave to the clock,—it's out of the question for me!"

"I'll show you if it's out of the question! You did something very wrong today, but I'm going to excuse you because it was the first day. Go back tomorrow and we'll see how it goes."

"It's impossible, Aunt Madge! If you'd only seen how the children behaved with me! I'm going to ask Zinha or another teacher to go instead."

"What? Do you think I'm to give you up after just one day? No, child, for mercy's sake, don't make me unhappy. You're the one hope of my life. Go and rest and go back tomorrow. I know you won't disappoint me."

I saw that it was useless to insist, said good-bye, and came running home. I arrived with a lump in my throat and fell sobbing on my bed. Mama came in.

"What happened, child? Did Aunt Madge scold you?"

"She didn't scold, mama. It's from rage at Aunt Madge! She drives me absolutely crazy! What will she think of next to torment me!"

"What happened? Tell me!"

"What I suffered today, mama, I think was almost as much as Jesus Christ."

"Horrors, child! How can you say such a thing?"

"But it was, mama. And Jesus Christ suffered because he wanted to but I'm suffering for no reason at all. I'd even like to break a leg not to have to go back to that school and not to have to endure those children; they're worse than demons. My head is almost splitting. I know I'm not going to be able to stand it even one more day and Aunt Madge is determined I'll stay two weeks! And on top of everything, the worst thing is not being able to say that Aunt Madge is mean and that she's doing it deliberately."

I told mama everything that had happened and she had an idea.

"Do you know something? We're going to make some caramels, right this minute. Tomorrow you can bribe the children, and I swear they'll behave better."

The two of us went to the kitchen and in a twinkling a batch of caramels was all made and wrapped up.

The next day I took them and started to leave and mama said, "It's better to take half today and leave the rest for tomorrow. Then we'll make some more."

So I did and went on to school. When I went in I found an awful uproar going on already. I hit the desk with the ruler and said, "Today I brought some caramels for those who behave well. Aunt Madge told me that I should punish those who are naughty and keep them after school."

They began to tell each other: "Oh! You're going to have to stay after school, too! Oh! It's serious, today." I sat down without having them sing. I handed out the copybooks but they didn't even do the writing lesson in peace. A shriek: "Teacher! Tonico's blotting my writing!" Another: "Teacher! Chico's pushing my arm!" "Teacher, look at what João's doing!" "Teacher!" "Teacher!" "Teacher!"

I was so discouraged I didn't even say a word. I took the copybooks; they were all dirty and badly written. I told them to sit down and study and it began again: "Teacher! Juquinha's planning to steal a caramel!" "Teacher, look at this; look at that!" I was silent and dejected. One of the bigger ones asked for "Permission," took the *taboinha* out in the yard, gave a horrible scream and stretched out on the ground. I ran to pick him up and he started laughing. I came back to the schoolroom and there wasn't a single caramel left on the desk.

I left the school and ran to Zinha's house, next door.

"Zinha, are you sick?"

"No, why?"

"Aunt Madge said you were."

"I told her that as an excuse."

"Zinha, I'm going crazy! Can't you do me the kindness of going in my place?"

"I knew you wouldn't be able to stand those little demons, Helena; it was mean of Dona Madge to do it to you. But I can't stand them either; that's why I told her I was sick."

"Zinha, let's go back together so you can teach me what I should do. You're so kind, have pity on me!"

"Very well, let's go."

We went in and Zinha said to the little devils:

"I've come to punish you for what you did to Helena. Not a peep out of you! I heard all the yelling from my house and now we'll see! Everyone in his place! Carlinhos, give me the book!" She opened the book and marked the lesson. "Júlio! Antônio! Maria Hilária!"

One by one they came up and went back to their desks with

the lesson marked. One of them gave a loud laugh. She got up, took him by the arm, gave him a good pinch, a box on the ear, and made him stand facing the wall.

She stayed a little while, put everything in order and said, "There, Helena. I have work to do. I'm going now, but if they as much as peep you call me."

She left. The minute she turned her back the one being punished left the wall. I ordered him back. He looked at me and laughed. I shouted and he paid no attention.

"Oh teacher! He's daring you!"

"He's making a face at you!"

I made a promise to say the rosary kneeling on kernels of corn if Our Lady would help me; then I ran to Zinha's house and fell sobbing on the sofa. Siá Donana came in from the kitchen to see what it was and Zinha said, "She's upset, mama."

"She has reason to be, poor little thing!"

I raised my head and said, "Siá Donana, I'll go crazy if Zinha doesn't take pity on me. I'm in such agony I think that only a lunatic could endure it. I'll end by going to the asylum, if Zinha doesn't take pity, and then she'll be sorry."

"*Coitadinha!*" said Siá Donana. "She's right! How mean of Dona Madge! She's so young and to try to struggle with those children, the worst in Diamantina! Only Dona Madge can handle them. She has a way with them; we have to admire her."

"That's it, Siá Donana, you know exactly. I'm suffering like this because I admire her so. Nobody else could do this to me. But Siá Donana, beg, please beg Zinha to go in my place. You're so kind."

"Go on, Zinha. Take pity on the girl! You're older, and she's so young!"

Zinha said, "All right; I can't help feeling sorry for her because I can see she's really suffering. How mean of Dona Madge! So many people needing to teach school and she goes and takes Helena away from her studies and sends her into this inferno.

All right, Helena, I'll go and get even with them for you. You can tell Dona Madge that it's for your sake I'm doing it."

I said thank-you to Zinha very gratefully and came up home. I met my father just coming from Boa Vista and asked him to speak to Aunt Madge for me.

And thus my sad experience came to an end.

Wednesday, August 21st

Today, for lack of a better subject I'm going to write about what happened at School.

I went into the second-year classroom and saw Sinhá looking through a hole in the window very intently. I felt like doing something foolish. I ran and stuffed an orange in the hole. Just then Seu Leivas came in, but I still had time to sit down without his seeing me. He always has to pry into everything, so he immediately asked who'd put the orange in the hole. Nobody answered. Just the same, we got a sermon. We all listened in complete silence. But when he went out and I thought he was far enough off, I said to the girls: "How our principal loves to preach a sermon, no matter what! An orange in a hole was excuse enough for that one! Why doesn't he get his crooked nose straightened and stay downstairs teaching the boys!"

Before I'd finished speaking, in came the old man again and turned on me and said, "I heard someone call me Crooked Nose. *My* defect is in plain sight. Many people have worse ones that they conceal." Isn't he mad?

After that I told the girls what had happened at Seu Mato's house, and I wish he'd heard that, too.

Saturday they gave a dinner there in honor of the Frenchman, Senhor Cugnin, of the Boa Vista Company. Seu Leivas went, and gave a toast in French. The man didn't understand a word of it. I think that Seu Leivas was invited just to give the toast. I saw the man was embarrassed and tried to translate the speech for him; and I was mean enough to tell him that Seu Leivas was our French teacher. He laughed a great deal and said he was very pleased to have one of Seu Leivas' pupils beside him, because otherwise he never would have guessed what he was saying.

Monday, August 26th

The day before yesterday something happened to me in which I see the finger of God.

Although I'm often of the last to arrive, I've never got to School and found the door closed before. Sometimes I'm in such a hurry to leave the house that I don't even have time for breakfast. And then yesterday I found the door already closed. I looked at the Cathedral clock: half-past six. I went up to take breakfast at grandma's and I found her sitting up in bed, very tired, and she said to me, "Daughter, I've been praying for you to come. You're my right arm. Take your coffee and milk and then hurry to Dr. Alexandre's and bring him here." I asked her why she didn't want to call Dr. Teles; she said he was in Medanha.

I didn't take any coffee. I went and brought Dr. Alexandre, whom I met just coming out of his house, like a flash. Grandma, sick as she was, when she saw I hadn't had any breakfast, wouldn't speak to the doctor until I went to eat something. My cousins say I flatter grandma. But how can I help but adore her the way I do?

I'm terribly worried today because grandma's worse. Mama, with all of us, Aunt Agostinha and Aunt Carlota, are all sleeping here; mama because papa's at the mine and the others because they don't have husbands. Aunt Aurélia's here, too, but she goes home at ten o'clock to get Uncle Conrado's lunch, at four to get dinner, and at nine, tea. She lives near here.

Grandma was sick three or four years ago and, when he came to Diamantina to visit the family, Dr. Felicio dos Santos operated on her bladder. He took a stone the size of an egg out of grandma. There was great rejoicing in the family. I remember when I saw the stone and saw grandma free of the pains she'd been suffering, it was a happy day for me. I began to realize how much she meant to me and how much I loved her.

I've made a great many vows, and I'm already dreading fulfilling them, even if we keep grandma with us. But I trust to God that I'll have to. Grandma's very strong, and everyone says that people often get over pneumonia, especially if they're treated the first day. And then God can't help but listen to the prayers of a family as large as ours, and all the Negroes' prayers besides. We're all praying all day long and burning a great many candles day and night on the altars, and we've taken many vows, too. God is good. I know He won't take grandma away from us, she's so good, so charitable to everyone.

Even though she's sick, grandma's sent me to a bedroom to study, but I can't do anything but write. It's impossible to study. I've been to School these days, too, because even in bed grandma doesn't forget me and my School work. I have to go to her room before I go out and when I come in, to kiss her hand.

Wednesday, August 28th

I'm fifteen years old today. What a sad birthday!

Even gasping for breath the way she is, poor one, grandma called me early and gave me a dress-length. She kissed me and said, "I know you're always going to be happy, my dear little girl, and that you'll never forget your grandma, who loves you so much." The tears ran down her face and I left her arms and ran here to my room to calm down and cry, away from everyone.

How it hurts me to see that even in bed, enduring such pain, grandma doesn't forget me and my affairs, and to remember that I haven't been as good to her as I should have been! But here and now I swear by everything that if grandma gets better I'll be an angel to her, and I'll dedicate myself to her because she's so good and she loves me so much.

I'm going to her room to see her now and I already know what she's going to say: "Have you done your lessons? Then go and lie down, but get something to eat first. Go with God."

Saturday, August 31st

Grandma's been sick a week today and everyone in the house is in a state of the greatest anxiety, because they say that if she shows improvement today by tomorrow she'll be saved.

I don't know why God let me know grandma! I might have been so happy, because my parents are both strong and healthy, if I'd never known her. If only she'd died when I was little the way the other one did!

I'm in agony today! Esmeralda came to help us and taught us some prayers that God can't possibly not listen to. We're all praying with such faith! We've done almost nothing else all day today. There wasn't even anyone to receive the callers.

I spent the day in anguish, seeing grandma in that condition, with nobody able to help her. The doctor comes and prescribes things, and goes away, and then she gets worried about herself!

What Mama says is always right. Sometimes I thought it was absurd when she said that life is made up of suffering. Now I see she was right. Life really is made up of suffering. These days since grandma's been sick I've forgotten all the joy I ever had and suffering is all I can think about. And since they said that tomorrow would be the crisis, I've been in such agony that all I can do is stay on my knees with the others, praying. When they get tired I take a walk around the garden, come back through the kitchen, the parlor, and go to every corner of the house, trying to find some peace, but I can't. And if I go in grandma's room, it's worse torture.

Why does God punish us all this way? We never hurt anyone. I wait for the day He'll remember and release grandma and us from this suffering.

Grandma died!

Oh dear grandma, why has God taken you away and left me all alone in the world, missing you so much! Yes, my dear little grandmother, I'm all alone, because weren't you the only person who's ever understood me up until now? Shall I ever find anyone else in this life who'll tell me I'm intelligent and pretty and good? Who'll ever remember to give me material for a pretty new dress, so I won't feel I'm beneath my cousins? Who'll argue with mama and always try to defend me and find good qualities in me, when everyone else only finds faults?

My dear little grandmother, I think I feel your loss more than all the other grandchildren do! I told my cousins that and they said, "You were the only one she loved." Why did you love me so much? Me, the most mischievous of the grandchildren, and the noisiest, and the one who gave you the most trouble? I remember now with remorse the struggle you had to get me in from play every evening and onto my knees, when it was time for the rosary. But here in secret I confess now that it was an hour of sacrifice you made me undergo. Even the rage I felt, when after saying the whole rosary and all the mysteries, my aunts and that hypocrite of a Chiquinha used to remember all our dead relatives and we had to say one more Our Father or Hail Mary for the soul of each and every one! I used to think that my prayers might even be sending souls back to hell, because I was always praying under protest. No one else could have made me do it. But I know, grandma, in spite of everything I did, you felt how fond I was of you and you saw the suffering written on my face when I saw you so sick. And I used to see how happy it made you when I came from School and ran to tell you my marks. Now that I'm unburdening myself here I remember all your tenderness, all your kindness. The thought of the day I compared you to Our Lady comes back to me.

On the anniversary of the Proclamation of the Republic* two officials came to grandma's to ask my aunts for two little girls, to make up the twenty to represent the States. They needed two more for the States of Piauí and Rio Grande do Norte. The girls were to walk in line, dressed in white, with red liberty bonnets on their heads and wide ribbons across their chests with the names of the States on them in gold letters. I followed all my cousins' preparations with great interest because it seemed to me it was an extremely important occasion. But I got sadder and sadder all the time because they hadn't even considered me.

The day of the celebration came and my aunts put my cousins up on the table so they could work over them better, arrange the dresses and the bonnets and tie the ribbons. They were both very proud, with everyone admiring them, and they were gloating because I was jealous. Somebody said, "How pretty they look!" Somebody else said, "Aren't they sweet!" I looked and listened in silence until I felt a lump in my throat and I ran out and threw myself face down on the grass behind the church. I was crying and sobbing when I felt your cane tap my shoulder. I turned over, frightened, because I was so well-hidden and hadn't expected anyone there. It was you, grandma! You'd been watching me and reading my soul, and you understood what I felt and had followed there in my steps. You'd walked there with the greatest difficulty, holding onto your cane with one hand and the walls with the other. I remember until now the kind words you said to me that day: "Get up, silly! You came here to cry because you're jealous of those homely little girls, didn't you?" I didn't have time to answer, and besides, I already felt comforted, and you went on: "I don't know why a girl as intelligent as you are doesn't understand some things. Don't you see that this holiday is for idiots, and that a girl like you, pretty, intelligent, and of English descent, couldn't take part in it? It's silly to celebrate the Proclamation of the Republic. The Republic is something for common people. It

* November 15th, 1889.

doesn't concern nice people. They know your father's a monarch-
ist, that he isn't one of the turncoats, and he wouldn't let his
daughter go out in the streets to play the fool in an idiotic celebration like that. Let the rest of them do it. Don't be jealous, because you're better than any of them."

Oh grandma, you can't imagine what your words meant to me!
You made me get up, took me around by the back door without
anyone's seeing us to wash my face, and you made me laugh and
waited until I looked cheerful again, so no one would notice I'd
been crying.

That was the day, grandma, I remember I compared you to Our
Lady and I thought to myself, "She's so good and so holy that
she can even guess what I suffer, to comfort me." But now who will
ever comfort me? I have my mother and father, my sister and
brothers, but none of them can be to me what you were. Why? Because you were more intelligent? Or because you loved me even
better than my own parents?

I don't know if I'll have any incentive to study, or if I'll ever
find anyone else to whom I'll have the courage to open my heart.
But, dear grandma, I know I'm going to miss you dreadfully!

Sunday, September 8th

Elvira didn't come here when grandma died because she's sick.
But she wrote me such a sincere letter! Today I answered it:

Dear Elvira:

I received your kind and friendly letter about the death of my
adored grandmother. I realized immediately that you were sick
when you didn't appear for the funeral. I never doubted your
friendship for an instant. On that day I must confess I didn't
notice anyone was missing. I was so grieved by the loss of my little
grandmother, and the house was so full, that I wasn't able to ob-
serve who was there.

I've read and re-read your letter, Elvira, and I marvel at the way you sensed, and knew how to write, so many things that are in my heart. It seems as if you'd even known grandma intimately. Only someone very close to the family could say the things that you say in your kind letter and that are the simple truth, I swear. I don't believe anyone could be better than grandma was. During the years that I knew her she only did good for whomever she could. I know every house in Diamantina and I never saw such a pilgrimage of the poor to any of them as grandma always had at her house; she always treated them all with such kindness that I was amazed. I used to get so upset by all the old women's complaints that came to her that many times I asked her if she wasn't bothered by all the lamenting. She used to say: "No, my child. *Coitada!* She has to complain to someone. And you shouldn't speak of it; it's being lacking in charity."

Everyone says that grandma lived a long time but I think she should have lived longer. You can't imagine what I suffer when I open my eyes in the morning and remember that grandma no longer exists. I even envy my other cousins whom she didn't appreciate as much as she did me. I ask myself constantly why she loved me so much and can't find the reason; I never did anything with the thought of pleasing and sometimes I rebelled against her excessive care. I have no remorse, fortunately, because in spite of my rash and disobedient nature, she saw the love I felt for her.

With gratitude, Elvira, from

Your faithful friend,
Helena

Tuesday, September 10th

Maria Balaio [Big Basket] called to me in School today to tell me that she'd gone to the seventh-day mass for grandma and that she and her mother had said a rosary for grandma's soul. I was so touched that I want to put her name down here, in my notebook. She's so kind!

On the way home to lunch we walked together almost all the way as far as the foot of Cavalhada and I told her more than once: "Maria, if I didn't just have my plate all ready and waiting for me on the stove, I'd invite you for lunch. I think it's a long way for you to go, to the Cross* and back again." She said, "Yes, it's a long way, Helena, but what can I do?" But when I told Seu Marcelo how sorry I was to see her going to the Cross every day for lunch, he was sorry and told Maria Antônia that she should take her home to eat lunch with them. How thoughtful that was! I couldn't have been more pleased if it had been for my benefit.

Thank heavens Maria Balaio is going on with her schooling. She only gets "passing" in everything, it's true; but she's not too intelligent and she can only manage to pass the examinations with great difficulty.

I'm the only one at School who knows about her life, because her mother, Siá Joaquina Balaio, is a woodcutter and mama always buys wood from her. I admire the efforts she and her mother make, *coitadas*, and if there's one walk I like to take it's to the Cross, just to go to their shack. If I said I envied their lot nobody would believe it; but they do lead the kind of life I like.

They live in a shack that's no trouble to keep tidy, and in the middle of a big field with the most wonderful view! I don't know how they came to think of building their little shack there. They're the only people there but they needn't have the slightest fear because they're protected by the Cross, which is very close. There's only one room, with a bedstead and a straw mattress for them both, and a wooden box to sit on. The stove is in the room, too, and they told me that in cold weather they keep themselves quite warm with cinnamon wood.

In order to write, Maria sits on the box and writes on the bed,

* Outlying district, named for the large cross there.

by the light of a wick in a clay saucer of oil. The bed is covered
with a patchwork quilt. The patches are so small that everyone
admires her mother's patience in having matched them and sewed
them together.

For studying she prefers the foot of the Cross, when it doesn't
rain. They told me that if only God didn't make it rain nothing
would bother them; but the rain makes it dismal, not only for the
mother, who has to look for firewood, but for Maria, who has to
go from the Cross to town and back. But in other ways their life
runs along like everybody else's.

Every day the mother brings to town a bundle of wood that she
sells for five hundred *reis*. Besides this they raise hens. When the
chickens are little, and it rains, they keep them in the room. The
hens wander around at large, roosting in the trees and laying in
nests around the shack. They eat some of the eggs and sell the
rest. Once in a while they eat a pullet; but her mother told me
that they raise them just for Maria's shoes; she uses up a pair a
month, at five *mil reis*. The wood brings in only enough money for
them to live on.

Sunday, September 15th

Mama's very happy; in any situation she immediately thinks—
I won't say of God, because I never see her calling on Him,—but
of the saints. Why is it, really, that nobody ever asks things from
God, since He's the sovereign? When it isn't from the saints, it's
from Our Lady. Grandma was the only one I ever heard say it
occasionally, like the time Uncle Joãozinho got into a fight,—"My
God, help me!" Usually it was a saint, or "Our Lady"; but "God,"
"Jesus Christ," "Eternal Father"—never. Mama's the most believing creature in the world and she never misses a chance to
make the most of any new saint's miracles. And anything new
in the church or in saints naturally came to grandma's house first,
because all the pious old women in town went there.

I've heard so much in respect to the protection of the saints and the souls in heaven, that I really do believe in invisible aid. At this moment the memory comes back to me of something that happened in my childhood, that confirms it.

I was perhaps seven or eight years old, I don't remember exactly. We found a guava tree loaded with fruit and climbed up, I and Luizinha. She ate more than I did or perhaps she'd already eaten something else that made her sick. We were in the shack at Boa Vista, at papa's mine, and Luizinha woke up in the night writhing with colic. Nobody could give her relief, not even with hot cloths, because the kitchen was separate from the house and it was raining hard.

Cacilda Pimenta had died just before this. She died of consumption at the Sisters' College and word immediately spread through town that she'd gone to heaven and that the priests and the Sisters believed she had turned into a saint, because she'd suffered with the greatest resignation. Cacilda's sanctity grew in such a way that very soon there were people who had seen the cloud carrying her soul up to heaven and the skies opening to receive her. The only subject of conversation was Cacilda's miracles.

This was when the colic occurred. Mama kneeled down and prayed to Cacilda, imploring her to make Luizinha better. I remember that I, since I'd known Cacilda, didn't have the same faith that mama had and I said to her: "Mama, pray to some more miraculous saint." She replied, "No. We'll see. Cacilda's the one who's performing miracles now."

After a little while Luizinha got better and I ended by having faith in Cacilda's miracles.

Sunday, September 22nd

Dindinha is the aunt who's most loved in our family, not only by her sisters but by all the nephews and nieces, who all call her Dindinha.

João Antônio, who's her nephew but whom she brought up like a son, tells how he heard Dr. Mata Machado speak about

Dindinha's beauty in his palace at Tijuca, in Rio de Janeiro, when
he was president of the Chamber of Deputies, at a table full of
ministers and politicians. João Antônio says that he almost burst
with pride when Dr. Mata told them how he was like her own son
and everyone looked at him.

Dindinha's been a widow for more than twenty years but she
sighs with longing for her husband until today. Sometimes when
there's silence in the room, Dindinha, who spends her life sitting
in front of her lace-pillow making the bobbins fly, heaves a sigh:
"Ah, Clarindo!" And her sighs are always so deep that they
break your heart.

Dindinha's story is so sad that I want to put it down in my notebook.

My grandfather accepted the husbands he liked for his daughters and married them off without consulting them. He had ten
daughters. Sometimes the suitors would ask for one of the daughters and he'd say, "No, not that one; she's too young. You may
have the older one."

They all asked for Dindinha but he kept her for the richest
farmer in the region. She loved a cousin and when she learned
that she'd been promised in marriage to another she wept without
stopping, day and night, making novenas and pleading with all
the saints. They said that she made all her trousseau in the parlor,
surrounded by slaves as was the custom, reciting the litany with
the slaves saying the responses, and begging God that something
would happen to the man so he wouldn't come to marry her.

The year came to an end and preparations for her wedding
and Aunt Carlota's began. Then grandpa wrote to the farmer,
setting the date, and telling him that he should be in Lomba for
Christmas, to get married. The man answered grandpa asking if
he could possibly give him another month to finish his harvesting,
that it was late that year. Grandpa wrote back breaking off the
marriage. The cousin seized the opportunity, proposed, and
grandpa accepted.

To hear Dindinha tell about their honeymoon at Guinda, the most beautiful country around Diamantina, is enough to make one envious. She would go with Uncle Clarindo, with their arms around each other, as far as his mine. Then she'd go back and make cakes or fry "dreams" to take him for his lunch, and they'd come home in the evening again with their arms around each other.

At the end of two years he died of a kind of cholera and left a little daughter, six months old. Dindinha returned to Lomba, went into her bedroom and wept for a whole year without stopping. The daughter got sick, she left the bedroom to take care of her better, but the little girl died, too.

Dindinha gave herself up to grief and never again thought of another man, in spite of having been widowed at the age of twenty-two. From that day on, her life has been a rosary of suffering. But she knows she was born to suffer and resigns herself.

Sunday, September 29th

I've just come back from Mass where I thought constantly of grandma and all her kindness to me. I remember something that happened when I was seven years old; in spite of grandma's efforts, I had a dreadful disappointment. At that age I was always envious of my cousins, not only because of being the poorest in the family, but because mama was so different from my aunts. Mama always wanted me to be better than my cousins at studying, and doing chores, and in manners, and she never realized how much I suffered, envying their dresses and shoes. But never was my envy so great as when I used to watch my aunts dressing my cousins as virgins, with little white dresses, ribbons in their hair and wreaths on their heads, and telling their older brothers, "You can go now, it's time!" Each one gave his hand to his younger sister and off they went, four couples, to church, and waited to go in at the side, each little girl with her lighted candle in her hand.

I never had a virgin's dress and I never hoped to have one. But I was so envious of my cousins that I see now it must have shown in my face, or it wouldn't have occurred to grandma to do what she did.

Just before one of the processions at the Mercês Church, grandma called the dressmaker and ordered a white dress for me. I'll never forget the anxiety with which I waited for the day when I'd go into the church with my cousins and get a fluted paper cornucopia filled with chocolates.

The longed-for day arrived. The night before, mama kept me sitting for a whole hour, wild with impatience, while she picked up little locks of my hair, wet them with a sour orange, and wrapped them in bits of paper. I don't know why mama did that; I was so much homelier with my hair in curls. The next day, right after lunch, we all went to grandma's, I, mama, and my sister and brothers. Renato was jealous because I was happy and he kept teasing me, "Look at her face, how pleased she is! She's going to look pretty silly, with that face like a sparrow's egg!"

I had freckles but I'd never minded, in spite of Renato's remarks. I'm not vain, even now. Shall I be, some day?

I was so happy that I lost my appetite and grandma threatened, "You can't go without dinner!"

I hurriedly swallowed down a plate of food. The nervous way I got dressed made them all laugh. My aunts were saying, "Get dressed quick; the bell's already rung the first time." I could scarcely breathe I was so excited. It came time to go and the boy cousins were waiting to take their sisters. At that moment grandma and mama suddenly thought: I had no one to take me because Renato didn't have any boots.

I was so disappointed when I saw my cousins leave without me that grandma felt obliged to make an effort that she'd only have made for me. She said, "Give me your arm, daughter." She took hold of my arm and her cane and started off, painfully, without my knowing where we were going. I was so unhappy I couldn't speak.

Grandma stopped at a neighbor's house and called out, "Excuse me, Mariana. Are you there?" Mariana appeared immediately and greeted grandma warmly, "What on earth is the Senhora doing here, Dona Teodora!" Grandma said, "I've come here after one of your boys, to take this girl in the procession, *coitadinha!*" Dona Mariana said that the only one at home was Betinho, and he was very small for grandma to trust. Grandma said that he'd do, that it was just to walk beside me; and putting her hand on the little boy's head she said, "Go get dressed quick and I'll give you a penny."

It was only then that I was able to speak. "Grandma, don't tell him to get dressed up because there isn't time. The procession's left already. I heard the bell ring." Grandma said, "You can get in the line when they pass by here."

When the procession went by I got in, and entered the church just as Seu Broa was giving out the cornucopias. They seemed bigger then than they do now, some filled with chocolates and others with almonds. Those with almonds were for the priests, the choir, and other important people. They were worth three of the other ones. But that nasty Broa passed me by without giving me anything. Betinho let go of my hand and ran to complain, but it was useless. He came back disappointed, telling me not to be sad, that he'd get one next day.

What I felt wasn't just sadness at losing a cornucopia, it was mortification. I could just hear my brother say, "Look at her face! Who'd give a cornucopia to that speckled face!"

It was the greatest disillusionment of my childhood.

Now I see that these childish disillusionments were useful in teaching me to have the patience to endure injustices from those teachers' pets at School.

Wednesday, October 2nd

Renato came home in a rage; he'd had a fight with a Portuguese who came here not long ago, who works as a clerk at Seu Cadete's store. He came in and said to me, "I fought with Cadete's Manuel because of you. From now on you go by there with a serious face. Don't go meandering along the sidewalk laughing all the time with the other girls the way you do. You're getting to be a young lady; you have to behave in the street. I hear these things from them and other people, too."

I was upset, without understanding anything.

Mama asked, "What happened?" He said, "I went into Cadete's store to buy a notebook and Manuel asked me, 'Who's that wench going by?' I looked, and it was Helena. Then I told him, 'That's my sister and I won't have you calling her a wench. If you say that again I'll smash your face.' He was very embarrassed and offered as an excuse that he spoke like that because in Portugal they call girls of good family 'wenches,' instead of 'girls.' But I saw perfectly well that he was just making it up as an excuse."

I told Renato that he was a nitwit and that he'd done something very stupid. At Seu Antonio Eulálio's house Seu Ramos, who's Portuguese, always calls the sister-in-law and the girls who go there "wenches" and nobody thinks anything of it.

Friday, October 11th

Today Maria Antônia invited me to go to her house to eat pequis. The only house where one can eat one's fill of pequis, mangabas, mangaritos* and other things from the country is Seu Marcelo's house, because he gets them by the bushel from some friends in Medanha.

I went with her. When we got there the shop was full of teachers. Seu Marcelo turned to them and said, "This little Eng-

* These are small, wild fruits, popular with children.

lish girl and Maria Antônia are inseparable. She's very lazy and Maria Antônia keeps trying to get her to study." Maria Antônia was embarrassed and she ran up the stairs with me after her. When we got in her room I said, "What kind of a story is this that your father's telling, that I'm lazy and you're the one who makes me study?" She said, "I don't say anything to him, it's his own idea."

I ate a lot of *pequis* and came home. She begged me to stay to dinner but I didn't want to; I wanted to make the most of being angry with her father and so I came home to put down some things I've been wanting to write but haven't had the courage, thinking it would be disloyal. But now I'm going to tell all.

Has anyone ever seen anything more foolish than that frame Seu Marcelo hung in the parlor with all Raimundo's marks in it, and just "passing," from the first year to the last?

And Siá Matilde's dizzy spells? And all because she eats too much; and the more she eats the more he wants her to eat. Siá Matilde is the luckiest woman I ever saw in my life. Seu Marcelo lives to please her, or else to stuff her with food. At home we still talk about what happened at Ilídia's wedding. Seu Marcelo asked for a little dish to send "Matilde's dinner" home in, and he went in the pantry to find one; he found a quarter-bushel measure, filled it up with everything and sent it home.

Uncle Conrado has a tomato plant growing in a box on the parlor balcony; it's more sacred to him than the holy wafer. But Siá Matilde passed by and saw the red tomatoes and immediately wanted them, and Seu Marcelo went and asked Uncle Conrado for them. There isn't a house where Seu Marcelo hasn't asked for a little something to "perk up Matilde's appetite." I'm there a great deal and I've seen her lack of appetite. Maria Antônia practically wakes up with the chocolate-stick in her hand so that the chocolate will be well beaten. It's chocolate with eggs in it, and milk, and I don't know what-all; I only know it's thick and delicious. Maria Antônia usually leaves a little in the pan for me and

I swear the only time that I'd like to be Siá Matilde is at choco-late-time in the morning. She's scarcely finished it when Seu Mar-celo is in the kitchen giving orders for "Matilde's lunch" to the cook. There are always three dishes for lunch and dinner: one a special rice dish, another with a chicken with blood gravy or with okra, and another of squash or *palmito* or some other vegetable. And she always says: "What an ordeal!" while she eats the three dishes and afterwards drinks a glass of wine "for sick people." Dr. Alvaro said that this wine was "good for sick people" and imme-diately it was separated from the rest and labelled "Wine for Sick People" on the bottles. After that she takes two eggs and another glass of wine on top. Wouldn't that give anyone dizzy spells? And the same greediness at dinnertime, and all the time complaining of having no appetite.

At night we all take *canjica* with brown sugar and she has a glass of milk Maria Antônia prepares; she puts three bottles of milk in the pan to boil down, and it makes two glasses.

And Lauro's piano? He knows how to play, but only on his own piano.

If I were to write down everything my notebook wouldn't hold it all. I'll leave the rest for the next time I get mad at them.

Monday, October 14th

A sister of Aunt Clarinha's daughter-in-law arrived from Montes Claros and went to call on Aunt Agostinha in Jogo da Bola Street. She is pretty, very nice, and dressed very well. Yesterday we all went to spend the day there, and the visitor from Montes Claros was the big event. All the aunts were admiring her beauty and the polite way she has of speaking. She speaks very clearly and very correctly. . . . I've never seen anyone speak so well; everything the way it's written, without swallowing a single *r*. We all were openmouthed and afraid to talk near her. Aunt Agostinha sent for a tray of grapes and asked her if she liked grapes. She replied, "I would appreciate a bunch of grapes exceedingly,

Dona Agostinha." At these words our jaws dropped. A girl from Montes Claros saying such a fine phrase! When she went out walking with the others Iaiá took the opportunity of eulogizing her and comparing her with us. She said, "Aren't you jealous to see a girl from Montes Claros, a much less civilized place than Diamantina, speak as nicely as that? You should profit by her being here and learn how. In my day it was Mariquinha Pimenta who taught us. It was she who taught us to say chamber-pot instead of the other word. We used to pay attention to her in order to learn really refined words. These days you don't pay attention to anything, and you speak like riffraff!" I answered, "These days we have a Portuguese teacher and we don't have to learn from other people. I'm going to use that phrase in my composition tomorrow, I want to see if the teacher's going to like it."

At dinner, to tease Iaiá, I and the cousins began to say, "I would appreciate the fried potatoes exceedingly," "I would appreciate a drumstick exceedingly."

Sunday, October 20th

When grandma died, Fifina had to look for a place to stay. She rented a little house for ten *mil reis* a month and found someone to live with her who'd pay half.

She only eats lunch at home and eats dinner every day at a different house. After lunch she takes some needlework to do and goes to someone else's house. She sits down in an armchair and stays there doing embroidery and drawn-work, and telling in the house she's at what she saw in the others. She takes her coffee at two o'clock, has dinner, and keeps on with her tales until nine o'clock when she goes home to sleep. That's her life.

After grandma's death she needed money and began to meddle in the things she'd had for a long time, and to sell anything at all. I've seen lace-edge sheets, embroidered towels, and even silverware that she's sold.

Today I went to Mass at the Carmo church. When Mass was

over I went down to Dadinha's house to pay her a visit. Going in, I found Fifina seated in an armchair in the parlor, with a cut on her head, streaming with blood and shaking frightfully. Dadinha and Podina didn't know what to do with her. I asked them what had happened and they said that Fifina had fallen and rolled down the hill, near their doorway, and some people passing by had picked her up and brought her in there.

I was dreadfully sorry for Fifina and went to get water to wash her face. In the kitchen I asked Dadinha, "Why don't you tell her to lie down on your bed? She's shaking so, poor thing!" Dadinha answered, "Don't you remember how your grandmother put her up for one night and she stayed there until your grandmother died?"—"But if it's your bed she knows it's yours and that you don't have another one, and she won't stay," I said. Dadinha said, "I don't trust to that. She'd pretend to be sick and then it would be hard for me to get rid of her. Even this shaking is put on. If you show her you're sorry, she gets worse."

Poor Fifina, to go from house to house, without having any place to stay! How she must miss grandma!

Sunday, November 3rd

My aunts planned to go and spend All Soul's Day, yesterday, at Curtume. Since Uncle Antonio Lemos and Aunt Florinda moved to Montes Claros, nobody's been back there. Curtume belonged to them and they went there every Saturday and came back early Monday morning.

From the time I was nine, they almost never went without me, he, because I was his favorite niece and she because she wanted me to do the work those days. I remember some happy days I spent there, in spite of all the hard work I had to do. Breakfast was pounded dried beef, with coffee. After breakfast I had to husk the rice, pick over the black beans, water the vegetable garden,—everything was left to me. Sometimes my uncle would come to the kitchen to take me away from work, to the tannery or the orange grove, saying, "Don't be silly, leave the work for them. Let's take a walk."

Because of this I was especially fond of him until the day Antenor died. At dinner papa and mama talked about nothing but my uncle and aunt's tragedy. "Poor things! They spent all they had on that boy's education, and now to have him die of yellow fever in Rio, away from his family, when he was just finishing his studies!" I listened to them, feeling very sorry for my uncle and aunt, particularly for Uncle Antonio who didn't use to let me work.

In the evening we went to their house. All the family was there, in the bedroom, crying, and Antoninho, the eldest son, was with them. They said that my uncle was a Mason and I was horrified to hear him exclaim: "I don't know how anyone can believe in such an unjust God as you believe in! If He wanted to kill one of my sons, why didn't He take Antoninho?"

Antoninho, right there, lowered his eyes, got up, and went out. I was so sorry for him that I went after him and told him, "It doesn't matter, Antoninho, everybody loves you very much." He said, "Helena, how did our family ever have a girl like you?" and he hugged and kissed me, with his eyes full of tears.

Curtume is abandoned now. We think it's too sad and decided not to go back there any more.

Thursday, November 7th

When I was writing about Uncle Antonio Lemos the other day I remembered something that made one of the deepest impressions of my life on me.

We were spending the days at Uncle Geraldo's and only going home at night to sleep because he was very sick; papa stayed there with him. Papa and that uncle are inseparable friends, always together. When papa isn't at the mine he's with Uncle Geraldo.

When he took sick he sent to the mine for papa, who came right away and stayed by his pillow day and night. There wasn't

enough to eat at this rich uncle's house for all of us, because
Dindinha was there, too, and Iaiá Henriqueta with Nico Spotted
Bull. I used to go to Aunt Florinda's house and work for her, because she didn't have anybody, her daughters were studying at
Normal School and couldn't help her. I remember it was the
hardest work I ever did in my life, carrying water from the yard
in a tin, up a long staircase, to fill two big barrels in the kitchen.
She just cooked lunch and then went to the parlor to chatter to
my uncle; the kitchen was left for me to clean up. But I ate well
there and I didn't go hungry, the way I did in the other house.

In the morning she told me to take breakfast to my uncle: a
plate of fried pork with manioc flour, two fried eggs, and a coffeepot full of coffee that he drank just like water. One day, when I
was taking in the coffeepot, Luizinha, who's always more inquisi-
tive than I am, said, "Let's go on tiptoe and see what he's doing
in that closed-up room all day long." We kept quiet as mice, left
everything on the staircase, and peeked through the keyhole.
What a shock! The window was closed and Uncle Antonio Lemos
was in front of the *oratório*; the *oratório* was always kept shut and
this was the first time I'd seen it open. He seemed to be saying
Mass. It was just like Mass: there were two candles lighted, a
chalice, and he was standing up making incomprehensible ges-
tures. We called him, he opened the window, blew out the candles, closed the *oratório* and opened the door. I asked him, "Uncle
Antonio, why is it that you keep your *oratório* closed? All of ours
are open." He said, "Mine's different."

Another time when we peeked he was burning a package of
barrusquês. Burning money! I was dumbfounded at such a mystery and went after grandma. "Grandma, I want to tell you a
secret that's going to give you a shock! Uncle Antonio's a wizard!"
Grandma began to laugh and asked me, "Why?" When I told
her what I'd seen she said, "I'll explain. He burns the *barrusquês*
because they aren't worth anything any more; nobody wants to

accept them. And that *oratório* must be something to do with Masonry; he's a Mason."

Sunday, November 10th

Today grandma's last African Negro died. He served her faithfully until her death. In a letter she wrote, grandma left him two hundred *mil reis*. She left five hundred for the Negro women. Although Joaquim Angola didn't need it. I think it was more to comfort him. This Negro came in from the garden every day to see her and on the day she died he cried so hard it was pitiful. Just the way all the Negro women did.

He was so fond of me that when I realized it I couldn't help but return it. Nobody else in the family had such beautiful big bunches of grapes and figs and peaches to eat as I did. He picked them for me and hid them under a bush. I knew about it, and when I came home from School I used to go to the kitchen to get his mug and give him some coffee and anything else I could find to go with it. When I got to the garden he would say to me, "Look, Sinhazinha, what your Negro* saved for you." Then I used to get the fruit and hide in a hole in the wall to eat it in peace.

Now I've done something that I know is bad; really awfully bad. But I couldn't seem to help doing it. Papa said he didn't even recognize me, he thought I was so brave and fearless. I told him yes, about the things of life; but about death, no.

The poor Negro didn't want to die without seeing me and he kept calling for me. Júlia, his daughter, came to get me at nine o'clock yesterday, so he could say good-bye to me. I don't know why, I didn't have the courage to go. I couldn't sleep well at night. At four o'clock in the morning, when the bell rang for Mass, Júlia, knowing that we always go to early Mass, came into

---

* "Your Negro" here is used to express affection and devotion. It is still occasionally used in this sense in Brazil, regardless of color.

my room and said to me, "Sinhá Helena, the Senhora isn't going to go to Mass without going to say good-bye to my father, so he won't die without seeing the Senhora? He talked all night about his 'Sinhazinha.' If the Senhora could only go right away, to put his mind at rest." Then I said, "It's impossible, Júlia. I don't have the courage." I ran to my father's bed and threw myself into his arms.

I never thought I'd be so afraid in my life. My father said that if I were a little girl it would be natural. But there's no excuse for a girl fifteen years old.

Thursday, November 14th

After grandma died, Dindinha asked mama if we would stay with her and Iaiá here in Direita Street, because the house is too big for her alone and also together we could support grandma's death better. Mama thought it was convenient, nearer the School and her brothers and sisters, and we could rent our house in Cavalhado Street, too. The house was rented immediately by the commanding officer of the battalion, because it's almost facing the barracks.

In spite of missing grandma dreadfully, our life goes along so-so. This is the meeting place of all the family and everything went peacefully until the day came to divide grandma's estate. Since they began to go over the inventory the house has turned into an inferno. Sometimes I'm afraid that grandma, there in the other world, sees what's going on in the family because of the money she left.

Iaiá, who's the most civilized and even reads novels and can tell us the stories word for word, turns into a demon when it's a matter of money. Only now am I beginning to believe mama's speeches about money's bringing unhappiness. But she's fighting, too, and doesn't want the others to get her share. Iaiá and Uncle Geraldo want to force mama to put some things grandma gave her before in the inventory: diamonds, slaves and everything.

Papa's always the same about everything. Mama tells him: "You ought to be more energetic, Alexandre, and protest!" But he doesn't do anything. He's like Saint Francisco of Assisi, watching a fight.

Today mama decided to go to Rio Grande for a rest from fighting with Iaiá. We spent the day there. When we came back I went into the fighting room to hear what Iaiá was saying to the others. Seeing that they were clearly getting together to take away mama's money, to which she has a right, I joined in the conversation. Iaiá yelled at me: "Get out of here, you long tapeworm, or I'll give you a whipping!"

I ran out and went to tell mama. She couldn't keep away and went and fought with Iaiá. Then she came back to the bedroom and locked the door. Iaiá, on the other side, almost broke it down.

Our life is an inferno. Fortunately the commander has promised to give up our house by Sunday.

Sunday, November 17th

The commander moved yesterday and we're already in our own house, thank God. It's almost time for exams. Right now I envy my classmates who study; they don't have to make all the vows I have to make. Everyone advises a different saint. I never made a vow to Saint Antônio because of the trick he played on mama. They tell me that he's only infallible for arranging a marriage; that if you put an image of Saint Antônio, with a string around his neck, in a water tank and leave it, the boy will propose. But this year, I'm even going to ask him for help.

There's a saying that goes: "God helps more surely than getting up early." God's helped me up until now, except when I had to repeat the first year. And I was a lot younger then. Mama's making a communion on our behalf, so that we'll do well. Her prayers almost never fail. I hope to pass the second year. I have doubts about Renato, though.

Friday, November 22nd

Today was my first examination of this year. It was the History exam. The other girls made "concertinas" for the written test, but I was braver and went without. I sat on a bench at the back, opened the book, and I was copying out the question peacefully when I looked towards the desk and saw Dr. Teodomiro looking at me and laughing. I had an awful shock, I shut the book and hid it in the drawer. He noticed I was startled, took a newspaper and hid his face in order not to see. And he didn't say anything.

How can anyone be so kind as our Dr. Teodomiro! And still my father says that dark people aren't any good. At School, at least, he and Seu Artur Queiroga are the best ones. The white teachers are really mean.

In the oral exam I only answered some dates, mumbled some things, and now I'm through with that one.

Tuesday, December 3rd

This time my bad luck was just too much! I never had time to think a minute about Physics, but Antonico Eulálio did something wonderful for us. He simplified the examination questions in such a way that by memorizing everything we could pretend that we knew. I memorized all the questions, I had them all on the tip of my tongue and I even had the apparatus in my head. I only skipped "hydraulic pumps" because I thought those machines were so complicated, it was the night before, and I didn't have time, believing it would be impossible that I'd get the only question I didn't know. I've always had such good luck!

The written test was a dream! It was "Archimedes' Principle," that I had on the tip of my tongue. I sat down in the first row and to make a good impression every once in a while I asked Seu Artur Napoleão how this or that name was spelt. Finally he said to me, "You're amazing me with your science. Who taught you so much?" I replied "Antonico Eulálio did," and went on writing down everything I had in my head. To be safe, I'd even memorized the lettering on the apparatus. I got three "excellents" in the written test and today I went for the oral.

At School I'm considered to be Artur Napoleão's pet. He treats me differently. I'm the only student whom he talks and jokes with. It was already a scandal that the examiners had given me three "excellents" for the written test. I never sat in the front row. I only answered the roll call and did crochet during classes. He knows better than anyone how lazy I am, and today he was the first person I met at the entrance and as I went up the stairs he said, "Wait a minute, Siá Laziness! Come here and tell me something: how did you make us think you were the laziest girl in the class all year and then have a paper like that? Whom did you study with?" And then he asked, "Do you know all about 'Hydraulic Pumps'?" I said, "Yes indeed!" He said, "I want to give you 'Perfect' and I'm afraid of 'Hydraulic Pumps'!" So I said, "Why should it be that question? There are so many. It might be anything." He said, "Maybe not!" How did he guess!

My life is full of surprises. I went up the steps thinking that it would be too awful if I got that question. I went in the hall and found my friends discussing my three "excellents"; Seu Artur had told Maria Pena. Some congratulated me, others said, "I don't believe it; only if you cheated." One said, "I know what it means. Seu Artur doesn't want her not to pass, and he's telling the story of the three 'excellents' so that in the oral exam, even if she doesn't answer a thing, she's safe. The Physics exam isn't like the History exam that you can pass without studying. But since everything's different for Helena here at School, and everyone loves her, even it could be."

I went in and waited for the roll call. I went to the desk, put my hand in the box, and what did I draw? Hydraulic Pumps!

It was a scandal. A lump came into my throat and I went back to my place in tears. It was at that moment I realized how much Seu Artur likes me. He got up, came over to me, and said in a low voice, "Come take your examination, foolish. Anyone who gets three 'excellents' can't fail." I said, "It's impossible! I don't know a word of the answer!" And I left.

However, it isn't such a tragedy. I'm taking the second term and I hope to get "perfect" then.

Sunday, December 8th

I came home from the *chácara* after having spent the day playing and dancing with my cousins, from early Mass until night.

Mama, who was there just a little while and thinks that everything is always too much, came into my bedroom and said,

"Daughter, do you think the world is coming to an end? That's what I think when I see you so anxious to amuse yourself. You're just beginning life, daughter. Don't be so greedy about it. Today, you all began this madness at six o'clock in the morning. I was there having coffee while you were all in the parlor, dancing. It worries me terribly; it isn't natural. Anything that isn't natural is scandalous, my child. You have to put a stop to this life and think about your studies more."

I let mama speak until the end. Then I said,

"Do you know why it is you're so nervous like this for no reason at all, mama? It's because instead of staying there watching us play and dance, you came home and shut yourself up in this dreary house, and worked all day long, and you should get the idea out of your head that life is made up of suffering. What harm could come to me, spending the day at my aunts' house, playing and dancing with my cousins? Think about it and tell me."

Mama said: "It's because it's too much. You don't do anything else lately, except play and dance. And you're taking exams. At this time of night your friends are poring over their books. Tomorrow, when you go to the examination you'll want me to stay here on my knees praying the whole time. Wouldn't it be better if you studied?"

Mama's always right. Tomorrow I have the oral exam in geometry, but I'm sure of it because of the mark I got in the written one. And after all, what use would it be for me to study for one day, and above all, Sunday?

Tuesday, December 10th

Everything went so well in the geometry exam it seems like a dream. Clélia gave me her notes and I copied them. For the oral, in the fifteen minutes that we have, Clélia took me into a corner in the other room and said, "Helena, for heaven's sake pay attention for these fifteen minutes so that you'll do well." She explained the theorems to me so clearly that I could repeat them for her perfectly the second time.

I went to the blackboard. Catãozinho, knowing me very well and realizing that I trust to memory alone, said, "Do you want me to ask questions or do you want to explain the problem?" I said I'd prefer to explain and I explained, one after the other, the three theorems, without his saying a word. When I finished the exposition he turned to the other examiners and said, "I'm satisfied. Do you want to ask her any questions?" They said no. I went out overjoyed.

In the evening, at Dona Gabriela's, Catãozinho said to me, "Look, I didn't give you *excellent* because you were very lazy all year. But I had to give you *very good*. Are you satisfied?"

What could I say?

Monday, December 16th

Today, if grandma were alive, she'd be eighty-five years old.

All the family went to Mass and we all, except the men, took communion for grandma's soul. On my part, more for the pleasure it always gave grandma to see me take communion; she used to sit in the window waiting for me to come out of the Rosário Church, to give me a glass of port. Not for a second because of the possibility that grandma's soul might still be in purgatory. She was so kind and lived just to do good. If she isn't in heaven, who is?

I spent a very sad day, in spite of trying to amuse myself. Our lives have changed so much! There aren't any more of those big dinners when all the family got together. There aren't any more of those suppers the Negroes used to make nights: a kettle of manioc and an enormous pan from the days of slavery full of chicken and okra, or blood sauce, or pork with tomato sauce.

Thank God the quarrels over the will didn't reach the point of breaking up the family. We're still friends. But how different it is now from grandma's time.

I hear people say there's no happiness in this world. But I know grandma lived a happy life. When something unpleasant happened she'd say "I never in my born days!" but right afterwards she'd add, "Better days will come." And now she must be happy in heaven and thinking that all her efforts and sacrifice were worth it.

Tuesday, December 17th

I've finished the second year examinations. I'll have to take Physics next term, but it's safe. Nothing went wrong in the others. I'm through the second year; now I'm going to enjoy the holidays. Papa wrote that he's putting the finishing touches on our new cabin, and since I've nothing to do until we go to Boa Vista I'm going to use the time enjoying myself and writing, in order not to get out of the habit.

Yesterday Bibiana gave a farewell dance, to the piano, for us. Besides the cousins the two *bicho** men were there. João Antonio told us we shouldn't be so friendly with them, that in Rio de Janeiro a man who runs a lottery is considered very low-class. But I told him, "What does it matter? They're considered low-class there but here they're considered to be quite all right and so

* *Jogo do bicho*, or lottery.

we can't be rude to them, because they're such nice, agreeable
boys." And besides, since they've come to Diamantina there's been
a little more money in circulation. Before the lottery there was
very little money around. This kind of gambling's a wonderful
idea! I'm only sorry I don't have enough money to bet every day.
Seu Costa is so amiable that when I complained about not being
able to bet every day he said I could bet on credit. I'm not doing
it, but it would be wonderful if I had the courage to.

I've noticed that the pleasure one has when one wins in the
lottery is a lot of nonsense. If only, after winning, one stopped
playing. I've won three times and lost all the money the next
time. When I win I mean to keep the money; but I buy something or other or else lose it again. They say that they aren't going to stay in Diamantina because the storekeepers are indignant
about them and want to send them away. Poor boys!

Everyone at the dance complained about our going to Boa
Vista. Nobody wanted us to. I confess I was proud to see how
they all miss me. But I'm thinking only of the country, that beautiful place where I've spent so many happy days.

Thursday, December 19th

We had a message from papa today saying that the cabin is
ready. Mama's cleaned house and is going to leave the key with
Siá Ritinha so she can feed the cat and the hens while we're away.
To make it up to her mama is leaving her the cucumber vines
loaded with little cucumbers, a pumpkin vine, also loaded, vegetables in the garden, and some bunches of bananas that are almost ready.

I swear they're the only things I don't like to leave. But I've
made the most of the cucumbers. I eat two or three small ones
with salt, for breakfast. I'm sorry for my cousins; they think cucumbers are poisonous. They only eat them cooked and have fits when
we eat them raw.

I never saw such nonsense as goes on at Uncle Conrado's. Life's so complicated there! Very different from us. When I say how we eat cucumbers they come back with a long song and dance about people who were poisoned, and if I believed it, it would make me deny myself one of the best things to eat there is.

Mama's already had Renato kill the chickens for us to take. Every family needs someone very courageous to do certain unpleasant things like killing chickens. If mama didn't have Renato, what would we do? I, like her and Luizinha, would be incapable of doing it under any circumstances. Everything's ready and early tomorrow morning off we go!

What bliss!

Saturday, December 21st

We left Diamantina at seven o'clock. We ate lunch on the way, we were all well-rested and enjoyed everything and got here about noon. We're in our cabin and everything is put away. We had to arrange everything and we still haven't gone out.

Papa rebuilt the cabin we stayed in last vacation which had to be torn down because it was very close to the mining. Uncle Joãozinho had one built of brick, with a lot of bedrooms, a good way from the mine, and he said it would be big enough for all the family. He's going to have a big *festa* for a housewarming and invite all the relatives. The cabin we're in is very small and only to sleep in. We have to go to take coffee in the other one, where Etelvina cooks. It's very pleasant and in front there is a big tree. From the door we can see the whole mine and the workmen washing the gravel. Papa and my uncle are very hopeful. Mama says that she isn't going to hope ahead of time because she's tired of getting her hopes up and then having them disappointed.

Papa says that it hasn't rained here and that the weather has improved, thank God. Today we went to get mangoes in Santa Maria. We didn't see anyone but Emídio left a message to bring them here. Papa brought some boards and made a table for me to write on. He loves to see me with a pen or a book in my hand.

But I don't expect to have time here. In the country I like to be
completely free.

How nice to wake up in Boa Vista tomorrow morning!

Tuesday, December 24th

Today we were all sitting, young and old, under the big tree,
pleased with life. It was the most beautiful afternoon, such as
there only are here in Boa Vista. A poor woman went by and
stretched out her hand to us and said, "Give me alms, please, for
the love of God!" Lucas, who was with us and who'll never over-
look anything, asked the poor creature, "You're still young; why
are you begging alms instead of working?" She answered, "Me
work? I'm so poor!"

We all laughed. Then I thought and said, "No. She answered
very well. Could she find a job as a cook? Nobody has cooks here.
Could she gather wood? Nobody would buy it here. What work
could she find to do? Poor thing!" The woman was pleased at
my taking her part and said, "Yes, that's it, she understands. You
have a little money, you buy some black beans, cook them yourself and eat them, and the work's all done in no time."

I was very sorry for the woman and offered her the job of staying with us and helping with the house, since that way at least
she'd get her food.

I'm not sorry for anyone's being poor; I'm only sorry when they
have no work. If anyone wants to punish me, it's to oblige me
to stay without anything to do. I think that my laziness in School
is mostly because I can't think of studying as work. I like to do
work with my hands that leaves my mind free to think about what
I'd like to do, and to build castles in the air. I adore building
castles in the air and they get more beautiful all the time . . .

*Wednesday, December 25th**

Mama's hired an old woman to work for us here, but she isn't much help. We have to do almost everything ourselves.

Renato brought the cart and the ram. When I haven't anything else to do I take him to the woods and fill the cart with firewood. I always look for spots where there is tender young grass for the ram to graze. We treat this ram like a brother; he eats what we eat and sleeps at the foot of my brother's bed.

Today when I got up I found mama with everything ready for us to go to the river to wash the clothes, piled up for more than a week. The old woman helped. She carried the bundle of clothes and the pans for lunch on her head, to the river. We went with Aunt Agostinha, Naninha, Glorinha and their maid, Benvinda; we to wash clothes and my brothers with other chores to do: getting wood, making brooms for the house, fishing, and setting the traps in hopes of catching doves. We went along happy as could be, and part way there mama left us to take papa's lunch to him at the mine. What she really likes is to go and stay right beside him.

When we got to the river we stayed on the bank and my brothers went into the woods. Old Luzia arranged the stones, made a grill, put the pot of black beans on it and built the fire. I and Luizinha filled the basin with clothes and started soaping them. My aunt and her girls did the same thing and Benvinda went to look for wood and helped make lunch.

We soaped the clothes and spread them on the rocks to bleach in a hurry because we had lots of plans and it was already almost time for lunch.

We sat on the riverbank with our plates of food heaped up like workmen's, with black beans and manioc, pork, fried eggs and rice, and for dessert, bananas and cheese. Delicious!

After lunch mama wouldn't let us set foot in the water because

---

* Christmas obviously was not celebrated.

she says it's bad for one. I always ask what harm it does but she never explains. I asked why it doesn't do the miners any harm; they go into the water up to their knees right after eating and stay in the water all day long, and she says it's because they're used to it. But she won't let us get used to it. Then we went down to the water's edge to find snail-shells and *cativos.**

But we had to return to reality before long; we had to attend to the clothes. We went back and found mama, finishing washing, wringing the clothes and singing such sweet songs, that only she knows how to sing. What a lovely voice mama has! Sometimes I even like her to be sad, so she'll sing. Not out of meanness, but when she's sad it's always because she's missing papa, even when sometimes he's just a little way off.

We put the clothes out to dry, and the job was done, since folding them up only takes a minute.

Then I looked for a pool behind a rock and got into it, wearing a cotton petticoat, to take a bath and wash my hair. I'd scarcely got in when I felt something nibbling my feet and legs. I looked and there was a whole school of *lambaris!* I ran to get rice and manioc flour. I sat down in the pool, put the food in my skirt, and immediately it was filled with *lambaris*. I got up and dumped them into a basin and kept doing it until I had a fine mess. Then I stopped, thinking of the work it would be to clean them. But I brought back enough for us all to have plenty.

It was a full day. Every day we discover something new and every day's better than the last!

Thursday, December 26th

I like Aunt Agostinha best of all mama's sisters. She's intelligent and she was married to an ignorant man, who constantly embarrassed her. Fortunately he's dead. Sometimes she tells us stories about their life in Lomba before they got married and I always love to hear her. Today I asked her, "Aunt Agostinha, tell us a

* *Cativos:* small, black, eight-sided crystals, the same form as diamonds.

story about the old days." She said, "I'm going to tell you something that seems like a coincidence that went through my mind just now. Something about Justino."

She went on, "As you know, he'd never had any schooling, and I struggled with him all the time. I didn't know him before the day of the wedding and I'd never talked with him. I used to see him and I thought he was handsome and well-mounted, with fine horses. The day of the wedding he arrived very well-dressed and I thought I might learn to love him. But when we went into our room and he put his hand around my waist and said, 'Agostinha, I'm mighty pleased. Ain't you?' I hung my head and saw in that one moment what our life was going to be and what it was. My life was unhappy from then on, and a constant shame to me. He said *l* instead of *r* and spoke all wrong. One day he came home and said, 'Know who I was with just now? Zoroasty.' I explained, 'It isn't Zoroasty, Seu Justino, it's pronounced *Zoroaster*.' He took notice. Another time he said, 'Well, I'm going out now. I'm going to the pharmacer's.' I said, 'It isn't pharmace*r*, it's pharmac*y*.' He said, 'I'll end up by never saying a word to you. You just torment me. If I say *ee* it's *er*, and if I say *er* it's *ee*. Let me talk the way I want.' "

My aunts tell about how they got married. The only ones who married for love, and knew their husbands, were mama and Aunt Aurélia, because they married after grandpa died. Grandpa chose the husbands he wanted for the others. Dindinha escaped marrying a stupid farmer only by a miracle. They used to peek through the keyhole and tell each other, "I think that so-and-so's mine."

Grandpa always managed so as to marry two at the same time. He gave a *festa* at Christmas and made marriage contracts for two of them. They spent the year making their trousseaus and were married the next Christmas. And that Christmas two more would get engaged.

Saturday, December 28th

A few days ago Renato came in and told mama that Salamão, a Negro who lives at Bom Sucesso and has eight children, had hired him to teach the children this vacation, at ten *mil reis* a month. He accepted because he's already made lots of walking-sticks and brooms and hasn't sold them, and he says it's better to be earning ten *mil reis* than to keep on making more things and not selling them.

Salomão mines all alone and always manages to find some little diamonds. His wife is named Margarida. They're a very clean and polite Negro family and always invite us to dinner every vacation, and offer us coffee and whatever they have whenever we go there. They have a nice clean house. The dining-room table and the benches are scoured with sand and shine like new. The water jar is covered with a lace-trimmed cloth and so is the tray of coffee cups. They have fruit-trees and a very well kept little vegetable garden, with all kinds of vegetables, and a henhouse full of hens that lay lots of eggs. They are better and more polite black people than lots of the white ones I know. The only thing at their house that shocks us is seeing the children all bitten by cockroaches. Papa asked him what it was and he said, "It's our affliction, Seu Alexandre. When we put out the light the cockroaches bite the little ones. We cover them up well, but they push off the blanket right away. You know how hard it is to manage children."

Renato went to teach them and he came back enchanted with the children's good behaviour. Margarida had a baby in her arms and was expecting another one soon. Renato says that when he got there he found Margarida waiting for him, with a switch from the quince tree on the table, and the children looking at their books, quiet and good. Today he arrived and found her in the same place, watching the children the same as the day before, but without a big belly, and with the new little pickaninny in her arms.

Aren't they different from us? If it had been a white woman, she would have stayed in bed a week, taking chicken broth. Margarida has been working since the day the baby was born and she says it's easier because now she feels lighter.

Sunday, December 29th

Today, Sunday, it's raining in Boa Vista, and I am thinking nostalgically of my First Communion. When all the little girls had studied the catechism a year, Father Neves told us that we were ready for our First Communion, which would take place in a month.

I was in raptures at this news and I told mama to begin to get everything ready immediately: the long white dress, the veil, the wreath, and the decorated wax candle.

On the evening of the great day, Father Neves brought all the pupils together in the church, and he went behind the grating of the screen to hear our confessions. The little girls knelt outside, confessing and then going away. My turn came and I knelt down with my list of sins all memorized: Gluttony, Envy, Luxury (the desire for pretty dresses),* stealing fruit from my grandmother, gossiping. I told everything and made my act of contrition, but I left the confessional with a small nail in my conscience.

There were lots of ex-slaves at grandma's who told nursery tales, tales of the spirits of the other world and the sins that had carried them off to purgatory and hell. If one stole an egg, for example, then the egg would turn into a hen, and one would have to spend as many years in purgatory as the hen had feathers. They also believed that it was an unpardonable sin to think that a priest was homely.

I listened to everything attentively and I couldn't have stolen an egg under any circumstances. But the sin of finding a priest homely haunted me all year long. Every time Father Neves came into church I thought to myself, "Am I really committing a sin?

* She is confusing *luxuria* with *luxury*.

I do think he's so homely!" I kept trying to put this wicked thought out of my head but it kept coming back again, and even at the end of the catechism class it hadn't left me.

When I went to confess that day, I reasoned, "No, I haven't committed a sin because I've never told anyone I think Father Neves is homely. It's better not to think about it any more."

I left the confessional very penitent but not quite as peaceful and relieved as one should be. I made a retreat all that day with as much contrition as a seven year old girl is capable of.

On the next day, the great day, mama woke me up early and helped me get dressed, giving me some last bits of advice on how to make a good communion. When I got to church I found all my playmates already in their places, just waiting for me for the priest to begin the sermon.

To give this sermon, Father Neves had asked an Italian priest, rather fat and red, who knew how to shout and make a big impression on little girls. The priest began:

"My children, this day is the happiest and most important of your lives. You are going to receive the body, blood, and soul of Jesus into your hearts. It is an amazing grace, my dears, that God grants you! But to receive it you must be prepared, and contrite, and you mustn't have concealed any sin whatsoever in the confessional. To hide a sin and then to receive communion is an abomination! I know of many horrible cases, but I am going to tell you just one as an example.

"Once a group of little girls were making their first communion just the way you are making it today. They received the host and went solemnly back to their places, and at that very moment one of them fell down and died. The priest said to the little girl's mother, 'God has taken her to Glory!' And all the others were envious of their playmate who had died in the grace of God. And then, what do you suppose they saw? The devil dragging the body of the miserable little girl behind the altar. Do you know why? Because she had concealed a sin in the confessional."

When I heard this I amazed everyone by bursting out howling. Father Neves ran to find out what was wrong. I said, "I concealed a sin in the confessional." Father Neves tried to comfort me very gently, "Don't be so upset, daughter; come and tell the sin and God will forgive you and you can take communion." I told him, "I want to tell the sin to the other priest, not to you, Senhor." He took hold of my hands, still very gently, and said, "You can't do that, little one; you confessed to me so you have to tell me the sin. Don't be afraid; the priest is here to listen to everything. Come on. I'll look the other way; you can tell me and go away in just a minute."

He took me to a corner of the sacristy and was very nice and insisted that I confess. Sobbing and horrified at what I was going to say I hung my head and whispered, "I confess to having thought that a priest was very homely." Father Neves said, "That isn't a sin, my child. What's wrong with thinking that a priest is homely?" I took courage and said, "But the priest is you, Father!"

Father Neves let go of my hands and got up, exclaiming, "I really *am* homely! And what of it? I can't stand such silly little girls! Here I spend the whole year struggling to get them ready for communion and at the end they come to me to confess that I'm homely. It's too much!"

Tuesday, December 31st

Today I'm thinking of grandma because since she died her soul has been protecting us.

How many times didn't she say to me, "You're the one who's going to save your family, child. You're so good and intelligent." I remember, too, how she always used to tell mama, "Carolina, I'll really have to die to make things better for you, daughter." She used to talk like that because she couldn't give us money while she was alive because Uncle Geraldo took care of her fortune and he wouldn't let her.

The money that grandma left for mama was very little and papa paid all his debts and kept on mining. But things changed immediately and our life has improved so much that I can only attribute it to grandma's soul watching over us. Papa joined the Boa Vista Company and the foreigners do everything through him because he's the only one who speaks English and who knows the mines well. We shan't suffer for lack of the necessities any longer, thank God.

But isn't it really grandma watching over us there in heaven?